Federalism and the Making of America

Though Americans rarely appreciate it, federalism has profoundly shaped their nation's past, present, and future. Federalism—the division of government authority between the national government and the states—affects the prosperity, security, and daily life of every American. In this nuanced and comprehensive overview, David Brian Robertson shows that past choices shape present circumstances, and that a deep understanding of American government, public policy, political processes, and society requires an understanding of the key steps in federalism's evolution in American history.

The most spectacular political conflicts in American history have been fought on the battlefield of federalism, including states' rights to leave the union, government power to regulate business, and responses to the problems of race, poverty, pollution, abortion, and gay rights. Federalism helped fragment American politics, encourage innovation, foster the American market economy, and place hurdles in the way of efforts to mitigate the consequences of economic change. Federalism helped construct the path of American political development. *Federalism and the Making of America* is a sorely needed text that treats the politics of federalism systematically and accessibly, making it indispensable to all students and scholars of American politics.

David Brian Robertson is University of Missouri Curators' Teaching Professor and former chair of the department of political science at the University of Missouri-St. Louis.

Federalism and the Making of America

David Brian Robertson

Routledge
Taylor & Francis Group

NEW YORK AND LONDON

First published 2012
by Routledge
711 Third Avenue, New York, NY 10017

Simultaneously published in the UK
by Routledge
2 Park Square, Milton Park, Abingdon, Oxon OX14 4RN

Routledge is an imprint of the Taylor & Francis Group, an informa business

Library of Congress Cataloging in Publication Data
Robertson, David Brian, 1951-
Federalism and the making of America / David Brian Robertson.
p. cm.
1. Federal government--United States--History. 2. United States--Politics
and government. I. Title.
JK311.R64 2012
320.473′049--dc22
2011009573

ISBN: 978-0-415-87918-7 (hbk)
ISBN: 978-0-415-87919-4 (pbk)
ISBN: 978-0-203-85212-5 (ebk)

Typeset in Garamond
by Taylor & Francis Books

Printed and bound in the United States of America on acid-free paper by
Edwards Brothers, Inc.

To My Students

Contents

Figures and Table

Figures

Table

Acknowledgments

This book has been a very humbling experience. It reflects the wisdom of many, many smart people who have reflected at length about American politics, history, and federalism. Their collective wisdom inevitably nurtured my understanding of American political development in ways I can never fully appreciate or properly thank them for.

Several anonymous reviewers for Routledge provided exceptionally informed, thoughtful, and incisive comments on both the proposal and many draft chapters of this book. I faithfully read and very seriously thought about every comment they made. I cannot thank them enough for their time and care. I would like to thank John Hoornbeek and R. Shep Melnick for their assistance. A 2009 conference on federalism at Central Arkansas University immensely sharpened my ideas. I especially appreciated the opportunity to learn from Gary D. Wekkin, Timothy Conlan, Virginia Gray, Robert Lowry, and Reinhold Herber.

My students have been particularly helpful in developing the ideas here. Students in my undergraduate Honors seminar in the Fall of 2010 involuntarily served as test mice for a draft of this book. They added immensely to it, and I hope they can see our conversations in the final product. These students included Ben Chambers, Jessy Chisholm, Jonathan Eftink, Alex Ellison, Durray Kauser, Gabriele Macaluso, Darren Olsen, Stephen Ordway, Stepan Tiratsuyan, Sherry Valdespino, Eric Vorst, and Rory White.

Friends and colleagues have shaped my thinking about federalism, politics, and the adventure of writing. Dennis Judd, my co-author on a book about federalism and public policy several years ago, has had a particularly long-lasting impact on my analysis of federalism. Among the many scholars in American Political Development, my intellectual home, I am particularly grateful for exchanging ideas over time with Margaret Weir, Suzanne Mettler, Richard Bensel, Elizabeth Sanders, Martha Derthick, Robert Lieberman, Bat Sparrow, Eileen McDonaugh, McGee Young, and Kimberley Johnson. David Webber is a durable influence on my thinking about federalism. Donald Critchlow, the Editor of the *Journal of Policy History*, has given me the priceless opportunity to experience the evolution of scholarship on all facets of the material in this book. Russell Hanson and Patrick Nugent are among the many other scholars who have influenced my thinking on federalism. Lana Vierdag, Raphael Hopkins, and Jane Allen helped in ways too numerous to mention.

Michael Kerns, my editor at Routledge, encouraged me to do this project and supported it throughout. Sue Cope did an outstanding job of editing the manuscript, preventing numerous errors and ambiguities and improving it immensely; I am most assuredly responsible for all remaining errors. Many thanks to Mary Altman and the rest of the Routledge staff. Thanks also to the inspiring music-makers who provided the soundtrack for this work: Antonio Vivaldi, Antonín Dvořák, Ludwig van Beethoven, the Dubliners, R.E.M., and the late Stevie Ray Vaughn.

And thanks to my wife, Cathie, and to my son Bryan, who taught me so much about everything. I'm incredibly lucky to have both in my life. I hope that the book lives up to the help and hopes of all who helped me write it.

1 Introduction

Federalism shapes Americans' lives because it has shaped the past and present of their nation. Federalism—the division of government authority between the national government and the states—affects the prosperity, security, and many everyday choices of each person living in the United States. The American states always have done most of the routine governing in the United States. State laws still regulate birth and death, marriage and divorce, crime and punishment, and commercial law, such as the purchase and sale of property. States manage education, prisons, highways, welfare, environmental protection, corporate law, and the professions. Because federalism's impact is so broad and so deep, political rivals have battled over federalism since the nation's founding. Federalism has influenced all the important political battles in American history. The United States, its government, and its public policy are a still-evolving legacy of choices powerfully influenced by federalism over time.

This book argues that federalism has played a pivotal part in the making of America because it has been a principal battlefield of political conflict. Political opponents have fought about federalism to advance or to stop government actions. Over time these political conflicts helped construct the unique path that the development of American government, politics, and public policy has followed.

Federalism has shaped American life most powerfully by converting many political conflicts over whether government should act into conflicts over which level of government—the U.S. national government or the states—should exercise power to resolve the conflict. The most bitter and spectacular political conflicts in American history have been fought on the battlefield of federalism, including states' rights to leave the union, and government power to regulate business, to institute political reform, and to respond to problems of race, poverty, pollution, abortion, and many more. The consequences of these choices played out over time and cumulatively have altered American political development. Federalism helped fragment American politics, encourage policy innovation and diversity, foster the American market economy, and place hurdles in the way of efforts to mitigate the consequences of economic change.

The Significance of American Federalism

Federalism is a long-lasting institutional arrangement of political power in which both a national government and regional governments within a nation each have separate authority to maintain order, make laws, spend public funds, and provide public services. Ronald L. Watts, a foremost expert on federalism, estimated that in 2002, forty percent of the world's population lived in nations organized around federalism; these nations include the United States, Argentina, Australia, Austria, Belgium, Brazil, Canada, Ethiopia, Germany, India, Mexico, Nigeria, Spain, and Switzerland. Many believe that the European Union is evolving toward a kind of federal system.[1]

Federalism emerged and endures because it offers an expedient way to harmonize separate smaller governments to achieve larger goals, especially to foster more commerce and better military security. In ancient Greece, Athens and other Greek city states created confederations to forge a stronger common defense against external threats. Swiss cantons organized a confederation in 1291. A Hanseatic League of cities in northern Europe, originally formed in the 1300s to foster trade, also developed overarching governing institutions and military power. A Dutch confederacy consisting of seven provinces emerged in the 1500s.[2] By the 1600s, such federations were recognized as a distinct form of government.[3] The American federation that emerged after the Revolutionary War changed concepts of federalism by creating a much stronger union than any of these earlier confederations. The U.S. Constitution left the American states with substantial authority, promised each a republican government, gave them equal representation in the U.S. Senate, guaranteed them a role in selecting the U.S. president, and required that any amendment to the Constitution would require ratification by three-quarters of the states. The more modern federalism created in the United States, in turn, strongly influenced many of the Federal nations that have developed since.

Today, although U.S. federalism is comparable to that in other former British colonies such as Australia and Canada, it differs from most of the other federal systems in the world. First, as political scientist Alfred Stepan has pointed out, while American federalism aimed to bring smaller units of government together, federalism in India, Belgium, Spain, and many other nations was instituted to help hold together polities with serious, geographically-based ethnic or cultural divisions. In these countries, some regional governments represent ethnic or religious minorities and exercise unique prerogatives of self-governance. In the United States, all of the states have equal legal standing and authority.[4] Second, in all other federal systems, the national government deliberately equalizes regional resources by redistributing more financial aid to the poorest regions. The United States is the only federal system that does not equalize state resources in this way.[5] Third, American federalism has proven extraordinarily elastic in comparison to federalism in other nations, in that it has adapted to enormous changes in physical size, population, race and ethnicity, the economy, and culture.[6]

American federalism now is so deeply rooted in American life that few Americans appreciate how much it shapes their lives and their government. The importance of state and local governments is best measured by the people and the money they manage. State and local governments each employ far more civilians than the Federal government.[7] About 2.7 million Americans worked in full-time Federal government employment in mid-2010, while 4.4 million worked for state governments and 12.2 million worked for local governments.[8] In 2008, prior to the spike in Federal spending driven by the recession that began in late 2007, the Federal government spent $2.9 trillion. In the same year, state and local government spending was about the same, totaling more than $2.8 trillion (including money received from Federal grants).[9]

States continue to shape American prosperity with substantial authority to encourage and to regulate business, and to supervise the public goods that foster economic growth, such as public education and highways. States regulate nearly twenty percent of the American economy, through insurance industry rules, occupational licensing, and health services laws. States issue ninety percent of all environmental permits and undertake three-quarters of all environmental enforcement actions.[10] One of the smallest American states, Delaware, maintains laws that are exceptionally favorable to private corporations, such as minimal regulation, no corporate taxes, and a separate court dedicated to business. As a result, many Fortune 500 companies that are headquartered in other states—including Wal-Mart, Google, McDonald's, Coca-Cola, United Parcel Service, the Walt Disney Company, Bank of America, and Verizon—legally exist as Delaware corporations.[11] State and local governments are major sources of investment capital in their own right; their employee retirement systems held $2.35 trillion in assets in 2010.[12]

States play a decisive role in education, criminal justice, and the regulation of everyday life. About fifty million students were enrolled in the public elementary and secondary education systems overseen by American states in 2007–8.[13] About three-quarters of students enrolled in higher education—eighteen million students in all—were enrolled in public institutions, either regulated or directly run by the states. State courts hold most of the criminal trials in the nation and produce most of the convictions. Today, thirty-five states maintain the death penalty. States executed 1,243 individuals between 1976 and mid-March 2011; Texas alone executed more than 464 people. In the same period, the U.S. government executed three individuals.[14] State and local laws regulate marriage, divorce, abortion, gambling, drinking, smoking, and drugs. States are the chief managers of welfare and health services for the needy.

The states even play an important role in responding to global opportunities and threats. A quarter of a million troops from state National Guard units served in Iraq and Afghanistan from 2001–7.[15] In 2002 the states "spent almost $200 million on export promotion, educational exchanges, and other international programs."[16]

States also shape political ambition and achievement in the United States. Governorships and U.S. Senate seats (as well as House seats in the seven smallest states) are contested statewide. All the U.S. House of Representatives districts are contained entirely within a single state. The states draw the boundaries of these districts, as well as their state legislative districts. Presidents have to win a majority of votes in the state-based Electoral College. Most U.S. presidents have been state office-holders before becoming president. Since the election of 1884, eighteen of twenty-two presidents won statewide election for governor or U.S. Senator before becoming president.[17]

Arguments for American Federalism

American federalism has five main virtues, according to its advocates. First, they argue, American federalism provides a bulwark for freedom, individual rights, and democracy because it prevents the national government from exercising too much power. Thomas Jefferson wrote that "the true barriers of our liberty in this country are our State governments."[18] In the *Federalist*, James Madison argued that the small state republics within the larger national republic would place "greater obstacles … to the concert and accomplishment of the secret wishes of an unjust and interested majority."[19]

> In the compound republic of America, the power surrendered by the people is first divided between two distinct governments, and then the portion allotted to each subdivided among distinct and separate departments. Hence a double security arises to the rights of the people. The different governments will control each other, at the same time that each will be controlled by itself."[20]

If a state acts unjustly, its policies could be quarantined without spreading to the rest of the nation. As British political scientist James Bryce put it, federalism is comparable to "a ship built with watertight compartments."[21] An unjust or despotic national action would mobilize resistance in the states and compel state leaders to use their powers to resist the law.[22] Alexis de Tocqueville, a French aristocrat who observed the United States in the early nineteenth century, wrote that "It is generally believed in America that the existence and the permanence of the republican form of government in the New World depend upon the existence and the permanence of the Federal system."[23] Today, states vigorously strive to protect their interests against the national government.[24] Further, a federal system can facilitate the expansion of individual and group rights. Those who seek the legal protection of rights can seek them at the national level, or, if they cannot influence the national government, at the state level, thus increasing the chance that rights will be established in at least a portion of the nation.[25]

Second, its proponents argue that American federalism makes government more responsive to citizens. In this view, states are much more likely than the national government to understand their citizens' needs and wants, and to respond satisfactorily to citizens' demands. Madison wrote that "the first and most natural attachment of the people will be to the governments of their respective States," because these governments would be much more familiar to citizens, would employ more people who would deal with them directly, and would provide and regulate "all the more domestic, and personal interests of the people," most especially civil and criminal justice.[26]

Third, American federalism fosters innovation, as James Bryce observed, because it "enables a people to try experiments which could not safely be tried in a large centralized country." As Supreme Court Justice Louis Brandeis put it eighty years ago, "a single courageous state may, if its citizens choose, serve as a laboratory and try novel social and economic experiments without risk to the rest of the country."[27] Political scientist Richard Nathan pointed out that the states keep policy innovation alive even in periods when support for national activism is low. The efforts of innovative states "have been tested, refined, debugged, and often diffused across the country" and sometimes evolve into Federal government policy. In this view, state innovations have laid the foundation for later national policy innovations.[28]

Fourth, advocates of American federalism argue that its responsiveness to citizens makes the nation more efficient at governing and effective at achieving results. At the Constitutional Convention, a number of delegates insisted that the country was too large and diverse for the national government to manage, and that the states were essential for good government. Connecticut delegate Oliver Ellsworth, for example, defended the state authority to maintain militias because national authority "could not sufficiently pervade the Union for such a purpose, nor could it accommodate itself to the local genius of the people."[29] Later, Tocqueville wrote that

> In the states ... all public authority and private energy is employed in internal [betterment]. The central government of each State, which is in immediate juxtaposition to the citizens, is daily apprised of the wants which arise in society ... This spirit of amelioration is constantly alive in the American republics, without compromising their tranquility; the ambition of power yields to the less refined and less dangerous love of comfort.[30]

More recently, James M. Buchanan and Gordon Tullock argued that federalism fosters efficiency because it allows citizens to move freely from one jurisdiction to another that provides a more desirable package of services and costs. In effect, state and local governments compete for taxpayers.[31] Aaron Wildavsky argued that states discover much sooner than national officials when a policy is unpopular or is not working as intended: the "crazy-quilt pattern of interaction" that characterizes decentralized policy frequently "generates more information on preferences, imposes fewer costs, inculcates more dynamism, and leads to more integrative solutions."[32]

Finally, some argue that American federalism nurtures national economic prosperity by protecting private enterprise and free markets. Barry Weingast contended that the federal system is "market-preserving," that is, it encouraged capitalist growth because the states have the ability and the will to compete with one another to foster their own internal prosperity. In doing so, they have a strong incentive to keep American economic regulations and taxes within limits that do not discourage investment and business expansion.[33]

Interpretations of Federalism

With all the evidence of federalism's impact, and all of these efforts to argue on its behalf, why is federalism not a more prominent topic in the United States? Americans do not fully appreciate how their federal system has shaped their nation, their government, and their lives because there are almost no efforts to provide a broad, systematic explanation of federalism's evolution and impact since the nation's founding. Most of the recent scholarship on federalism neglects its broad political origins and development. Instead, recent books on American federalism generally limit themselves to describing the way that local, state, and national governments manage public policy. These works simplify the development of federalism by describing the eclipse of an older model of "dual" federalism (a period when the Federal government and the state governments had very limited responsibilities) by a more complex mixture of responsibilities.[34] These works frequently use political scientist Morton Grodzins's metaphor comparing dual federalism to a "layer" cake, and more contemporary federalism to a "marble" cake.[35] David B. Walker's *The Rebirth of Federalism* (2000) stands out as the most careful analysis of the historical development of federalism. Walker's discussion, however, still emphasizes the description of administrative problems.

Scholars use the term "intergovernmental relations" to describe these administrative relationships in the United States. Timothy J. Conlan's *From New Federalism to Devolution: Twenty-Five Years of Intergovernmental Reform*, which focuses on three Republican efforts to reform the federal system, provides the most insight into the politics of intergovernmental relations.[36] Deil S. Wright's inclusive inventory of intergovernmental relationships exhaustively describes the stages of these relationships.[37] Edited volumes survey important scholarship and the contemporary state of intergovernmental relations.[38]

Scholars in other fields have laid the foundation for a more political and evolutionary understanding of American federalism, but have not completed the framework. Several historians have emphasized the importance of the states in the evolution of American government and politics.[39] Legal historian Alison LaCroix has published a thoughtful study of the ideological origins of American federalism, and political scientist Samuel Beer wrote about the political theories that informed it.[40] Political scientist William Riker, a pioneer of rational choice approaches to understanding politics, proposed that federalism results from a bargain between politicians who seek more centralized power, and politicians whose power depends on smaller constituent units. Political parties in a federal system like the United States play a critical role in maintaining the federal bargain by battling over the level of government that should control policy. Riker, however, never fully developed this argument, or fleshed out these observations with a systematic analysis of the development of American federalism.[41] Many scholars have analyzed federalism's important role in the development of public policy in other nations.[42] Recently, comparative politics scholars have published excellent studies of federalism, especially in Europe and Latin America, and this work provides very helpful ideas for the analysis of the origins of federalism and its consequences more generally.[43]

All these promising lines of scholarship must inform a systematic political analysis of American federalism, but it is the field of American political development that must bring these strands together. The field of American Political Development, or APD, has emphasized a very broad and realistic view of politics since its emergence in the 1980s. APD aims to study systematically the evolution over time of American government, politics, and public policy. APD scholars trace continuity and change in policies, laws, and enduring institutions such as the states, the U.S. Congress, the Supreme Court, the presidency, and the executive agencies. Leading scholars Karen Orren and Stephen Skowronek define political development as "a durable shift in governing authority," and they define "governing authority," in turn, as "the exercise of control over persons or things that is designated and enforceable by the state."[44] Political development, then, examines the use and control of government authority as it changes over time. Because federalism is so important for the evolution of government authority in the United States, federalism should be a central concern of APD research.

Indeed, APD scholars have provided great insight into the role of American federalism in many specific areas. For Robert Lieberman, federalism is an important part of the explanation for the way the United States has dealt with race over time.[45] For Suzanne Mettler, the decentralized aspects of the Social Security Act helped create an inferior American welfare state for American women.[46] For Kimberley Johnson, American national policy-makers enlisted the states in its policy efforts and laid the basis for cooperative federalism and intergovernmental relations long before the 1930s.[47] For Richard Bensel, sectionalism has been a critical driver of political change in the United States.[48] Martha Derthick brought an unparalleled political insight to specific cases of intergovernmental relations in the last half-century.[49] My own work has examined the origins of federalism in the U.S. Constitutional Convention and the impact of federalism on the development of American public policy, business, and labor relations, and early efforts to initiate public health insurance.

But American Political Development (APD) has yet to produce a fully elaborated narrative of American federalism. It is essential for APD to bring its insights to bear on federalism because APD is especially well-suited to answer three kinds of questions. First, how has government capacity changed over time? The American states have played a major role in governing Americans and in organizing their politics from the start. The evolution of this role needs to be more clearly understood to better appreciate this capacity today. Second, how have the relative powers of the state and national governments changed over time? All sides agree that national powers have expanded (whether they believe that to be good or bad), and that states play a more secondary role to the national government. On particular policy issues, however, the states have been at the forefront of political conflict, whether on slavery in the nineteenth century, or on climate change and gay marriage in the early twenty-first century. The ever-shifting balance of institutional relationships strongly affects the outcomes of political struggles in the United States. Third, APD emphasizes government's cumulative effects on the composition of society, the allocation of wealth, and the distribution of power in the United States. Conflicts over economic power and race have been a foundation of politics in the United States since its independence, and federalism has helped define and determine the results of these conflicts. For all these reasons, it is a good time to take a broad perspective on American federalism as one of the defining factors of American politics, policy, and life.

Federalism and Politics

This book develops three themes about American federalism. First, federalism is fundamental to the conduct of political conflict in the United States. From the start, political opponents have fought about federalism because it affects who wins and who loses a particular fight. The states produce different policy results than the national (in this book, also the "Federal") government. These different levels of government face different opportunities, constraints, and circumstances. Some of the state governments almost always have responded to public problems rapidly, and often act before the national government deals with an issue. State policy experiments often influence national policies. None of the states have as many policy tools as the national government, however. State officials must be very cautious about enacting pathbreaking innovations in public policy because they are keenly aware of intense competition for business investment from states with lower taxes, fewer regulations on business, and less generous social benefits.

Federalism therefore has played a part in every major political conflict in American history. Opponents have used federalism as a strategic weapon, either as a shield against change, or as a sword to bring change about. Public debates may evoke highly principled arguments for or against federalism or national power, but these philosophical assertions usually cloak the real purpose behind the struggle over state versus national power: to get government to do something that they want it to do, or to prevent government from doing something they want to prevent. In many ways, federalism resembles a "common carrier" like a railroad, but one that is used to transport a wide variety of political pressures instead of cars full of freight. Both liberals and conservatives, and both Democrats and Republicans, have used federalism as an expedient political weapon to deal with controversial issues such as labor, the environment, education, abortion, and gay rights. Their support for federalism is almost invariably contingent on their calculations about the different results that the states or the national government are likely to produce. Virtually no conservatives or liberals hesitate to jettison federalism when it interferes with more substantive political priorities. Efforts to treat federalism as an abstract philosophical question divorced from political reality, or as a purely administrative issue without political implications, are misguided and misleading.

Because federalism is most important as a political *instrument*, federalism's *consequences* can be very difficult to specify in a simple way. Federalism's results are inconsistent; federalism has been used by and against Republicans as well as Democrats, liberals as well as conservatives, and innovators as well as those who resist change. Although today's liberals typically are associated with support for Federal power, and today's conservatives are associated with decentralization and returning power to the states, the record is much more complicated. In American history, liberals and advocates of social change have relied much more on federalism and the states, and conservatives have relied much more on centralized national power, than they recognize.

Federalism and Path Dependence

The book's second theme emphasizes that federalism's impact on American politics, policy, and life has developed cumulatively over time. The expanding scope of economic and social life inevitably drove change in American government. Change helped nationalize public affairs and made the growth of Federal government influence in American life—driven by Americans of all ideological persuasions in one way or another—impossible to stop. Efforts to reform public policy and change government institutions have been irrepressible. Periods of sweeping, durable reforms—the Progressive Era (from the 1890s through the 1910s), the New Deal (1930s), the Great Society (1960s), and the conservative era beginning in the 1980s—changed American federalism and, along with it, the path of American political development.

American political development shows how institutions, once established, influence the decisions and changes that come later. Government institutions like federalism resist change and change slowly. People adapt to these institutions over time, and in this way the institutions gradually shape the development of government, politics, and public policy. Political scientist Paul Pierson explains this process as "path dependence," a tendency for an established way of doing things to become self-reinforcing for most people.[50] Federalism, like other institutions, endures because all Americans are accustomed to it, many have benefited from it, and some tenaciously have resisted changes in it.

To better understand the United States, it is essential to understand the way federalism has influenced politics and policy in American history. Federalism has worked gradually, rewarding the interests of individuals, political parties, pressure groups, government officials, and others who learn how to use it effectively. Once its framers fixed federalism in the U.S. Constitution, for example, Americans got used to its role in the new government and built it into their expectations and use of American government. Federalism also affected the new institutions, such as the political parties and interest groups that began to emerge soon after the new government started operating in 1789. Once established, such new institutions and policies created new reasons to defend federalism and states' prerogatives. An APD scholar trying to understand the nation's racial problems, for example, would study the key turning points in conflicts about state prerogatives in the 1960s, the 1930s, the 1860s, and the 1780s to reconstruct the path that brought us to where we are today.

The United States, its government, and its public policy are a legacy of choices strongly influenced by federalism. Federalism helps explain why American public policy has been more fragmented, uneven, and often limited than policy and politics in comparable nations.[51] American political parties and powerful interest groups, such as business and labor, also are more fragmented than those abroad because they have learned to adjust to American federalism. Together, the cumulative impacts of federalism help explain some of the most important features of the United States, most notably conflict over racial policy, economic development driven by free markets, and the prominent role of the states in national reform movements.

Federalism and the Sequence of Change

The book's third theme emphasizes that expanding government activism was constructed atop the foundation of federalism, resulting in a durable, thriving intergovernmental system today. State and local governments have remained active, influential, innovative, and indispensable. Federalism offered a bundle of strategic possibilities for anyone who wanted to bring about policy change. Many new initiatives—including alcohol prohibition, business regulation, social welfare programs, and environmental protection—were established in some of the states before they became Federal policy.

Federalism, then, has played a crucial role in the *sequence* of events in the growth of American government activism since the late nineteenth century.[52] It is particularly important that the Federal government enjoyed broad authority to raise money long *before* the surge in government activism, but was conceded the authority to police domestic affairs only *after* the growth of government activism was well underway. The Constitution clearly gave the U.S. national government the legitimate power to impose import and other taxes. The Constitutional authority to levy a Federal income tax in the early twentieth century expanded Federal revenue capacity. But Federal court decisions continued to set strict limits on Federal regulatory authority into 1937. This sequence had two important consequences when industrialization increased demands for more active government in the late nineteenth century. First, the states took the lead in instituting regulations to control business and social policies to mitigate the effects of industrialization. Second, the Federal government adapted creatively to its powers and their limits. It provided grants-in-aid to states to carry out purposes such as highway construction and vocational education. By the time the Supreme Court in the late 1930s allowed more Federal regulation of the domestic economy, Federal–state grants were becoming a wider and more deeply embedded part of American government activism.

In a sequence of events that drove American political development along a path that could not be predicted in advance, prior arrangements shaped major policy change by shaping the subsequent strategic opportunities and constraints of the advocates of government activism.

(1)   Progressive Era reformers inherited a system of broad state authority and national authority, and changed the federal system to increase the engagement and professionalization of governments at all levels.

(2)   The New Deal inherited a system of governments that were more active than they had been in the nineteenth century, and changed the federal system to establish Federal leadership in actively mitigating the problems that resulted from market-driven economic growth.

(3) Post-World War II liberals inherited a New Deal system of inter-governmental activism, and changed the federal system to expand rights, equalize opportunity, and reduce risk nationally.

(4) Conservatives in the 1980s inherited a very active federal–state system of regulations and social welfare benefits, and used the federal system to promote market-driven economic growth and traditional social values.

Federalism and Strategies for Reform

In each of these periods, reformers employed three strategies to overcome the hurdles that federalism placed in their path. While these strategies often limited the range of the states' actions, each strategy also reinforced the intergovernmental system and the strength of the states in some way.[53]

First, advocates of policy change battled for *partial national rules* to set legal limitations on some of the actions of all the states, often to place a uniform limit on the uses of state authority. These rules have taken the form of Constitutional amendments (such as the Eighteenth Amendment that prohibited the manufacture and sale of intoxicating liquors in all the states, or the Twenty-Fourth Amendment that banned states from imposing poll taxes), congressional laws (such as rules banning legal segregation based on race or that limit automobile exhausts), or Federal court rulings (setting basic national rules for state capital punishment or for abortion regulation). The Federal government subtly reinforces state authority even when it constrains it, because Federal rules generally allow and expect the states to exercise residual policy discretion, and the states' exercise of this discretion often has politically significant consequences for Americans. For example, the diverse state laws enacted since the 1973 Supreme Court abortion decision, *Roe* v. *Wade*, make access to abortion uneven across the states.

Second, reformers employ *layering*, a tactic of placing new responsibilities on the states to produce desired outcomes, usually in return for a conditional grant of money or some other benefit. Layering is the most common approach to expanding government activism, because it provides the least disruption of existing arrangements, the least threat to diverse centers of power, and often generates less conflict than national rules. For example, when the Morrill Act of 1862 authorized Federal land grants to the states to provide higher education in science, engineering, and agriculture, the law supplemented existing state colleges and did not replace them. Many of the reforms of the Progressive Era, the New Deal, and the Great Society typically were layered on top of deeply rooted older institutions. To motivate state action, the Federal government has initiated grants in every area of state responsibility from highways and policing to health, education, and welfare. The history of public policy toward medical care is a history of layer after layer of supplemental policy, from Federal grants for maternal and infant child care in the Progressive Era, to tax breaks for business health insurance after World War II, to grants for medical care to the poor during the 1960s, and finally the effort to create an overarching framework for the many existing health care institutions in the Patient Protection and Affordable Health Care Act of 2010.

Third, reformers who confront obstacles at the state level sometimes try to *bypass* existing state government and political institutions by energizing new institutions that are more likely to produce the outcomes they seek. During Reconstruction, the Federal Freedmen's Bureau attempted to bypass Southern governments to help newly freed slaves become self-sufficient and acquire lands in the former Confederacy. In the 1930s, the New Deal attempted to bypass state governments by creating grants programs that encouraged states to establish new agencies with professionals in highway construction, welfare services, and other areas who would share the mind-set of national professional leaders and Federal administrators. In the 1960s War on Poverty, the Federal government bypassed state and local governments and funded new Community Action Agencies, which were created by local residents, provided services in poor areas, and helped mobilize the poor politically.

Federalism as a Contributor to American Political Development

While federalism has played a powerful role in shaping American political development, it is not the only factor that has driven the development of the nation. Far from it. Scholars have shown that many other factors also have shaped the United States. The sheer size of the United States and its population posed a huge obstacle to universal Federal control of public policy. American culture and ideology treasure decentralization and distrust strong central government, inhibiting the scope of Federal power. Its multiple ideological traditions played out in different ways, in different times and places. The unique circumstances of history—such as charismatic leaders and unprecedented disasters—have shaped the critical junctures of American political development.

Federalism has not been a singular cause of American political development, but rather a contributing factor. This book argues that it is an important factor that too few appreciate. It integrates the many factors that drove the nation's history into a narrative intended to reveal federalism's importance.

The Plan

These themes enliven our understanding of the politics of federalism and its effects on Americans. This book consists of three parts. The first part, "Bringing American Federalism to Life," discusses the Constitution and the role of political parties and interest groups in the development of the federal system. Chapter 2 shows how supporters of strong national power clashed with defenders of state prerogatives at the Constitutional Convention of 1787. These delegates compromised, producing a Constitution that allowed the states tremendous responsibility to govern Americans, while it also denied the states some of the tools that any national government could use, such as restricting trade or printing money. It also set limits on the scope of the national government's power, limits that American leaders struggled to surmount from the first. Chapter 3 examines the impact of federalism on political parties and interest groups, especially on the exceptional fragmentation of these institutions in the United States. Political parties emerged soon after the Constitution took effect, sparring over national versus states' prerogatives. Leaders of the parties have used federalism for strategic reasons, to gain advantages in conflicts with their rivals. Interest groups, too, have used federalism strategically to help ensure that the government most responsive to their needs has the responsibility to make policy in the area of their concern. American political parties and interest groups themselves mirrored federalism and evolved into exceptionally fragmented institutions.

The second part of the book, "Enduring Fault Lines of American Politics," examines the two deepest and most lasting sources of political conflict in American history: race and economic power. Racial equality and economic power have been the most momentous, consequential, and hotly contested issues influenced by federalism. Both of these enduring struggles have produced results that have set American government, politics, and policy apart from other industrial democracies. Conflicts over the terms of citizenship for racial minorities played out in clashes over slavery, legal segregation, and civil rights. These political struggles cemented the power of states' rights as a strategic political weapon in American politics. These conflicts helped make race such an agonizing "American dilemma" in the mid-twentieth century, and produced new battles over affirmative action, educational opportunity, and other areas of racial disparity. The struggle to industrialize the United States helped produce the large independent corporation, the economic institution that distinguished the American economy from others. The limited tools of the national and state governments encouraged policies that nurtured the national expansion of free markets, but impeded efforts to mitigate the consequences of that expansion for economically vulnerable Americans.

The third part of the book, "The Construction of Active Government," shows how federalism has influenced the path of government growth since the beginning of the twentieth century. Chapter 6 shows that reform-minded progressives, constrained by existing limits on national power, made a virtue of the necessity of federalism. Their national, state, and local reforms changed public policy, while they widened the gaps among the states and fragmented policy further. The seventh chapter shows how the New Deal pushed for nationalized policy with more success than the progressives. The New Deal designed most of its permanent national initiatives to layer national activism on top of state discretion. Chapter 8 explores the way that liberals in Congress and the White House used federalism to extend rights, regulations, and equal opportunity in a variety of areas in the 1960s and 1970s, and the way that some of these efforts bypassed the state governments. These national efforts, and the difficulties of national-state cooperation, sparked substantial political dissatisfaction with the liberal agenda. Chapter 9 shows that conservatives ascended to power with the election of Ronald Reagan and utilized federalism strategically to achieve different goals. These conservatives, however, expanded Federal government power as often as they decentralized it.

The final chapter argues that liberals and conservatives, Democrats and Republicans, still use federalism principally as an expedient tool to deal with difficult issues such as corporate behavior, the environment, education, abortion, and civil rights. It reassesses the arguments for federalism, concluding that American federalism has shored up democracy and fostered market-driven economic development, but has had ambiguous consequences for rights, innovation, responsiveness, efficiency, and effectiveness. It also has hindered efforts to mitigate the consequences of economic growth. For the foreseeable future, federalism will continue to shape American democracy, prosperity, and public life by organizing politics into two battlefields, sustaining divided power despite fundamental change, and shaping the results of most of the divisive conflicts in the nation.

Part I

Bringing American Federalism to Life

2   Federalism at the Founding

No one at the Constitutional Convention of 1787 fully anticipated or welcomed the federal framework they placed in the U.S. Constitution. The specific rules of American federalism in that document resulted from the delegates' conflicts over the direction of American political development. Most of the Constitution's framers were skilled republican politicians who agreed that the national government needed more power, but they strongly disagreed about how much power the national government needed, and how much power the states should keep. Supporters of broad nationalism, like James Madison of Virginia, aimed to create a very powerful national government, exercising complete power to tax, govern commerce, and defend the nation. These delegates sought to reduce the states to a small, secondary role in American government. Supporters of narrow nationalism, like Roger Sherman of Connecticut, insisted that the new national government needed only a few additional, limited powers. They believed that the states should continue to govern most of American life, and that the national government should supplement, not supplant, most of the existing powers of the states.

These clashing visions produced a federal framework built by a series of political compromises that included elements of both broad and narrow nationalism. Advocates of narrow nationalism won many limitations on national power and protections for the states, while supporters of broad nationalism won many new national powers and elastic authority that could be expanded to meet future national needs. The Constitution gave the national government the tools to manage national sovereignty, but made it difficult for the national government to use these powers. It gave the states the power to manage everyday American life, but it amputated some of the states' tools for dealing with public problems. The Constitution left the dividing line between national and state power ambiguous, inviting endless political conflict over the rules of federalism in the United States.

The Self-Governing States in 1787

By 1787 the states were strong, vigorous, independent-minded political societies. Most were more than a century old. Physically isolated from the

British monarch and distant from one another, the colonies gradually established their own taxes, judicial systems, and laws governing commerce, crime, and morals. Long accustomed to such self-rule, the colonies readily declared their independence and transformed themselves into separate, self-governing republics even while they battled the British. Eleven states adopted a new, written constitution laying out the basic rules for exercising state government authority (Rhode Island and Connecticut continued to govern under their written colonial charters of the 1660s, which had established a strong measure of self-government). Each state mounted its own military defense, maintained internal order, and established its own tariff, currency, land, trade, and debt policy. Each created relatively democratic governments in which a large share of white males could elect the state legislators who made state laws.[1]

But because each state's history, economy, and culture differed from the rest, each state had different—sometimes opposing—political interests. The Southern states (Georgia, South and North Carolina, and Virginia) nurtured a plantation economy. These states had extensive, fertile lands and a long growing season, and so grew vast quantities of crops like tobacco, rice, and indigo to ship in bulk abroad. These crops, in turn, encouraged large plantations, and the plantations became dependent on slaves. In the middle states (Maryland, Pennsylvania, Delaware, New Jersey, and New York), smaller farms raised more diverse crops, and manufacturing began to develop. New England had relatively poor soil and a harsh climate that made farming more difficult and less profitable. Compared to the South, New England governments fostered fishing, shipbuilding, and commerce to supplement agriculture.[2] By the 1780s, American leaders recognized that New England and the South already had fundamentally different, and conflicting, interests driven by climate, slavery, commerce, and culture.[3] But many other conflicts among the states cut across these issues. Delaware, Rhode Island, Connecticut, and New Jersey resented the abundant lands that the geographically large states, such as Virginia and Pennsylvania, had at their disposal. The slave *trade* divided the South: Georgia and South Carolina demanded more slaves and the continuation of the slave trade, but Virginia and North Carolina already had an adequate population of slaves and were much more supportive of banning the slave imports. States with large ports, such as Philadelphia, New York, and Boston, angered their neighbors in Connecticut, New Jersey, Delaware, and Maryland, whose farmers had to ship and receive goods through these ports and pay other states' taxes.[4]

In the mid-1780s, the states' diversity and self-serving policies seemed to be breaking the newly independent nation apart. States seemed to benefit themselves at the expense of other states and the nation. An acute economic slump in the 1780s made the problem worse. In response to angry voters, several states relaxed debtors' obligations to lenders and liberally printed paper money. Rhode Island legally limited interest rates, printed an enormous amount of paper currency, and punished creditors who refused to accept this paper money for debts. Creditors in Rhode Island and in other states were outraged. Massachusetts pursued a much more cautious policy, keeping taxes high and enforcing debt obligations. Local sheriffs foreclosed on financially strapped small farmers who could not meet their obligations. Here, anger spilled over into outright rebellion when Revolutionary war veteran Daniel Shays led a small army of outraged western Massachusetts debtors in seizing towns and burning courthouses. Shays's Rebellion seemed to foreshadow a firestorm of anarchy across the nation.[5] Some leaders and newspapers anticipated the crackup of the nation and its reorganization into smaller confederacies.[6] Like other prominent leaders, George Washington blamed the state governments. Their pursuit of narrow self-interest was making "the situation of this great Country weak, inefficient and disgraceful."[7]

Instead of grappling with these problems, the national government seemed paralyzed by them. The Articles of Confederation of 1781 had established national governing authority in a Confederation Congress. The Articles, however, severely restricted Congress's powers. Each state cast a single, equal vote in the Congress, and the rules allowed a few states or even a single state to block Congress from taking action. Only an extraordinary majority of nine states could enact any major defense or financial policies, and only a unanimous vote of the states could change the Articles. The Confederation government had no executive and no court system. Unlike the states, Congress could not impose taxes (though it could borrow money). Its funding depended on "requisitions," that is, requests to the state governments that the states provide Congress with a particular amount of funding. Congress had no power to compel the states to pay these requisitions, however, and by 1786, Congress was broke because states did not pay their share. Though a large majority of states supported efforts to authorize the Confederation Congress to generate revenue by taxing imports, individual states objected to these plans and killed these proposals by denying them a unanimous vote. Powerful European nations posed a potential threat to the United States by land and sea, but Congress could not defend the nation effectively because it could not pay for an army and navy.

Broad and Narrow Nationalism at the Constitutional Convention

By 1786, many American leaders believed that it was urgent to strengthen the national government. Public support was growing for Constitutional changes that could strengthen property rights, increase national security, and stabilize the economy.[8] An inconclusive meeting in Annapolis, Maryland in 1786 called for a Convention of states in Philadelphia in the next year to "render the constitution of the Federal Government adequate to the exigencies of the Union."[9] All the states except Rhode Island sent delegations to the Constitutional Convention, which met from late May to mid-September, 1787.

Fifty-five prominent political leaders, chosen by their state governments, participated in the Constitutional Convention. State governments chose these delegates to be trustworthy stewards of their own interests as well as those of the nation. Nearly all the delegates had served in state legislatures, and some had served as state governor, attorney general, Supreme Court justice, or other prominent state office. Over half had represented their states in the Confederation Congress. The most active leaders of the Convention occupied most of their time with politics and government. Many, such as thirty-six-year-old James Madison and thirty-year-old Alexander Hamilton, were rising young political leaders, ambitious to build and lead a more potent national government.[10] Most went on to prominent careers in the national government they created.[11]

Broad Nationalism

Some of the delegates insisted that the national government be given broad and strong authority to exercise all the important powers of government, and that the states should be reduced to a minor role in American governance. James Madison of Virginia was the chief spokesman for this broad nationalism. Madison had been battling to increase national government power since his arrival in the Confederation Congress in 1780.[12] A skilled and experienced political leader as well as a natural political strategist, Madison believed that the states' autonomy, power, and selfish parochialism were the fundamental flaw in American government. The states were subverting the national interest, crowding out national power, and threatening basic rights.[13] For Madison, the state legislatures' schemes were the "great evils" about which Americans complained the most, and a new national government with broad national powers was the cure.[14] Madison tried to frame the Convention's fundamental choice in stark terms between two alternatives: "a perfect separation & a perfect incorporation, of the 13 States." If the states went their separate ways, "they would be independent nations subject to no law, but the law of nations" and would have "everything to fear from the larger states." But if the Convention recommended a single strong government, the states "would be mere counties of one entire republic, subject to one common law" and the small states "would have nothing to fear" from the larger ones.[15] He believed that the national government should control all commercial and military power, and should have the power to impose any taxes as needed.[16]

Madison was largely responsible for the Virginia Plan, a set of proposals for a complete restructuring of American government that was introduced at the very start of the Convention. The Virginia Plan proposed a revamped government and a vast expansion of national government power. A new national legislature, composed of two houses (eventually named the "House of Representatives" and the "Senate") would have the authority "to legislate in all cases to which the separate States are incompetent, or in which the harmony of the United States may be interrupted by the exercise of individual Legislation." It also would have the remarkable power to veto "all laws passed by the several States, contravening in the opinion of the National Legislature the articles of Union." Madison believed that this national veto was "absolutely necessary to a perfect system" to "control the centrifugal tendency of the States; which, without it, will continually fly out of their proper orbits and destroy the order & harmony of the political system."[17] Unlike the Confederation Congress, the seats in the new House and Senate would be distributed on the basis of population, so the larger the state, the more votes it could cast in each chamber. The voters, not state governments, would directly select members of the new House of Representatives, and the House then would choose U.S. Senators (from a slate of nominees put forward by state governments). Congress would choose the national executive and national judges, thus almost completely eliminating any state role in selecting national leaders.[18]

Madison's allies endorsed this broad nationalism and sharply criticized the states. Gouverneur Morris of Pennsylvania viewed "State attachments, and State importance" as "the bane of this Country. We cannot annihilate; but we may perhaps take out the teeth of the serpents."[19] For Alexander Hamilton of New York, the United States could not create a true national government unless the states surrendered all their authority to the nation. "The general power, whatever be its form, if it preserves itself, must swallow up the State powers," said Hamilton. "Otherwise it will be swallowed up by them."[20] Charles Pinckney of South Carolina proposed to expand the national veto of state laws by authorizing the national government to veto "all laws" that the new Congress "should judge to be improper"; he emphasized that the states "must be kept in due subordination to the nation."[21]

Narrow Nationalism

But other delegates were just as determined to protect most of the existing state government powers and to grant only narrow, limited authority to the national government. These delegates aimed to shield most of the states' self-government that already had existed for decades, and that the states had strengthened since 1776. The advocates of narrow nationalism wanted a stronger national government, but they wanted specific, narrow new powers rather than the broad authority Madison sought. The national government, for example, should have the power to defend the nation when necessary, but the states should control the militias they already had constructed. The national government should administer commerce between the United States and other nations, and among the states, but the states should control commerce and taxes within their borders.

The most passionate opponents of broad nationalism represented the small, economically vulnerable states wedged in between populous Virginia, Pennsylvania, and Massachusetts. Leaders from New Jersey, Connecticut, Delaware, and Maryland, particularly Roger Sherman and Oliver Ellsworth of Connecticut, mounted the most tenacious opposition to Virginia's proposals. These delegates had legitimate worries. Their states lacked ample lands for expansion, good ports for trade, and a large population to ensure their future prosperity. A strong national government controlled by the large and Southern states could harm the rest. States with large ports like Boston, New York, and Philadelphia could legislate a monopoly for themselves, damaging their neighbors.[22] Any national commercial agreement with another nation could give special treatment to the products and industry of a particular state, and impair the market for the products of other states. Delaware's Gunning Bedford accused the Pennsylvania and Virginia delegates of wishing for a government in which their states "would have an enormous & monstrous influence." Bedford asked, "Will not these large States crush the small ones whenever they stand in the way of their ambitions or interested views?"[23]

These opponents of broad nationalism immediately questioned the Virginia Plan, and emphasized the importance of accepting the existing states as established polities that could not be cut out of the nation's fabric. The states "do exist as political Societies," said Connecticut's William Samuel Johnson, and "a Government is to be formed for them in their political capacity, as well as for the individuals composing them."[24] The states were entrenched in American life, with deep roots that could not be destroyed arbitrarily. These advocates of narrow nationalism soon argued that it was not only necessary to take the existing state governments into account, but also that the states were a great national virtue. The states, in their view, had thriving republican governments that American citizens enthusiastically embraced. Ellsworth insisted that the survival of republican government depended on maintaining the vital role of the states, and he doubted that republican government could exist on a national scale, or maintain the happiness of the citizens.[25] He also doubted whether the national government could deal adequately with the local tasks on which domestic happiness depended. Ellsworth said that from the states "alone he could derive the greatest happiness he expects in this life. His happiness depends on their existence, as much as a newborn infant on its mother for nourishment."[26]

The delegates devised a new form of federalism for the United States, using all their political ingenuity to agree on a series of specific compromises between broad and narrow nationalism. This struggle was fought out piecemeal, and no delegates expected the specific results. Two issues especially divided the Convention: the states' representation in Congress, and the extent of power required by the national government.

Inventing Shared State and National Sovereignty

At first, the advocates of broad nationalism seemed to have the upper hand because it was widely assumed that, by definition, sovereignty—public authority in a geographical area—was supreme and could not be shared among different governments. Conventional wisdom held that a new national government, then, would have full sovereignty in the nation, and this sovereign power could not be shared with the states.[27] Hamilton, for example, insisted that "Two sovereignties cannot co-exist within the same limits."[28] "There can be no line of separation dividing the powers of legislation between the State & General Governments," said John Dickinson of Delaware; it was "inevitable that there must be a supreme & august national Legislature."[29] Elbridge Gerry of Massachusetts "urged that we never were independent States ... The States & the advocates for them were intoxicated with the idea of their *sovereignty*."[30]

Proponents of narrow nationalism directly challenged this conventional wisdom, and advanced the innovative idea that the state and national governments should and could *share* sovereignty. Roger Sherman argued that the national government need only be given "power to legislate and execute within a defined province." National government authority should be limited to "defense against foreign danger" and internal upheavals, "treaties with foreign nations," and "regulating foreign commerce, & drawing revenue from it."[31] Two weeks into the Convention, representatives from Connecticut, New Jersey, Delaware, Maryland, and New York constructed an alternative to the Virginia Plan that proposed a power-sharing arrangement for the national and state governments. This "New Jersey" Plan (named for the home state of the delegate who initially presented it to the Convention) proposed to maintain the Confederation Congress, to add a national executive and a supreme court, and to authorize a limited set of new national powers very similar to those Sherman advocated. New Jersey's William Paterson defended the plan, linking state sovereignty to equal state representation in Congress. The success of the new government, said Patterson, depended on "the quantum of power collected, not on its being drawn from the States, or from the individuals," so that it did not matter which level of government exercised power.[32] These arguments moved some advocates of the Virginia Plan, such as Virginia's George Mason, to concede that the state governments required some Constitutional defense.[33]

When the Convention rejected the New Jersey plan, its supporters dug in and focused on protecting equal state representation in Congress. All the delegates believed that, if the state governments chose the U.S. Representatives and Senators, these legislators would serve as agents of state interests. Narrow nationalists viewed equal state representation as an essential safeguard for the less populous states, but broad nationalists saw it as a prescription for ensuring the parochialism that had brought the

Confederation to its knees. This debate on representation, meanwhile, gradually was forcing the delegates to clarify the novel concept of shared state and national sovereignty. If the states were to "retain some portion of sovereignty," they needed representation in Congress to preserve it.[34] By late June, even Madison's close ally James Wilson agreed that "There is a line of separation" between state and national powers.[35]

Once the delegates had accepted proportional representation in the House of Representatives, Oliver Ellsworth pressed harder for equal state representation in the Senate, summarizing the idea of shared national and state sovereignty with the phrase, "We were partly national; partly federal." For Ellsworth, "proportional representation in the first branch was conformable to the national principle & would secure the large States against the small," while "An equality of voices was conformable to the federal principle and was necessary to secure the Small States against the large."[36] Delegates like Benjamin Franklin were beginning to accept this logic.[37] On July 2, the Convention deadlocked on the issue and delegated it to a special committee. This committee (which included Sherman but not Madison) proposed the "Connecticut" or "Grand" compromise that included proportional representation in the House and equal state representation in the Senate. After much more wrangling, the Convention adopted this solution on July 16.

The approval of this compromise on representation, in turn, instantly made some delegates recoil from the idea of broad national power. Madison understood from the first that the issues of representation and authority depended on one another. He believed that, if the large states and the rapidly growing Southern states enjoyed more voting power in the new Congress than in the Confederation, their "principal objections" to transferring power from the states to the national government would disappear.[38] Madison specifically predicted that the failure of proportional representation in the Senate would cause the Convention to withhold "every effectual prerogative" of national authority.[39] On the day the compromise was accepted, Randolph observed that "all the powers" proposed for the national government in the Virginia Plan "were founded on the supposition that a Proportional representation was to prevail in both branches of the Legislature."[40] The next day, Gouverneur Morris feared that equal representation in the Senate "would mix itself with the merits of every question concerning the powers."[41]

As he anticipated, some delegates who had supported Madison now began to advocate narrow national powers and extensive state authority. Southern delegates were especially worried about their ability to protect slavery. When the Convention revisited earlier language that authorized Congress to "legislate in all cases to which the separate States are incompetent; or in which the harmony of the U.S. may be interrupted by the exercise of individual legislation," South Carolina's John Rutledge called for a committee that would enumerate national powers, to constrict national authority and leave existing state prerogatives in place.[42] The next day, Sherman urged the Convention to approve a list of enumerated national powers and to prohibit the national government from interfering "with the Government of the individual States in any matters of internal police which respect the Government of such States only, and wherein the General welfare of the United States is not concerned."[43] When a Committee of Detail drafted a preliminary Constitution in early August, it dropped the Virginia Plan's broad warrant for national authority, specified a list of specific powers authorized for the national government, and added another list of powers that the states were not allowed to exercise.

This Committee of Detail report seemed to end all hope for broad national authority. The powers enumerated were written into the final Constitution.[44] For the rest of the Convention, proponents of broad nationalism had to fight to show that national authority on any specific issue should be expanded, and state authority diminished. While Madison sought to make the states prove that their powers did not harm the nation's interest, the Committee of Detail draft decisively placed the onus on the national government to prove that it required specific powers to pursue the national interest. States would retain prerogatives not granted to the national government.

Dividing Power

The delegates, then, designed American federalism by compromising on a series of disagreements about the specific powers of the national government. Narrow nationalism prevailed in protections for state power to tax, maintain a militia, and commercial power. Broad nationalism prevailed in new national taxing, military, and commercial authority, and in flexible powers that could be expanded in the future.

The Convention turned shared sovereignty from a theory into a reality when the delegates decided how to divide important government powers. Slavery was the foremost example. Southerners defended slavery more tenaciously as proportional representation in the Senate slipped away. Pierce Butler of South Carolina insisted that "The security the Southern States want is that their negroes may not be taken from them, which some gentlemen ... have a very good mind to do."[45] Narrowing national power and protecting state prerogatives could protect slavery. As Abraham Baldwin of Georgia put it, slavery, as "one of" Georgia's "favorite prerogatives," was an issue "of a local nature" that should be out of the reach of the national government.[46] Three provisions in the Constitution protected slavery in the Southern states. First, Southern delegates nailed down enough Southern seats in the House of Representatives to hamper any congressional move to do away with slavery. Three-fifths of the Southern slaves would be counted as part of the state population when it came time to allocate seats in the House of Representatives.[47] This three-fifths rule was a straightforward political compromise between Northern states, which did not want slaves counted at all (a formula that would increase Northern House seats), and Southern states, which wanted the slaves counted fully (thus increasing Southern House seats). Second, the Convention protected the slave trade by providing that Congress could not stop it until 1808, thus allowing South Carolina and Georgia to import slaves legally for a generation. Third, the Convention protected slavery by adding a "fugitive slave" clause, a provision that slaves who ran away from their owners—even across state lines and into the North—had to be returned.[48]

The delegates also narrowed national power by protecting most of the states' taxing, commercial, and military powers. Although the Constitution banned states from interfering in commerce by taxing imports and exports, they protected the states' power to levy other taxes. As Sherman put it, the states "retain a concurrent power of raising money for their own use."[49] Similarly, national authority over commerce included commerce with other nations and among the states, but not commerce *within* the states, which would remain under state authority. Further, the Constitution restricted national power to favor one region over others by requiring that all national commercial rules be uniform across the country.[50] The delegates refused to authorize additional specific national powers to encourage economic development, such as the power to charter corporations, construct canals, and establish a national university.[51] Finally, supporters of narrow nationalism largely shielded state militias from national control. Sherman argued that these militias were crucial: "the States might want their Militia for defense against invasions and insurrections, and for enforcing obedience to their laws. They will not give up this point."[52] Sherman complained that the idea of national appointment of top militia officers was "absolutely inadmissible."[53] In the final Constitution, the national government was required to get state permission even to intervene in internal state rebellions.

Though the supporters of narrow nationalism won key battles to protect important state powers, advocates of broad nationalism won many key points as well. Most important, they ensured that the Constitution authorized the national government to expand its power substantially. First, the Constitution firmly established that it and national laws "shall be the supreme Law of the Land," binding judges and overriding state laws where state and Federal law conflicted. The national courts would serve as watchdogs, defending national supremacy against state incursions. Second, the Committee of Detail gave the national government potentially broad authority to make all laws "necessary and proper" for executing all its enumerated powers.[54] The delegates did not contest this "necessary and proper" clause, because it seemed essential to give the national government some latitude. George Mason refused to sign the Constitution because he worried that provision allowed Congress to "extend their powers as far as they shall think proper; so that the State legislatures have no security for the powers now presumed to remain to them, or the people for their rights."[55] Third, a committee that considered proposals for additional national powers recommended more elastic language, expanding national authority "to provide, as may become necessary ... for the well managing and securing the common property and general interests and welfare of the United States," in a way that would not "interfere with the Governments of individual States in matters which respect only their internal Police, or for which their individual authorities may be competent."[56] The committee that wrote the final Constitution expanded this "general welfare" clause and dropped any protection for state powers. The preamble to the Constitution also reflected a vision of broad national government responsibility "to form a more perfect union, to establish justice, insure domestic tranquility, provide for the common defence, promote the general welfare, and secure the blessings of liberty to ourselves and our posterity."[57] The delegates did not contest this language.

The Constitution broadened national power by authorizing far-reaching military, taxing, and commercial authority for the U.S. government. Though the delegates protected the state militias, they refused to impose strict constraints on the national military, and defeated an effort to limit its size.[58] The national government would levy tariffs, and the delegates expected that these tariffs would provide a strong financial foundation for the government. The delegates also authorized a very broad national "power to lay and collect taxes, duties, imposts and excises."[59] The delegates refused to prohibit or put a time limit on the national government's power to levy direct taxes. To be sure, these direct taxes (such as taxes on property) had to be levied equally on a per capita basis, and this rule made it more difficult to design a national direct tax that met the Constitution's requirements.[60] But the restriction that direct taxes be applied per capita did not apply to national excise taxes, that is, taxes on specific goods (such as alcohol).[61] By the end of the Convention, even the most engaged delegates found it hard to understand the limits of the national taxing power.[62] Finally, the Constitution protected national commerce by limiting the states' powers to interfere in commerce among the states, by stabilizing currency, and by providing for more conservative regulation of credit.

Ratification and the Tenth Amendment

When the Convention delegates made their Constitution public, most returned to their states to fight for its ratification. Critics of the Constitution (the "Anti-Federalists") slammed the document for proposing so powerful a national government, warning that it would evolve into a centralized tyranny if the Constitution were approved. In their view, the strengthened national government would not accept competition from the states, but would soon consolidate power and swallow up the states. They repeated the conventional wisdom that sovereignty could not be shared, and criticized the Constitution for lacking safeguards such as a bill of rights to protect the states and the people.[63]

These criticisms forced leading delegates to further defend the notion of shared sovereignty and to show how the states would and could defend their prerogatives under the Constitution. Madison contributed the most thoughtful defense of state authority in his essays in the *Federalist*, published to advocate ratification in New York. Writing anonymously under the pen name "Publius," Madison assured readers that the states were "regarded as distinct and independent sovereigns" in the Constitution. He also assured them that

> The State Governments will have the advantage of the [F]ederal government, whether we compare them in respect to the immediate dependence of the one on the other; to the weight of personal influence which each side will possess; to the powers respectively vested in them; to the predilection and probable support of the people; to the disposition and faculty of resisting and frustrating the measures of each other."[64]

Madison noted that "the powers delegated by the proposed Constitution to the [F]ederal government, are few and defined. Those which are to remain in the State governments are numerous and indefinite."[65] Ellsworth, writing as "A Landholder," wrote that "State representation and government is the very basis of the congressional power proposed," and that the powers given placed "into the hands of your [F]ederal representatives," were general powers "such as must be exercised by the whole or not at all, and such as are absolutely necessary ... "[66]

Madison helped add the Bill of Rights to the Constitution, including the Tenth Amendment, another Constitutional defense for the states. When Virginia ratified the Constitution, it proposed an additional list of guarantees against national power, including a rule "that each state in the Union shall respectively retain every power, jurisdiction, and right, which is not by this Constitution delegated to the Congress of the United States, or to the departments of the [F]ederal government."[67] Madison promised the Virginia voters who elected him to the first House of Representatives that he would propose a similar bill of rights, and he did so a month after the new Congress began its session. Madison's list of rights included a version of the protection for the states, and his suggestion became the Tenth Amendment: "The powers not delegated to the United States by the Constitution, nor prohibited by it to the States, are reserved to the States respectively, or to the people." This amendment seemed to strengthen the case that the national government bore the burden of proof for exercising any authority not enumerated in the Constitution. But the Tenth

Amendment provides no guidance about the precise boundary between state and national power. Madison himself did not think this amendment was necessary at all.[68] Subsequently, opponents of expanded Federal power have used other provisions of the Constitution, rather than the Tenth Amendment, as the basis of their arguments.[69] The Tenth Amendment, then, did little to settle but much to encourage conflicts over the legitimate authority of the national and state governments.

The Constitution of Power in American Federalism

While many ideas and philosophies shaped the framers' notions of federalism, the specific Constitutional provisions that established the foundations of American federalism, then, were the product of power struggles at the Constitutional Convention.[70] More than anything else, the delegates aimed to build governing institutions that would shape the use and pursuit of power in the future. They knew these institutions would, in turn, create opportunities for those Americans who wanted to pursue and use government power. Because a series of ingenious and expedient compromises produced American federalism, it is futile to try to find a single, logical blueprint for federalism in the Convention debates or the Constitution. In the end, advocates of both broad and narrow nationalism could claim some success in its design, because they had created a government that was "partly federal, partly national." Madison described this new form of federalism as "compound republic" in the *Federalist*.[71]

The key to understanding the original design of this compound republic lies in the way it distributed the tools of government power between the states and the national, or as it quickly became known, the Federal government. American federalism distributed the tools of everyday governing to the states, allocated the tools of sovereignty to the national government, injected state interests into national politics and policy-making, and created a double political battleground in American politics.

States' Powers: The Tools of Everyday Governing and their Limits

First, the Constitution allowed the states to keep the powers of everyday governing, that is, to retain most of the policy tools for governing everyday American life. During the ratification debates, "A Freeman," writing in support of the Constitution, pointed out how extensive these tools were. States would retain power over taxes (except on imports or exports), militias, criminal law, property, and contracts, "corporations civil and religious," and the creation of cities, counties, courts, schools, "poor houses, hospitals, and houses of employment." They could regulate vices, manage politics and elections (including elections to national office), promote their own manufactures, and build roads and canals.[72] Within their borders, then, the state governments had power over labor (including slave labor), capital, land, natural resources, and energy—all the basic elements of a productive economy. With the blessing of the Constitution, then, the individual state republics had the power to manage and nurture the growth of social relationships, their economies, and their politics.

The states' powers in the compound republic, in turn, profoundly shaped every major step in American political development. Most of the major public policy conflicts of American history, whether over race, economic development, political reform, social welfare, education, health, the environment, or dozens of other explosive issues, initially have been fought out at the state and local level because states had the power to deal with them. Since each state had different resources, cultures, histories, and many other qualities, each state has done things differently. The power to make policy is the power to do things differently. As political scientist Aaron Wildavsky wrote, federalism is all about inequality: the encouragement of diversity "lies at the heart of federalism. ... It is inequality of result, not merely in income (some states choosing high tax, high services, others the opposite) but also in lifestyle, that distinguishes federalism as a living system from federalism as a front for a unitary power."[73] Thus some states apply capital punishment for crimes, or discourage trade union organization, or ban gay marriage, while others do not. American public policy is fragmented and varied as a result of this state power.

Moreover, because the states lacked the full set of powers that sovereign national governments always have used to respond to these conflicts, state policies have been more limited than policies abroad. The Constitution amputated important powers of sovereignty that nation-states could use. These policy tools included printing money, taxing imports, and restricting trade. Immediately after the Convention ended, Sherman and Ellsworth explained how these clauses worked together to protect free markets:

> The restraint on the legislatures of the several states respecting emitting bills of credit, making any thing but money a tender in payment of debts, or impairing the obligation of contracts by ex post facto laws, was thought necessary as a security to commerce, in which the interest of foreigners, as well as of the citizens of different states, may be affected.[74]

National governments have used these powers to balance the costs and benefits of national policy. These tools also can delay, shift, or even conceal the adverse impacts of public policy. American states were denied a full toolbox of policy instruments, and without them, states—the principal economic policy-makers for most of American history—found that any policy that harmed businesses or interfered with markets had much more immediate, visible, and politically costly effects than the same policies enacted by a national government that could make use of the full range of economic tools. The Constitution exposed each state to national market competition from enterprises in other states, and it largely prohibited each state from inhibiting the expansion of the American market economy. State policy-makers, then, came under strong pressures to help private enterprise and facilitate market-driven economic growth. Businesses quickly and routinely complain about any regulation or tax that seems to disadvantage them in national competition. Sometimes, these businesses threaten to move to other states with more favorable policies. From the beginning, then, the short-term interests of entrepreneurs and speculators weighed very heavily in most state decisions about taxes, business regulations, land use, and natural resources.[75]

National Power: The Powers of National Sovereignty and their Limits

Second, the Constitution authorized the national government to exercise the powers of national sovereignty, that is, the tools of diplomacy, commerce, and national security exercised by other sovereign national governments. The Federal government could go to war, build alliances, and manage trade to the advantage of the nation. But the Constitution did not give the national government the full toolbox of policy powers needed for managing the development of the nation, its politics, and its economy. States, not the national government, had and kept the power to govern their own culture, politics, and economy. Because Federal policy-makers lacked the authority to regulate everyday life, they gradually learned to use Federal revenues as an instrument for exercising a limited measure of national action. Federal grants-in-aid to the states aimed to induce state governments across the nation to undertake new policy activities in specific fields (see Chapters 6 and 7).

The compound republic also made political cooperation difficult to build and maintain across the whole nation. The Constitution's framers deliberately infused federalism thoroughly into the institutions of national policy-making. The delegates built a national policy process that assumed and encouraged robust republican politics organized around state and local interests. National institutions supported different, sometimes conflicting policies because they represented different geographical interests in different ways. The U.S. House of Representatives, elected every two years, constructs public policy around a majority of relatively short-term, sub-regional interests. The U.S. Senate, elected by states for six-year terms, constructs public policy around a majority of state interests. Only an extraordinarily large geographical majority could win approval in both the House and Senate for any public policy measure. No law could be passed in the 1st Congress without, at a bare minimum, the consent of representatives of fifty-five percent of the American population.[76] Additionally, the state-based Senate plays a larger role in governing than the House because it alone approves treaties and presidential appointments. The Constitution, then, created a complicated national government that protected the delegates' diverse state constituencies by filling the policy process with potential veto points: the Senate and House effectively could veto each other, and the president could veto any bill on which they could agree.

The Unsettled Boundary of Government Powers

Third, the unsettled dividing line between state and national power animated substantive political struggles throughout American history. The politicians who negotiated American federalism deliberately left the power-sharing details blurry and the line between state and national authority imprecise. They left the ensuing boundary disputes for future politicians to work through. The framers of the Constitution therefore built enduring conflict over federalism into the government by authorizing both the states and the national government to expand future policy and by leaving the boundary between state and national authority so ambiguous. Madison expected such conflicts, and in the *Federalist* essays, he celebrated this potential conflict as a check on national power.

> In a single republic, all the power surrendered by the people is submitted to the administration of a single government; and the usurpations are guarded against by a division of the government into distinct and separate departments. In the compound republic of America, the power surrendered by the people is first divided between two distinct governments, and then the portion allotted to each subdivided among distinct and separate departments. Hence a double security arises to the rights of the people. The different governments will control each other, at the same time that each will be controlled by itself.[77]

Here, Madison argues that the states can check the national exercise of power, and invites them to do so. This ambiguity, combined with the provision that states would exercise powers not specifically granted to Congress, "amounted to a standing invitation to contest the [F]ederal government's power," according to historian Ronald P. Formisano.[78] "The political logic of federalism," concludes legal historian Herbert Wechsler, "thus supports placing the burden of persuasion on those urging national action."[79]

The Double Battleground of American Politics

Fourth, this unsettled frontier of power, combined with political conflict over the control of power, turned American federalism into an arena of political conflict. The Constitution's prestige as the nation's source of fundamental law, combined with its ambiguity, has made federalism an irresistible battleground in American political conflict because it gives political adversaries the incentive and the opportunity to use the Constitution as a shield and a sword. Those who oppose more national power to deal with a particular problem often have invoked specific constitutional provisions as a shield against interference with state prerogatives, as has often happened in racial or economic development disputes in American history. Those who want change often invoke national supremacy and elastic power as a sword to establish national prerogatives against the states.

These contested provisions have divided and complicated American government and politics by creating a double battleground. The first battleground—the political battleground that exists in every nation—involves whether the government should act to deal with a public problem or not. In every nation, many fundamental political battles are fought over whether the government should do something about health, welfare, the economy, morals, or any of the thousands of specific situations that some define as a public problem deserving government attention. But the second battleground turns on which level of government should have the power to choose whether to act. As the following chapters make clear, this second alternative has had a far-reaching impact on the nation's evolution.

The Framers' Legacy

The Constitution's framers created a resilient republic that has endured wrenching social change, economic catastrophe, war, and extraordinary growth. This resilient republic was a political compound: the Federal government had the authority to lead the nation into its future, while the states kept the authority to maintain most of the governing arrangements that existed when the Constitutional Convention met. Advocates of narrow nationalism won a limited, enumerated list of national powers, state control of substantial policy authority, and political weapons that states could use to fight the unwanted aggregation of national power. Advocates of broad nationalism won some explicit new national powers with elastic potential, a Constitutional guarantee that national law would be supreme, and Constitutional language that could be used to expand national power on a case-by-case basis.

A century later, Woodrow Wilson explained that Constitution's unfinished framework of federalism shaped the development of America fundamentally.

> The question of the relation of the states to the [F]ederal government is the cardinal question of our constitutional system ... It cannot, indeed, be settled by the opinion of any one generation because it is a question of growth, and every successive stage of our political and economic development gives it a new aspect.[80]

Meanwhile, Americans were forging this unfinished Constitutional framework into a set of weapons for conducting political warfare.

3 Federalism, Political Parties, and Interests

Politics energized the new U.S. government that convened in 1789, just as it had energized the states before the Constitution took effect. Over the next two centuries, those who sought to use the new government built alliances with others, organizing themselves into coalitions that could apply more pressure to the different parts of government. Sometimes great social movements consisting of a fervent mass of people arose almost spontaneously and swept across the national landscape. The strongest social movements, such as the Populist movement of the late nineteenth century or the civil rights movement of the twentieth, compelled government to respond. But such social movements are too rare, and often too unfocused and fleeting, to energize government action over the long term. In a *republican* government like the United States, political parties and interest groups have been much more durable forces that organize demands for government action. Even in its infancy, American government encouraged parties and pressure groups to emerge.

But while its republican features fostered political parties and pressure groups, federalism rewarded political organizations that were fragmented and decentralized. The federal system's distribution of policy-making authority made it difficult for political parties and interest groups to centralize their power around a clear, broad national program. Parties and interest groups naturally had to focus on influencing the diverse state and local governments that governed everyday life. In response to federalism, political parties became nationally diverse, poorly disciplined, internally divided, united more by office-seeking than a clear agenda for using government power. While federalism encouraged parties that were too broad to pursue coherent national programs, it rewarded those pressure groups that focused on very limited policy goals. The American political system thus encouraged "pluralism," an interest group system in which many relatively narrow interests compete to influence limited slices of government activity. Federalism, in short, contributed to the development of political parties that were too broad, and pressure groups that were too narrow, to stand for a clear, wide-ranging national policy agenda.

The Constitution and Political Factions

By building a *republican* national government for a people with many diverse and sometimes clashing interests, the Constitution's framers deliberately installed politics as the engine of the government machine. In a republic, the people rule. If the people disagree among themselves about the things government should do, republican theory mandates that a *majority* of the people should determine what government does. But majorities do not form automatically. Political leaders must build coalitions of legislators to create a majority, and organize voters to support these legislators by electing them to office. Politics, then, brings American government alive, energizes it, and makes it work. Vibrant, dynamic republican politics already permeated American state legislatures in 1787.[1] Individual legislators each represented different constituencies within each state, and each constituency had somewhat different interests from the others. Groups of these state legislators organized into thriving political factions. The Constitution's framers fully expected the new government to work the same way.

But these factions deeply troubled the Constitution's framers, because factions often abused power when they took control of government. During the Constitutional Convention, James Madison observed that any civilized society naturally divided itself "into different Sects, Factions, & interests, as they happened to consist of rich & poor, debtors & creditors, the landed, the manufacturing, the commercial interests, the inhabitants of this district, or that district, the followers of this political leader or that political leader, the disciples of this religious sect or that religious sect." When these factions become a majority "united by a common interest or passion," they would endanger the rights of others.[2] Wicked schemes to gain majority power would be common in the new government, as they were common in the states. Alexander Hamilton warned that "When a great object of Government is pursued, which seizes the popular passions, they spread like wild fire, and become irresistible."[3]

Political factions were inevitable, but Madison believed that federalism and the separation of powers would fragment the government so thoroughly that these factions would find it hard to use the government for their selfish, destructive purposes. In the *Federalist*, Madison argued that these two institutional firewalls reduced the danger that a selfish political faction would gain control of government and abuse public power. Within the national government, members of the House, the Senate, and the executive branch would have the power and the motive to block other branches that might be controlled by a faction. It would be very difficult for one faction to overcome the separation of powers to achieve a majority in the House and Senate, and at the same time control the presidency and the Supreme Court. Federalism provided an equally important firewall against factions. The states and the national government would have the power and the motive to check each other. In the United States, a nation with such a "great variety of interests, parties, and sects ... a coalition of a majority of the whole society could seldom take place on any other principles than those of justice and the general good," that is, on an interest so widely shared that it would generate little or no disagreement in any of the separate jurisdictions.[4] Federalism could help factions resist national power and public policy, and advance their interests at the state level.

Madison emphasized that the states would fight the national abuse of power, and that the states enjoyed many advantages in any such fight. First, the U.S. Senate, the House of Representatives, and even the presidency each would "owe its existence more or less to the favor of the State governments" because of states' influence in selecting the people who filled these offices. These elected national officials would need to maintain political support within their states. Second, because states would do most of the governing in the nation, citizens frequently would encounter state and local officials, and rarely deal with national officers. State government, then, naturally would enjoy more citizen loyalty in any conflict with the national government. Third, because the members of Congress would owe their careers to the states, and because of the people's attachment to the states, the members of Congress inevitably would be motivated by a "local spirit," or a parochial sensibility. Members of the House and Senate would kill proposals that intruded too heavily on the states. Congress would lack the motive "to invade the rights of the individual states, or the prerogatives of their governments." Madison worried—with justification— that "[m]easures will too often be decided according to their probable effect, not on the national prosperity and happiness, but on the prejudices, interests, and pursuits of the governments and people of the individual States." Finally, the states could defeat the expansion of national power when they desire to do so, because objectionable national action would arouse anger in both the citizens and the state officials who owed their offices to these constituents. State officials could refuse to cooperate, build coalitions of resistance to national power, work to defeat legislators who supported undesirable national initiatives, and act in other ways that would make the unwanted usurpation of state powers politically suicidal.[5] Federalism, in short, would be a crucial obstacle to national political cooperation.

Federalism as a Central Battlefield of American Politics

As Madison expected, federalism became a major battlefield in American politics, a site of nearly every important conflict over the use of government power in American history. American federalism is a political battlefield because it widely disperses public authority and political opportunity, unlike a fully centralized government that concentrates power.[6] State public offices have different powers than national offices, and state office-holders use their power in different ways than national policy-makers. Since each state has distinctly different constituencies, cultures, leaders, histories, and economic situations, state officials confront different political opportunities in each state, and they guide each state government toward policies that differ in some ways from other states. For example, in a state with con-servative voters, such as Utah, state officials have pursued conservative policies, while Massachusetts officials, with a much more liberal electorate, have pursued more liberal policies than Utah. If the states are responsible for implementing public policy, the resulting policy effort across the nation is likely to be more varied, and on the whole different, than a public policy implemented nationally by the Federal government.

State policy discretion produces unequal outcomes.[7] The more states control government action, the more a given public policy will differ geographically. Some states ban concealed weapons, for example, while others allow citizens to carry concealed weapons. State governments have significant discretion in implementing unemployment compensation, even though it is part of the U.S. Social Security Act. Because each state has a different set of qualifications, benefits, taxes, and rules for unemployment, compensation differs in important ways across the country.[8] In contrast, the Federal government completely runs the Social Security Old Age, Survivors, and Disability Insurance (OASD) Program, and its benefits and rules are the same across the nation.

Because state-controlled public policy decisions tend to produce different results than nationally-directed policy decisions, any political faction that wants to influence policy in the United States can fight on two political battlefields: first, the usual political battlefield in all nations, whether government should act, and how; and second, the political battlefield in a robust federal system like the United States, whether and how much authority the *national* or the *state* governments should exercise over public policy. Today, for example, while many opponents of abortion would prefer a national ban on the practice, they have become adept at lobbying for state laws that complicate and discourage abortions, such as Nebraska's law restricting abortion after twenty weeks of pregnancy. Many envir-onmentalists turned their attention from the national to the state level to advance environmental protection laws after Republicans won a majority in the U.S. House of Representatives in 2010.[9]

American political opponents routinely choose to fight on the second of these battlefields, over the role of the states versus the national government, because they are likely to get better results at one level of government than the other. For example, in the mid-nineteenth century, abolitionists suc-cessfully pressured for laws in Northern states that defied Federal laws requiring fugitive slaves to be returned to their owners. A century later, leaders in the Southern states countered demands for a national law ending racial segregation by denouncing national interference with state segregation laws and asserting "states' rights." These civil rights conflicts show how opponents use federalism to reframe issues as conflicts over national rules versus "local control." Federalism allows one side to narrow the scope of conflict to the states, and potentially to a few states rather than all of them.[10]

The political battlefield of federalism thus has shaped both the *tactics* of many American political conflicts as well as the *results* of those conflicts. States are not just laboratories of policy innovation, but laboratories of political innovation as well. Political combatants can use their state experiences to test out new means for achieving their ends, through new allies, new ways of framing issues, and new ways to mobilize voters. Often, conflicts that are fundamentally about the scope of government power in other nations have been displaced in the United States by the tactic of framing the conflict as a fight about which level of government should have authority. American federalism has redirected enormous time, money, and energy into such contests over state versus national government authority. In 2010, for example, conservative state attorneys general who opposed the Obama administration's proposed national health care plan challenged it in court as, among other things, an unconstitutional expansion of national power.[11] Liberal lawyers argued just as forcefully that the proposed mandate was constitutional.[12] Sociologists David Meyer and Suzanne Staggenborg point out that in a federal system "conflicts can be prolonged for a very long time as switches in venue make it very difficult for one opposing movement to vanquish the other."[13]

The political struggle at the heart of conflicts over federalism is the struggle for control over the use of government, and the results of government action. As legal scholar Herbert Wechsler put it, "Federalism would have few adherents were it not, like other elements of government, a means and not an end."[14] "State's rights" inevitably became a major weapon in American politics because it makes a difference. The rest of this book shows that the conflict over the control of public policy in this battleground of federalism has been endless, vigorous, and bipartisan. Ideological liberals and Democrats are just as quick to invoke states' rights as conservatives, and ideological conservatives just as ready to invoke national uniformity and power, if it serves their political purpose. During the 2004 presidential election, for example, President George W. Bush, a conservative Republican, called for a national rule to ban gay marriage across the nation, while his liberal Democratic challenger, John Kerry, argued that the states should determine the rules for gay unions.[15]

Constructing Factions in the American Federal System

Some of the most sweeping national changes in American politics have occurred when there are sustained efforts by a large number of ordinary people to change the way authority is being used.[16] Such "social movements" have formed around the abolition of slavery before the Civil War, the grievances of farmers in the 1890s, women's suffrage in the early 1900s, and the civil rights movement of the 1960s. Social movements can pressure the national government and many state governments simultaneously. For example, prohibitionists strategically pressured local and state governments to restrict alcohol, eventually leveraging a Constitutional amendment prohibiting alcohol manufacture and sales nationwide.[17]

But social movements are the exception in American politics because they are hard to sustain. Federalism affords counter-movements many more opportunities to overcome, fragment, and block these social movements.[18] Often, when the initial social movements lose momentum or pass away, they leave behind change that is incomplete, uneven, and unfinished.

There are two much more durable ways of constructing factions. One way to construct a faction is to build a durable coalition of individuals who seek and hold public offices. These coalitions can evolve into stable political parties that organize Congress, the presidency, state legislatures, and state executive offices. Because they are organized around controlling the use of government, political parties develop broad policy agendas. A second way for interests to organize is to directly focus on the decisions made by key policy-makers. These factions can evolve into durable interest or pressure groups. These pressure groups generally seek much more specific government responses than do political parties, so they have narrower policy agendas, and do not seek direct control over offices with general, broad policy-making powers. Unlike political parties, then, interest groups do not run candidates for office (although they often provide support for specific candidates who support their policy objectives).

In the United States, federalism has powerfully shaped the development of both political parties and interest groups. First, American federalism impeded national cooperation among potential political allies. Second, it prolonged political conflict by providing opponents an additional set of venues in which to fend off challenges, develop counter-strategies, and obstruct the momentum of change. In part because of federalism, the United States failed to develop the coherent national parties and strong, inclusive, and centralized business and labor organizations that influenced governments in many other wealthy democracies in the twentieth century.

American Political Parties

In electoral democracies like the United States, political parties organize conflict, manage the competition for political office, help obtain popular consent for public policy, and organize the opposition to incumbents. Political parties are indispensable factions in any democracy because they offer voters competing coalitions of office-holders. Any political party consists of candidates who run for office under a common label, officials who are elected or appointed to office and adhering to this label, voters who regularly vote for the party's candidates, and officials who manage the party organization but are not in government. Political parties aim to win elective offices, build a majority in government, hold on to that majority in future elections, and use it to make public policies. Political parties can offer an agenda on a wide range of government choices, and they make the political choices more simple and government decisions more lasting. Without parties, legislative politics would be much more unstable, unpredictable, and chaotic.[19]

Parties grew muscular in the United States before they did in other nations because the United States allowed so many citizens to participate in politics so early in its history. State laws entitled more than half of adult white males to vote even at the time of the Revolution, and ninety percent of the adult white males met eligibility requirements in several states by 1788. Suffrage expanded further in the early nineteenth century. New states joined the union with nearly universal adult male suffrage, and older states gradually expanded the franchise in twenty-one of twenty-four states by 1824.[20] States removed remaining restrictions on white adult males by the 1840s, although state residency requirements, poll taxes, and voting restrictions for women and African Americans limited the electorate well into the twentieth century. Abroad, suffrage expanded much more slowly.[21] Political parties mobilized these mass electorates in the United States before they emerged in other nations.[22] Fueled by broad suffrage, the factions that already had emerged in American politics matured and greatly intensified the competition for control of government. A century ago, foreign observers marveled at the organizational sophistication of American political parties.[23]

In the twentieth century, however, political parties in many other industrializing democracies became much stronger, more disciplined, and more centralized than political parties in the United States. By the middle of the twentieth century, centralized parties united by a common policy agenda and strong party discipline were the norm in Western Europe.[24] Meanwhile, political scientist V.O. Key suggested that "Perhaps the outstanding characteristic of American party organization, viewed from the national aspect, is its decentralized nature."[25] In the 1990s, political scientist Kenneth Janda compared political party characteristics across nations and concluded that "American political parties are clearly less centralized than the European norm, and they are certainly among the most decentralized parties in the world."[26]

Federalism helps explain both the strength of nineteenth-century American political parties and the fragmentation of these parties in the twentieth century. American political parties naturally grew strong at the state and local levels rather than at the national level because state governments controlled most of the domestic policy in the nineteenth and early twentieth centuries. Because the states differed greatly over fundamental issues like slavery and economic development, political competition evolved differently in each state. But these parties did not change as dramatically as did European parties when politics transformed in the industrializing nations.

Federalism ensures a continuing political debate in American politics because it encourages state leaders to build an opposition to national officials. Because state politicians can build a career with the help of only a fraction of the nation's constituents—and only rarely a representative fraction— they have strong incentives to diverge from their own national party leaders and platforms when it serves their political purposes. Because the states have many independently elected executive offices, different state leaders can put forward several alternative agendas at the same time. For example, some state Attorneys General have been very active in promoting consumer protection, financial reform, and environmental protection.[27] As political scientist David Truman put it, federalism created state governments that offered political aspirants "separate, self-sustaining centers of privilege, power, and profit."[28] States organize conflict over most of the offices in the United States, including seats in the U.S. Congress, and also states manage elections. Collectively, political party successes in the states can provide "a sheltering place for the losing party" at the national level by allowing a party that loses the presidency and Congress to use state governorships, Attorneys General, legislatures, and other offices as a platform for criticizing the party holding power in Washington, and to develop policies and strategies to dislodge them.[29]

This robust federal political system, then, exerts a very strong decentralizing pull on party competition. In this way, federalism helps make it difficult to develop an agenda for using Federal power that party adherents all across the nation could accept. Party leaders often have kept their agenda for the Federal government to a minimum so that state and local parties could tailor their appeals and candidates to the specific interests and culture unique to each state. When the national government gradually expanded its domestic power in the twentieth century, the long-established state and local parties resisted the full surrender of political control to national party leaders.

The politics of federalism, then, has encouraged the parties to maintain the policy authority of state and local governments. When more centralized and disciplined national party organizations developed in other wealthy democracies in the twentieth century, the very decentralization that helped make American parties strong and modern in the nineteenth century made it much more difficult for American parties to follow suit. These patterns continue to be very difficult to overcome, despite determined and partially successful efforts by party leaders to centralize control over parties after 1968.[30]

As a result, economic, social, and other differences have rewarded state political parties for tailoring their programs to different state constituencies, so that the actual policy goals of a "Republican" or "Democrat" varies widely across the United States.[31] In Utah, Democrats can only win if they take positions attractive to the conservative, largely Mormon, electorate of that state. In Massachusetts, Republicans can only win if they can attract moderate to liberal Massachusetts voters. Some states like New York or Ohio have long been known for intense and balanced party competition. But until the 1960s, Southern states had one-party electoral systems in which a substantial proportion of economically disadvantaged white voters and most blacks were kept from voting. Southern Democrats had no need to promote popular democracy or policy reform in the Southern states. Conservative state policies therefore resulted from the absence of party competition in that region.[32]

Decentralized American parties, in turn, reinforced their geographical diversity using patronage appointments rather than a clear, coherent national platform to tie their national coalitions together. Political scientist Martin Shefter observed that the United States expanded mass democracy before it developed public bureaucracy that existed in many western European nations, a fact that encouraged party-building based on the control of public jobs. Abroad, professional administrators developed strong, independent, professionalized public agencies before the advent of mass democratization. In the intense competition of American politics, in contrast, parties at all levels became accustomed to building themselves and maintaining power through filling these administrative posts with party loyalists, and replacing incumbents whenever a new party took power. Patronage appointments helped these parties win and retain public offices in spite of their internal differences over divisive issues such as race. Thus, a decentralized spoils system rather than a fully developed and coherent policy agenda became the critical instrument for maintaining political parties in the United States. The control of offices provided the principal glue for holding each political party together.[33]

Observers in the nineteenth century recognized how much American political parties depended on patronage and how little on a unifying policy agenda. These observers found it very difficult to distinguish the policy positions of the Democratic Party from those of the Republican Party.[34] Stephen Skowronek later described American government in the nineteenth century as a "state of courts and parties" and little else. Political parties coordinated national government through their control of political appointments, while Federal courts—insulated from direct election—tried to define what state and local governments could do.[35]

The perception that American political parties lack broad, coherent policy programs remains common. Although political scientist John Gerring has demonstrated that the national parties have taken contrasting positions on some major issues for a century and a half, these areas are more limited than the policy platforms of parties in other democracies. Equally important, in comparison to most other nations, American national parties have little control over who is nominated for office, or over members who are unfaithful to even the most basic party positions.[36]

Federalism and the Development of the Parties

Federalism has played a crucial role in the development of two major American political parties since the 1790s. Strong and durable national political parties in the modern sense did not emerge in the United States until the 1830s, but by that time, factions of those seeking and holding office had been organizing at the national and state levels for decades.[37]

The Democrats

In the early 1790s, when Treasury Secretary Alexander Hamilton proposed an ambitious national economic program that threatened agricultural regions, Thomas Jefferson and James Madison used federalism to construct a faction to oppose him.[38] Madison argued that the states, not the national government, should manage most of American economic development.[39] When Congress debated Hamilton's proposed new national bank, Madison argued that the Constitution did not give the national government the power to create such a bank, that a national bank would interfere with state powers, and that it would set a precedent for even more national action at the states' expense.[40] After Madison failed to stop the bank, he and Jefferson set about to organize Hamilton's opponents more effectively; they made states' rights and national organization the cornerstone of this new political effort.[41] In newspaper articles, Madison urged all Americans who were "jealously attached to the separate authority reserved to the states" to work "to maintain the various authorities established by our complicated system, each in its respective constitutional sphere."[42] During the presidency of John Adams, this "Democratic-Republican" party mounted fierce opposition to the Federalists, the faction that coalesced behind Adams and Hamilton. Madison's Virginia Resolution of 1798 expressed his state's vehement opposition to the Adams administration's policies, declaring that national authority was limited to a list of specifically enumerated powers. When national officials abused their authority, states were "duty bound" to stop them, and to maintain "the authorities, rights and liberties appertaining to them." Virginia called on other states to join in declaring the objectionable actions of the Adams government unconstitutional.[43]

For these Democratic-Republicans, federalism offered a winning political formula. They united their coalition selectively by advocating low national tariffs to increase agricultural exports. They used "states' rights" to decentralize the divisive issue of slavery to jurisdictions in which different elements of the party could control policy outcomes. The doctrine of states' rights appealed to farmers and small entrepreneurs, and it nurtured a coalition across states with different political economies and at different points of development. States' rights in an agricultural nation also could promote a kind of equality, as least for white males—even though states' rights in the South inherently protected slavery, and Madison knew it.

As the party evolved into the Democratic Party led by Andrew Jackson and Martin Van Buren in the 1820s, it stood steadfast against the expansion of national power at the expense of the states—a position that cemented its coalition of the Southern planters and less affluent farmers and artisans in the North. In 1830, President Andrew Jackson vetoed a bill to construct a part of a national turnpike in Kentucky, and wrote a veto message that balanced regional interests in the party by keeping the need for national revenues—and the tariffs the Southern states opposed—to a minimum. At the same time, it limited national power to interfere with state governments' efforts to promote their own internal economic development.[44] For most of the rest of the nineteenth century, the Democratic Party continued to emphasize the states' autonomy and limited national government power.[45]

By the final years of the 1800s, this states' rights platform was causing internal problems for the Democrats. Large corporations and banks now seemed oppressive to many farmers, especially in the South, the Great Plains, and the West. Resentment among these farmers sparked "Populism," a social movement that demanded more national government intervention to protect the freedoms of the common man. In 1896, the Democratic Party embraced many of the principles of this Populist movement and expanded its coalition by seeking to extend the reach of the national government. Much of the activist public agenda of the Progressive Era, and many national reforms, including banking reforms, the income tax, antitrust, and farm, labor, and education measures, had roots in these agricultural movements.[46] But by no means did the Democrats abandon federalism and the states. The Democrats still protected the right of Southern states to enforce legal segregation, and many of their national initiatives underwrote state authority.

In the 1930s, President Franklin Roosevelt's New Deal simultaneously accelerated the expansion of national and state government activism. Roosevelt's administration nationalized the regulation of important sectors of the economy, such as stock markets, but it still left the states great responsibility. For example, the Roosevelt administration underwrote existing state arrangements for regulating the production of oil, the fuel that increasingly drove American prosperity. The New Deal laid the basis for a large, national program of Old Age insurance in the Social Security Act, but used grants-in-aid to the states to expand other social welfare programs. These grants allowed state diversity despite national action, notably in the South, where state governments could deliver New Deal programs without disturbing racial segregation.

Since the 1940s, the Democrats have broadened their commitment to use national power to advance social justice and equal opportunity. The party expanded the scope of its national agenda to address problems like poverty and discrimination.[47] The party gradually committed itself to civil rights for African Americans, a commitment that split its coalition. Southerners began to drift away in 1948, when a "States' Rights Democratic Party" (better known as the "Dixiecrats") temporarily broke from the national party. Gradually, the Democratic Party lost its long-lasting dominance in the South. Even during this period, many Democratic programs for government activism heavily depended on grants and delegated enforcement.

The Republicans

Andrew Jackson's Democratic Party initially drew organized opposition from the Whig Party, which was committed to a more active national encouragement of economic development. Slavery helped divide and wreck the Whig Party, however. In the 1850s, former Whigs such as Abraham Lincoln formed a new Republican Party that shared the Whigs' support for a strong national government that could foster economic expansion.[48] Its broad conception of national power allowed the Republicans, once in control of the presidency and Congress in the 1860s, to justify not only war against the Southern secessionists, but also to use Federal power to promote homesteading, continental railroads, and land grant colleges.[49] From the 1860s until the New Deal, Republicans cemented their coalition with high tariffs that protected manufacturing, the national enforcement of free markets, a strict monetary policy based on the gold standard, and Federal pensions for Civil War veterans.[50] Republicans used federalism strategically in these years. In 1876, Republicans withdrew Federal troops from the former Confederate states and permitted the Southern states to govern themselves. This policy allowed the Republican Party to focus on building its strength in the North and West, virtually abandoning the South to the Democrats.[51] Support for national power in the Republican Party peaked during the presidency of Theodore Roosevelt. In 1912, Roosevelt temporarily fractured the party by running for president as the candidate of the Progressive Party, whose platform promised a substantial expansion of Federal activism and criticized the Democrats for their "extreme insistence on States' rights."[52]

While twentieth century Democrats embraced a more active national government, the Republican Party grew increasingly critical of government activism, especially national government activism.[53] Republicans began to advocate more decentralization to the states, in part to blunt national activism and in part to relocate policy battles to the states, where their business allies exercised considerable power. After the New Deal, each Republican president who immediately succeeded a Democrat soon announced a major institutional initiative to redirect power and resources to state and local governments. From the 1970s, Republicans viewed decentralization as a tool for cutting back the welfare state and government activism.[54] At the same time, elements of the Republican Party advocated substantial expansion of national power for the military, for internal security, for the expansion of private markets, and for the protection of traditional social and religious values.[55]

Interest Groups

"A striking feature of American politics," wrote political scientist V.O. Key half a century ago, "is the extent to which political parties are supplemented by private associations formed to influence public policy."[56] These private "interest" or "pressure" groups are organizations that attempt to exercise power in the public policy-making process on behalf of their members. Traditional membership groups have individual members who share a common concern; examples include groups of teachers, doctors, farmers, retired people, environmentalists, civil rights advocates, opponents of abortion, and gun owners. Unlike political parties, these groups do not seek responsibility for running the government, and do not run candidates for office. Instead, these groups directly try to advance their interests by influencing the decisions of national, state, and local legislators, elected executives, administrators, and courts. Interest groups provide information and expertise about policy choices (sometimes, they even write legislation), press for government to give more attention to issues important to them, support government officials, offer campaign contributions and other support for those running for office, and monitor the implementation process. Often, interest groups are particularly effective in opposing and stopping some proposed government action. To achieve their policy goals, interest groups sometimes form coalitions with other groups or align themselves with one of the political parties.[57]

Interest groups have been strong and politically engaged since the beginning of the United States. Early in American history, foreign observers noticed Americans' inclination to join groups. Alexis de Tocqueville wrote that "In no country in the world has the principle of associations been more successfully used or applied to a greater multitude of objects than in America."[58] At the state level, businesses lobbied legislatures for canals, railroads, highways, bridges, and other beneficial public policies. New England cotton textile manufacturers lobbied Congress for favorable national tariff laws as early 1816.[59] Lobbyists kept Congress functional in the 1870s.[60]

By the late nineteenth century, groups at the state and national level pushed for more government action. In the 1870s, the Granger movement, organized by Midwestern farmers, successfully pressured states for laws regulating railroads and warehouses. Trade unions lobbied for new labor agencies and regulations across the nation. Interest group efforts to pressure government at all levels accelerated dramatically around the beginning of the twentieth century, an era of avid organization.[61] Sociologist Elisabeth Clemens showed how farmers, workers, and women effectively organized into pressure groups in this period.[62] Reformers in the 1910s, the 1930s, and the 1960s repeatedly turned to interest groups as a policy instrument that could surmount the parochialism of state and local governments and political parties. By the late 1920s, political scientists estimated that there were three hundred or more effective lobbying organizations in Washington, and the numbers increased with the activist government agenda of the New Deal years. By the 1960s, there were more than a thousand Washington lobbyists, and by the twenty-first century, there were over fourteen thousand (these lobbyists spent over three billion dollars to influence policy). The state capitals experienced a similar growth in lobbying.[63]

Federalism and the Development of the American Interest Group System

Federalism and the separation of powers have made it very difficult to construct and maintain strong, nationally disciplined interest groups with a broad, clear policy agenda. This institutional fragmentation has had particularly important consequences for the organization of the conflict between business and labor, "the mainspring of politics in most industrial polities."[64] According to political scientist Graham Wilson, the most fundamental distinction between the American interest group system and interest groups in comparable nations is its fragmentation, the relative weakness of American economic interests and the relative strength of other kinds of interests.[65] The Constitution helped narrow interest groups by weakening the political parties, allowing groups to focus on limited, specific policy aims instead of working within a larger, broader coalition.[66] In comparable nations, national organizations of business and labor became strong and powerful actors who influenced policy across a wide range of areas.

As American interest groups developed in the nineteenth century, they naturally strengthened at the state level, because states controlled most of the everyday governing in the nation. Typically, strong state organizations preceded the consolidation of national associations, and once strong statewide or functional organizations were in place, it was hard for many national organizations to leverage control over their activities.[67]

In the mid-twentieth century, with many states dominated by one political party and lacking experts in public service, political scientist Grant McConnell wrote that "a great number of interest groups and narrowly-based factions of different kinds have flourished to provide such political organization as most states have."[68] In some states, particularly the larger and wealthier states with a diversified economy, a well developed and competitive interest group system allowed a balance of power among interests, such as labor and business. In a few states, a single interest often dominated public policy, as did the Anaconda Company in Montana, the oil industry in Texas, the coal industry in West Virginia, the gaming industry in Nevada, and the Mormon Church in Utah.[69] Across the states, it appears that interests in the field of communications, manufacturing, health, legal services, and welfare services had expanded considerably by the end of the 1990s. In the last two decades of the twentieth century, "state interest communities" have "become increasingly crowded."[70] Groups that represent existing economic institutions, especially businesses and labor unions, often have had the most wide-ranging impact on the organization of politics.[71]

Business

Business generally is a powerful, and often a dominant, influence in public policy decisions in capitalist democracies. From the outset, federalism strongly shaped the development of American businesses' approach to politics. States governed almost everything that was crucial to business except for the national tariff. States granted businesses corporate charters and set the rules for basic business behavior. State and local laws also set the framework for the market—for contracts, for property, and for regulation. States governed the key means of production—the acquisition and use of land, rules about labor, and the terms of loans and debts.[72] States contracted with private concerns to develop roads, bridges, canals, railroads, and other infrastructure projects that fostered economic growth. While the nation industrialized, business grew politically influential at the state level.

Business interests are the strongest interests in the American states today.[73] In the twenty-first century, general business groups (such as a state chamber of commerce) rank as the most influential interests across the fifty states, followed by teachers' organizations (such as the National Education Association and American Federation of Teachers) and utility companies (such as electric, gas, water, and telecommunications companies).[74]

Federalism strongly influenced the features of American business that distinguished it from business in other wealthy democracies: the early emergence of the individual large corporation that could secure its policy interests independent of broad business alliances, and the relative weakness of collective action by businesses as a group. The corporations that were sheltered by state laws flourished in key industries, such as chemicals, oil, automobiles, steel and other primary metals, and paper. These large companies were bigger and more dominant in their industries than were comparable business enterprises abroad. As a result, the large American business corporation "effectively enjoyed a monopoly of the political and institutional power without parallel in the capitalist world in the twentieth century."[75] At the same time, the opportunities that federalism offered to individual businesses and industries also fractured business interests geographically and functionally. Business leaders in different states and regions and different industries had different interests, internally dividing business leaders across industries and within them.[76]

Because federalism helped fracture business interests, it weakened American businesses' incentives to cooperate in building strong "peak" organizations that would advocate a broad, coherent, and clear program of business priorities for national action. The "peak" organizations of

American business, such as the U.S. Chamber of Commerce, are much weaker than their counterparts in many European nations. Industrial relations scholar Rogers Hollingsworth viewed "weakness of associative institutional arrangements" as "the distinctive feature of collective governance in the American case."[77] At the end of the 1980s, despite two decades of efforts to strengthen their influence in national policy-making, American "peak" organizations remained fragmented, competitive, and lacking in authority.[78]

Organized Labor

Trade unions are the strongest and most durable counterweight to business influence in capitalist nations. As with business, federalism provided strong incentives for trade unions to organize in the United States in a way that left them fragmented geographically and functionally. States controlled trade union law until the 1930s, and states still have important powers to discourage union formation through "right to work" laws, which in twenty-two states ban a requirement that employees join a union or pay union dues. Like business, the decentralization of trade unions encouraged individual unions to pursue their own goals independent of other unions. Unions representing the railroad brotherhoods (the locomotive engineers, brakemen, firemen, and conductors) were among the strongest of the American unions, but they refused to join the American Federation of Labor (AFL), the supposed "peak" organization of labor founded in 1881. During the New Deal, several major unions, most notably the then powerful United Mineworkers of America, spun off the Congress of Industrial Organizations (CIO) because of fundamental differences with the craft-based AFL. The AFL and CIO merged in 1955, but rarely has the AFL-CIO represented all the major unions. Several large unions, such as the Teamsters and the Service Employees, formed "Change to Win," a rival of the AFL-CIO. In contrast, European central labor organizations, such as the British Trades Union Congress (TUC) and the German *Deutsche Gerwerkschaftsbund* (DGB), generally enjoy a monopoly status as trade union associations (though these peak organizations exercise varied degrees of control over their member unions).[79]

The fragmentation of trade unions, combined with laws in some states that discourage unions, helps explain why American unions have been weaker than trade unions in comparable nations. Continental European collective bargaining has tended to be more centralized, and therefore to provide security to a large majority of workers. Officials in European governments often play a more active role in brokering conflicts between employer associations and unions and in extending agreements industry-wide.[80] At the beginning of the 1990s, collective bargaining agreements covered fewer than one in five American workers. This percentage constituted less than half that of any other major member nation of the Organization for Economic Cooperation and Development (OECD) except for Japan.[81] Trade union weakness, in turn, has contributed to the distinctiveness of the American political party system.

Uniquely among the industrialized nations, no distinct "labor" or "socialist" party has ever received extensive, sustained electoral support in the United States.[82] Instead, federalism and the separation of powers taught American labor leaders to be opportunistic, supporting public officials of either party who support unions' agenda. By the early 1900s, the AFL generally tied itself to the Democratic Party, and organized labor has remained an important part of the Democratic coalition ever since.[83] But at the same time, organized labor has followed a policy of rewarding its friends and punishing its enemies, and has supported some Republican candidates where it is expedient. Individual unions, such as the railroad brotherhoods, coal miners, Teamsters and some of the building trades have supported Republican candidates more often and more enthusiastically.

Pluralism

The combination of so many different economic interests and the exceptional number and influence of non-economic groups makes for an unusually fragmented interest group system in the United States. Analysts commonly describe the American interest group system as "pluralistic," a system in which organized interests are much more numerous, narrow, dispersed, and competitive than is true in comparable nations.[84] Non-economic interest groups in the United States "have been mobilized on a scale unmatched in any other democracy," and "more successful in challenging economic interest groups than their counterparts in other countries."[85] This American interest system appears to have a "hollow core" that differentiates it from the interest group system in much of Europe.[86]

American federalism strongly reinforced this pluralism. As David Truman pointed out, "Groups that would be rather obscure or weak under a unitary arrangement may hold advantageous positions in the State governments and will be vigorous in their insistence upon the existing distribution of powers between States and nation."[87]

Pluralism, in turn, further has weakened American political parties, because pressure groups can fill the gaps left by the parties' inability or unwillingness to pursue clear, coherent, national agendas.[88] American pressure groups "do not consider the national parties critical factors in their attempts at policy influence" because they neither compete with nor consult with the parties with significant frequency.[89] Comparing analyses of group strength across several nations, Clive Thomas found that stronger political parties seem to co-exist with strong economic interest groups, notably business and labor, in nations as varied as Japan, Israel, Australia, New Zealand, Britain, and Sweden. Weak parties in the United States, in contrast, are related to its weaker and more fragmented economic interests and its more variegated system of non-economic interest organizations.[90]

Fragmented Parties and Interests

Parties and interest groups make republican government take action because they build majorities necessary for government decisions. Federalism is one of several factors that have contributed to the fragmentation of American political parties and interest groups. Other factors such as diverse economic interests, racial antagonisms, immigration, cultural variation, and relatively strong but diverse religious affiliations, also have complicated the development of political parties and pressure groups in the United States. The sequence of events that allowed patronage parties to take root before bureaucracy had a major impact on American party development.

American federalism has helped decentralize and narrow political organization in the United States, making it more difficult to construct majorities on behalf of a clear, coherent, wide-ranging political agenda. It contributed to relatively weak political parties, relatively narrow interest groups, and a relatively pluralistic political system. Parties and interest groups were essential for *sustaining* states' rights and federalism.[91] States still exercise a strong centrifugal force on both parties and interests. These distinguishing features of American politics, in turn, profoundly shaped American policy toward enduring and pervasive problems such as race and economic development.

Part II
Enduring Fault Lines of American Politics

4   Federalism and Race

Federalism's powerful influence on American political development is most clear in the enduring political battles about race and the government's role in the economy. These two issues have been the most basic, persistent, far-reaching, and passionate conflicts in American life. In turn, the relentless use of federalism in these conflicts legitimized it as a weapon in all other major conflicts. This chapter and the next focus on the way federalism affected the way the United States has grappled with these issues over its history.

Conflict over the place of African Americans in the United States has been an agonizing "American dilemma" for generations, from battles over slavery until the 1860s, then racial segregation and white supremacy until the 1960s, and remedies for the consequences of this history ever since. Race has permeated American politics from the beginning.[1]

Federalism has had three effects on the politics of race in America. First, it decentralized key choices about the status of African Americans. In the early American republic, slave owners used state government authority to strengthen their domination of slaves. But while slavery thrived in the South, it withered in the Northern states, where opposition to slavery inspired Northern state laws that defied it.

Second, federalism allowed the slaveholding states to prolong the exclusion of blacks for generations, even after abolition and the military defeat of the slave states in the nineteenth century. The Civil War settled the issue of state secession but it did not permanently remove the states' authority legally to subjugate African Americans, or the political incentives for the Democratic and Republican Parties to allow the Southern states to continue to subordinate their black residents. In the late nineteenth century, the former slave states all but eliminated the voting rights of blacks, and they segregated blacks into inferior roles in Southern society. The Federal government left the Southern states' racial order intact as it became more active in the first half of the twentieth century.

Third, federalism severely complicated efforts to overcome the cumulative consequences of this heritage, and helped produce widely varied results for the legal, social, and economic inclusion of African American citizens. As demands for an end to legal segregation gathered strength after World

War II, segregationists dug in behind the bulwark of "states' rights" to resist and delay these changes. The civil rights laws of the 1960s finally eliminated legal segregation, but the cumulative effects of decades of the legal subordination of blacks left African Americans excluded from full participation in American life. New, more active government efforts to incorporate blacks into the American mainstream have yielded very uneven results, with strong protections for voting and employment rights, but continuing disadvantages for minorities in sharing in American prosperity. Federalism remains an important battlefield for efforts to deal with the consequences of America's racial history for employment, housing, and education.

Why Race Matters

Americans' struggle with racial exclusion has been intense and continuous, and has strongly influenced the development of American culture, the nation's economy, its political parties and interest groups, its public policy, and all its governing institutions. In the words of political scientist Robert Lieberman, "Race—particularly the color line dividing white from black (or white from everything else)—has always been central to American political life."[2] As political scientist Rogers Smith pointed out, while America lacked the feudalism that created a hierarchy of nobles and commoners in Europe, race and gender constituted equally important hierarchies in the United States. White European men built the American republic, and they assumed that white male descendants of Europeans would control it. Though these men treasured freedom, equality, and democracy for themselves, they viewed blacks, Indians, and women as inferiors. The white men who built the American republic did not fully incorporate members of these groups into the nation's civic life.[3] Race always has divided Americans, and it has often divided Americans with otherwise similar economic interests. Political scientists identify race as a major dimension of political conflict in the United States, one that cuts across economic divisions, the other major dimension of political division in American history. James L. Sundquist showed how race contributed to fundamental realignments of American politics in the nineteenth and twentieth centuries. In their landmark study of 70,000 congressional votes from 1789 to 1985, Keith T. Poole and Howard Rosenthal found that racial conflicts often constituted a fundamental cleavage in American politics.[4] As Americans cope with the enduring consequences of racial exclusion today, many still retain clear personal and family memories of legal segregation and the civil rights movement. Racial discrimination is burned into the American memory. The effects are evident in many areas of fundamental importance to the American future, including employment, housing, education, and the distribution of wealth.[5]

America's struggle with race was fought out on the battlefield of federalism. No conflicts in American history involved federalism more openly. No conflicts did more to mark out the boundaries of Federal and state power in the nation's formative years. Southern states used their policy discretion to ensure whites' control over slaves before the Civil War, and to ensure white dominance over freed blacks after it. Southern leaders forcefully invoked "states' rights" to fend off national interference with slavery and racial segregation. Laws, institutions, and precedents set in this period became the deeply entrenched state racial laws that were surmounted with difficulty in the twentieth century. Ironically, laws in other states that aimed to erase barriers to black citizenship laid a foundation for the national civil rights revolution of the 1960s. In the United States, then, federalism and race have been deeply and inseparably intertwined.[6]

Federalism, Citizenship, and Slavery in the Early Republic

In the early United States, the states defined who was fully included in and who was excluded from the American community.[7] No state treated African Americans, Native Americans, or women as equals of white men. States restricted the right to vote, an essential part of participation in the political society, and as late as 1855, only four New England states allowed blacks to vote. In the same period, voting rights for Native Americans were limited, and New Jersey, the lone American state that had permitted suffrage for women, restricted voting rights to men in 1807.[8] Native Americans were distinctly inferior if they lived in the states, and considered dependent nations if they lived beyond it.[9]

The enslavement of Africans in the Southern states made federalism an incendiary political issue for over seventy years after the Constitutional Convention. The U.S. Constitution coupled slave ownership to power in Congress, allowed the states to govern slaves as they wished and import slaves for a generation. Yet, while delegates were hammering out the Constitution in Philadelphia, the Confederation Congress in New York enacted a Northwest Land Ordinance that banned slavery in the territory that became Ohio, Michigan, Indiana, Illinois, and Wisconsin. As the Northern economy developed and nurtured small family farms, cities, and manufacturing, slavery became unnecessary in the North.[10] Northern states increasingly committed themselves to treating all workers as "free labor," that is, free to be hired, to be fired, and to quit as individual workers and employers chose.[11] By 1804, Pennsylvania, New York, and all of New England provided for the elimination of slavery by state constitution or state law.[12] While the South was using law to strengthen slavery, Northern states were using state power to expand commerce and industry (see Chapter 5).

While slavery faded in the North, slaves became ever more indispensable in the South. Blessed with abundant land and water, a favorable climate, and increasing demand for cotton from the booming factories of England and the Northern states, the South doubled down on its commitment to produce cotton and collect its extraordinary profits. The hunger for cotton drove the plantation economy and the expansion of slavery westward across Alabama, Mississippi, and Louisiana. By the early 1860s, there were nearly four million slaves in the United States. The value of these slaves amounted to three billion dollars, or forty-four percent of the South's entire wealth. The per capita income of free Southerners had grown faster and exceeded the income of Northerners between 1840 and 1860. Southerners never had a greater stake in protecting their regional economy than they did when at the outbreak of the Civil War.[13] Northern and Southern states were developing along radically different—and incompatible—paths.

From 1787 to 1861, Southern states used their legal authority to safeguard slavery and tighten control of their slaves. Southern slave codes aimed to reinforce complete white domination. State law allowed masters virtually unlimited power to punish their slaves. While many slave states made it illegal to mistreat a slave and required that an owner provide adequate food, clothing, and shelter, there are few recorded trials of violators of these laws. In effect, then, there was little or no limit to the violence that an owner could impose on his slave. Slaves could not own property, and they could be bought, sold, inherited, and repossessed like physical property or real estate. Laws prohibited them from marrying, from learning to read and write, and from assembling together. They could not vote or serve on juries. In states like Virginia, South Carolina, and North Carolina, slave patrols limited slaves' movements, harassed slaves, and mistreated innocent blacks (and sometimes whites).[14]

The U.S. Congress, designed to balance the representation of slave and other states, tried to smooth over the disparate interests of the South and North as they grew apart. With no debate and little opposition, Congress in 1793 enacted a law that required the return of runaway slaves. Slave owners or bounty hunters could cross state lines, seize an escaped slave, and appear before any magistrate to obtain a certificate permitting the transport of the recovered slave back to the owner. Any interference with this process could be prosecuted as a Federal crime.[15] The emerging Democratic-Republican Party used federalism tactically to deflect controversies over slavery that could divide its Northern supporters from its Southern ones. In 1797, four North Carolina blacks freed by their owner petitioned the House of Representatives for help. A new North Carolina law required them to be re-enslaved. Representative James Madison and other Democratic-Republicans successfully argued that these petitioners should take their claim to the North Carolina courts because the dispute was a state problem outside of Congress's responsibility.[16] Congress banned slave imports in 1808, as soon as the Constitution authorized it to do so. The elimination of legal imports, however, limited the supply of slaves as the Southern economy expanded, so it increased the value of slaves and the wealth of those who already owned them. Illegal slave smuggling survived, and occasionally some free blacks in the United States were kidnapped and sold into slavery.[17]

When the addition of new Western states made it impossible to avoid conflict over the balance of slave and free state representation in Congress, national legislators used federalism to work out political deals that perpetuated slavery westward. Missouri, a slave territory, asked Congress for statehood in 1818, and when it did, conflict over slavery exploded onto the floor of Congress. Admitting Missouri as a slave state would tilt the balance of power in Congress to the South. When a Northern Representative proposed to phase out slavery in Missouri as a condition of its admission, defenders of slavery argued that Congress had no authority to restrict the new state's right to govern slavery as it wanted. The legislators compromised, perpetuating the fragmentation of African Americans' status. Missouri was admitted as a slave state, and Maine as a free state, thus maintaining the balance of slave and free-state power in Congress. This Missouri Compromise banned slavery in territories north of Missouri's southern boundary.[18]

The bitter debate over Missouri's self-governance decisively coupled "states' rights" to race, and it crystallized the deeply felt idea that the South was a distinct, exceptional section of the nation.[19] Americans came to believe that the "North and South had evolved separate societies with institutions, interests, values, and ideologies so incompatible, so much in deadly conflict that they could no longer live together in the same nation."[20] When the Congress passed a high tariff in 1828 (the "Tariff of Abominations"), the South went to the brink of revolt. Southern plantations required a very low tariff on imported goods, so that other nations would reciprocate with low tariffs and import more cotton from the Southern plantations. The higher Tariff of Abominations thus posed a very serious threat to the Southern states. South Carolina's leaders, including U.S. Vice-President John C. Calhoun, argued that it was "impossible to deny to the States the right of deciding on the infractions of their powers." Its sovereignty allowed a state like South Carolina to "interpose" itself between the national government and its people by "nullifying" the law, or refusing to allow it to be enforced within the state if it believed the law unconstitutional. According to historian Daniel Walker Howe, Calhoun turned his exceptional political talents "to immobilizing the [F]ederal government in the service of a slave economy."[21] In 1832, a South Carolina convention declared two national tariffs unconstitutional and unenforceable within the state, threatening secession if the national government used military power to force the state to comply. President Andrew Jackson responded by threatening to send troops—but he also agreed to reduce the tariff. With tariff cuts, the nullification crisis passed. But the possibility of state secession continued to haunt the nation.

The relentless expansion of the nation made it impossible to find a political accommodation that could cushion the growing conflict over slavery indefinitely. In the North, a strengthening social movement demanded abolition. While the United States was acquiring half a million square miles of Western land in the 1840s, David Wilmot, a Democratic

U.S. Representative from Pennsylvania, proposed to ban slavery in all these new territories, just as the Northwest Ordinance had excluded slavery. This Wilmot Proviso never passed Congress, but it created a bitter division between Southern and Northern Democrats.[22]

When California's application for statehood threatened to tilt the congressional balance of power against the South, Democratic leader Stephen A. Douglas of Illinois proposed a new political bargain, the Compromise of 1850, which became law. California joined the Union as a free state, but Utah and New Mexico were allowed to choose for themselves whether or not to permit slavery (that is, to exercise "popular sovereignty"). Congress also added a stronger Fugitive Slave Act in 1850, providing punishment for all Federal, state, and local law enforcement officials who refused to arrest a runaway slave.[23]

Angered by this interference with their state prerogatives, most of the Northern states passed "personal liberty" laws that obstructed enforcement of the new Fugitive Slave Act within their borders. These Northern personal liberty laws guaranteed suspected escaped slaves a fair judicial process, and limited the role of state officials in helping recover slaves. These laws established the legitimacy and practicality of legal language that found its way into the Fourteenth Amendment to the U.S. Constitution.[24]

The terms of statehood for Kansas and Nebraska finally wrecked the increasingly fragile balance of state power in Congress. These two territories were north of the Missouri Compromise line, and if they were admitted as free states as the compromise required, they would give the anti-slavery states a decisive majority in Congress. Douglas's Kansas-Nebraska Act, enacted in 1854, repealed the Missouri Compromise and allowed "popular sovereignty" in both states. Pro- and anti-slave settlers poured into Kansas, and their struggle to control the state deteriorated into armed violence. When the Whig Party collapsed over the slavery issue, coalitions of anti-slavery Whigs and Democrats formed new party alliances in each Northern state. These parties convened as the Republican Party in 1856, and their election victories quickly made the Republicans the strongest party in the North. In 1857, the Supreme Court, with loyal Jacksonian Democrat Roger Taney as chief Justice, made animosities much worse. In *Dred Scott* v. *John F. A. Sandford*, the Court concluded that blacks "have for more than a century been regarded as beings of an inferior order, unfit associates for the white race" and thus "had no rights which white men were bound to respect." In his majority opinion in this case, Taney wrote that blacks were not entitled to Constitutional protections and that Congress had no authority to prohibit slavery in any of the Federal territories.[25]

Statehood for Minnesota (1858) and Oregon (1859) finally gave the free states a majority in the Senate for the first time in the nation's history. The Democrats split into factions in the 1860 presidential election, and none of the three Democratic presidential candidates could compete effectively across the North. The Republican candidate, Abraham Lincoln, was not even on the ballot in most Southern states, but he won outright majorities in fifteen Northern states. After seventy-three years, the Southern states no longer could use the presidency or the U.S. Senate to defend their prerogatives. Eleven Southern states declared their independence of the United States when they lost their political defenses in the U.S. Congress.

Civil War and Reconstruction

The ensuing Civil War marked a critical turning point in American political, economic, and social development. The Emancipation Proclamation of 1863 freed slaves in Confederate territory, and the Thirteenth Amendment of 1865 ended slavery completely. Wartime devastation, the evaporation of the wealth held in slaves, and reduced demand for Southern cotton retarded the economic development of the South for generations. For decades after the Civil War, the Southern states resisted change while the rest of the nation changed dramatically.[26] The South isolated itself from the dynamic investment and economic growth that were driving industrialization and urbanization in the North. Cotton plantations were divided into smaller, low-income tenant farms. With a policy of poor education for blacks and a practice of tightly restricted job opportunities, low wages were rooted in the Southern economy. By the 1870s, "the South was a low-wage region in a high-wage country." Income per capita in the South fell to half the level of the North, and remained there until World War II.[27] The South remained outside the economic mainstream of the United States, one with a self-conscious regional identity forged in war and remembered in symbols like the Confederate flag.

For an exceptional period from 1865 through 1877, "Radical" Republicans dominated Congress and pursued a policy of reconstructing the Southern states by imposing extensive national protections for African American citizens. The Federal government placed the South under military control and imposed new state governments that protected civil rights, voting, and office-holding for African Americans. Enforcement Acts established Federal supervision of elections and allowed the president to declare martial law in areas where the racist Ku Klux Klan intimidated blacks. The Federal Freedmen's Bureau attempted to bypass Southern governments to help newly freed slaves become self-sufficient and acquire lands in the former Confederacy. The Fourteenth Amendment (1868), inspired by the pre-war Northern personal liberty laws and the *Dred Scott* decision, designated "all persons born or naturalized in the United States" to be "citizens of the United States," and of the State wherein they reside." No state could "abridge the privileges or immunities of citizens of the United States," nor could any state "deprive any person of life, liberty, or property, without due process of law; nor deny to any person within its jurisdiction the equal protection of the laws." The Fifteenth Amendment (1870) specified that neither the national nor the state governments could restrict voting rights "on account of race, color, or previous condition of involuntary Servitude" (but the Amendment did not prohibit laws that denied women the right to vote). The Fifteenth Amendment enfranchised more than a million black men outside the South, encouraged vibrant African American communities in Northern cities, and laid the groundwork for building black participation in political party coalitions as well as interest groups (most notably, the National Association for the Advancement of Colored People, or NAACP, founded in 1909).[28] The Civil Rights Act of 1875 made it illegal to discriminate in schools, jury selection, hotels, restaurants, railroad cars, and other public accommodations (but it suggested that racially separate schools that provided equal educational advantages to all children could be legal).[29]

The fragmentation of American government made it impossible for Congress to ensure that the other branches of government and the states would adhere to its Reconstruction policy faithfully and permanently. First, Lincoln's successor as president, Andrew Johnson, was a Tennessee Democrat who slowed Reconstruction in its most important phase, immediately after the war. Johnson, likely aiming to reconstruct an all-white political coalition of Northern Democrats and Southern conservatives, used his powers to slow and frustrate important reforms such as land redistribution and the elimination of ex-Confederates from state and local offices in the South.[30] Second, the Republican Party needed to build a durable presence in the South to ensure that Reconstruction would endure. But after Northern support for Reconstruction waned, the party failed to sustain its Southern wing.[31] Third, the Federal courts interpreted Reconstruction narrowly, upholding extensive state authority and limiting the scope of national rules. The *Civil Rights Cases* drastically limited the reach of the Fourteenth Amendment by declaring that Congress could not prohibit legal racial discrimination because such a national law violated state authority. The Federal government, said the Court, could only legislate after a state took a specific action that abridged the protections listed in the Amendment.[32] Largely in response to the ruling in the Civil Rights cases, eighteen Northern and Western states enacted their own laws banning racial discrimination in public accommodations by 1900 (these laws were not very effective, however).[33]

After the 1876 election, Republican President Rutherford Hayes withdrew Federal troops from the region, and Southern Democrats gradually returned to power in the Southern states.[34] These states regained control of managing race, and used their power to ensure the economic, political, and social supremacy of whites over blacks.

Southern State Restrictions on African American Citizenship after Reconstruction

As Federal protection of African Americans evaporated, the former slaveholding states extended their subordination for another century. State governments in the South began to legislate white supremacy in 1881, when Tennessee enacted the first "Jim Crow" law, mandating the segregation of whites and blacks in railroad cars. These "Jim Crow" laws spread across the Southern states, requiring racially separate facilities in trains, ships, streetcars, and waiting rooms. Blacks were legally banned from white hotels, restaurants, saloons, restrooms, and courtrooms—that is, anywhere blacks and whites could come together.[35] In states with a significant Hispanic population, such as Texas, such laws also were applied to Latinos. By 1890, all the former Confederate states legally segregated their public schools by race, as did Oklahoma, Missouri, Kentucky, West Virginia, Maryland, and Delaware. Four other states (Kansas, Arizona, New Mexico, and Wyoming) permitted locally segregated public schools. Northern states banned legal segregation in schools, but many localities physically closer to the South segregated schools anyway, and gerrymandering of school districts and residential segregation established de facto segregation in many other places.[36]

Most of the South also ensured white supremacy and black subordination by virtually eliminating African Americans' voting rights.[37] Thirteen states enacted such laws as literacy tests, poll taxes, and "grandfather" clauses (that exempted voters from educational requirement and poll taxes if their grandfather had been eligible to vote, that is, if they were not former slaves) and the all-white primary election. Hostile local election officials, fraud, violence, and intimidation ensured these laws were effective. Black voting was virtually non-existent in the former Confederate states by 1912.[38] The suppression of black voting weakened the potential strength of working class voters, undermining their ability to challenge wealthy elites for control of Southern governments.[39]

In *Plessy* v. *Ferguson* (1896), the U.S. Supreme Court confirmed that the U.S. government would uphold states' rights to control the quality of American citizenship for racial minorities. Homer Plessy, who was seven-eighths white, was required by Louisiana law to sit in a racially segregated railroad car, and was arrested for violating the law. Plessy challenged Louisiana's law as a violation of the Thirteenth and Fourteenth Amendment. The Court overwhelmingly ruled that Louisiana's segregation law was consistent with the Constitution. The majority opinion stated that the Fourteenth Amendment "could not have been intended to abolish distinctions based upon color, or to enforce social, as distinguished from political, equality, or a commingling of the two races upon terms unsatisfactory to either." Thus, laws that required racial

> separation in places where they are liable to be brought into contact do not necessarily imply the inferiority of either race to the other, and have been generally, if not universally, recognized as within the competency of the state legislatures in the exercise of their police power.

Legal segregation:

> as applied to the internal commerce of the State, neither abridges the privileges or immunities of the colored man, deprives him of his property without due process of law, nor denies him the equal protection of the laws within the meaning of the Fourteenth Amendment.

The states had "a large discretion" to decide what laws were reasonable, given established customs and the need to preserve order.[40]

The South, the Democrats, and Government Activism

With uncontested political control reinforced by legal segregation, conservative whites overwhelmingly dominated the Democratic Party in the South. The Democratic Party controlled Southern politics from Reconstruction until the middle of the twentieth century. In 1880, the first presidential election after Federal troops left the South, all of the former Confederate states voted for the Democratic presidential candidate. These same states voted overwhelmingly for Democratic presidents for the next sixteen presidential elections, through 1944. Because Republicans could win the presidency and congressional majorities without winning the South, Republicans wrote off the region and did little to challenge the Democrats there. National Democratic leaders, in turn, refused to challenge the South's segregation laws directly, because Democrats could not win the national election for president or a majority in Congress without the solid block of Southern support.

When Democrats took charge of the Federal government in the 1910s and in the 1930s, they activated the Federal and state governments without disturbing the Southern states' racial arrangements. Soon after progressive Democrat Woodrow Wilson, a Virginian by birth, won the presidency in 1912, he put Southern Democrats in charge of the Post Office, the Treasury Department, and the Navy. These cabinet officers imposed segregation in their departments. Photographs were required of all applicants for Federal civil service positions, a rule that made it easier to exclude blacks. Supervisors in the South were empowered to fire black employees. During World War I, the Army segregated blacks and assigned them to minor roles; the Marine Corps did not accept black recruits. The Republicans who succeeded Wilson in the 1920s sustained this segregation.[41] By the late 1930s, ninety percent of blacks employed by the Federal government in Washington, DC were custodians, and almost all the rest were clerical employees.[42]

Franklin Roosevelt's New Deal in the 1930s greatly expanded Federal and state activism, and these efforts reached African Americans. Several New Deal initiatives included provisions that banned racial discrimination. The Civilian Conservation Corps enrolled blacks and provided literacy programs. The Roosevelt administration opened a Civil Rights Division in the Justice Department and appointed liberal appointees to the Federal courts. When civil rights marchers converged on Washington in 1941, the president responded by creating a Fair Employment Practices Committee.

But the New Deal also reinforced white supremacy and the low wages of the Southern states, as well as the practice of racial segregation in the North, by allowing state and local officials to discriminate against blacks and other minorities in many New Deal programs. Farm workers and domestic workers—an especially important part of the Southern low-wage workforce—were not included in the old-age insurance or unemployment insurance titles of the Social Security Act, or protected by the National Labor Relations Act, which guarded the right to unionize, or covered by the Fair Labor Standards Act, which established minimum wages and maximum working hours. Southerners objected to the Fair Labor Standards Act because "you cannot prescribe the same wages for the black man as for the white man."[43] As Robert Lieberman put it,

> Where African Americans were potentially included among a policy's beneficiaries, Southerners demanded institutional structures that preserved a maximum of local control. Conversely, strong, national social policy institutions [such as the old-age insurance title of the Social Security Act] were politically possible only when African Americans were excluded from the center.[44]

The Federal Housing Authority reinforced the bias in access to housing, home loans, and residential segregation outside the South, institutionalizing discrimination in its own underwriting manual.[45] While Roosevelt viewed the underdevelopment of the South as the "the nation's No. 1 economic problem" in the late 1930s, and initiated a massive effort to bring modern prosperity to the region, the administration's leading effort to develop the South, the Tennessee Valley Authority, ultimately reinforced segregation in its agricultural programs.[46]

During World War II, segregation endured despite the unprecedented role of the national government in American life. Racial segregation persisted in the armed forces and in defense industries.[47] According to historian Patricia Sullivan, "[b]y most measures, the war exacerbated racial discrimination and repression in the South and underscored [F]ederal complicity with Southern racial mores."[48] After the war, veterans, both white and black, had access to housing and education benefits through the GI bill. Existing racial obstacles to higher education and employment, as well as local administration, severely limited the ability of African American veterans to take full advantage of the GI Bill.[49] Meanwhile, the political foundations of legal segregation were weakening.

The Civil Rights Revolution

As the nation changed at an accelerating pace in the 1940s, leaders reconsidered Southern segregation. The crusade against Nazism in World

War II compelled some Americans to acknowledge the gap between the ideals of justice the United States espoused and the reality of the legalized black subjugation in the South.[50] During both World Wars, millions of blacks moved to Northern cities, attracted by higher wages and better conditions. Many of these African Americans could and did vote, and Democrats and Republicans began to compete for the allegiance of black voters in large, closely contested Northern states.[51] President Harry Truman reached out to African Americans in part to solidify the Democrats' weakened post-World War II electoral position.[52] Meanwhile, the system of low-wage farm labor in the South declined because of New Deal policies, the development of more manufacturing, the modernization of farming, and the migration of low-wage workers to Northern factories.[53] Within the South, some reformers had very cautiously begun to question the practicality of some elements of the Jim Crow order.[54] In 1944, the U.S. Supreme Court struck down the white primary, opening the choice of candidates in the South to African American participation.[55] When Southern Democrats walked out of the party in 1948 and ran South Carolina Governor Strom Thurmond for president as the candidate of the States' Rights Democratic Party (or the "Dixiecrat") Party, Thurmond was only able to win South Carolina, Alabama, Louisiana, and Mississippi, losing the rest of the South to Truman.[56]

States outside the South were beginning to lead the way to more forceful action against segregation in their borders. By 1941, half the states banned discrimination in their civil service, and a third of the states banned discrimination in public works employment. New York initiated the nation's first law against discrimination in employment based on race, creed, color, and national origin (but not gender) in 1945. By 1964, twenty-five states had enacted such laws.[57] In 1945, New York state also enacted the first fair employment practice act. New York formed a Committee on Discrimination in Housing in 1949, and in 1961 enacted a state fair housing law banning discrimination in housing. By 1968, twenty-two states had enacted fair housing laws.[58]

All these developments encouraged proponents of racial inclusion to step up their efforts to destroy legal segregation, but the uneven advance of civil rights in the states made the campaign for racial inclusion difficult, costly, and lengthy. Black churches became organizing cornerstones against Jim Crow locally in the South.[59] The NAACP filed lawsuits in Federal courts against segregation in the public schools, and won cases against segregation in public colleges.[60] In 1954, the Supreme Court's *Brown* v. *Board of Education* ruling struck down laws that segregated education. The majority opinion in *Brown* stated that "education is perhaps the most important function of state and local governments" and "is a right which must be available to all on equal terms ... Separate educational facilities are inherently unequal." While its decision struck down segregation laws in seventeen states, the District of Columbia, and the four states that allowed local segregation, it did not lay out a plan for implementing its decision. In a later decision, the Court urged that desegregation proceed with "With all deliberate speed." Missouri, Kentucky, West Virginia, Maryland, and Delaware soon complied with the *Brown* decision.[61]

The former Confederate states bitterly fought the Brown decision, however, using "states' rights" as their first line of defense. Evoking John C. Calhoun, the state of Mississippi declared interposition against the Federal government in 1956, vowing to take all measures to "void this illegal encroachment." The same year, Mississippi set up a State Sovereignty Commission, explicitly to "resist the usurpation of the rights and powers reserved to this state and our sister states." During the next seventeen years, this Commission actively spied on civil rights activists and funneled money to segregationist groups.[62] Ninety-six Southern U.S. Representatives and Senators signed a "Southern Manifesto" in 1956, in which they promised to use "all lawful means" to reverse the *Brown* decision as unconstitutional and because it "is destroying the amicable relations between the white and Negro races that have been created through 90 years of patient effort by the good people of both races. It has planted hatred and suspicion where there has been heretofore friendship and understanding."[63] Georgia, Alabama, and Virginia prohibited desegregation regardless of Federal court rulings.[64]

Slowly but surely, political imperatives trumped white supremacy. The highly publicized Montgomery bus boycott (1955–56), protesting segregation on public transportation in that city, accelerated a broad social movement for civil rights and elevated the national influence of its leaders, most notably the Reverend Martin Luther King. African American students defied segregation by sitting in whites-only sections of lunch counters, and "freedom riders" defied segregation on intercity Greyhound and Trailways buses. The Federal government established a Civil Rights Commission in 1957 and strengthened the investigative authority of the Civil Rights Division of the U.S. Justice Department. Presidents Eisenhower and Kennedy sent Federal troops to intervene when Southern governors fought the desegregation of Central High School in Little Rock, Arkansas in 1957 and the University of Mississippi in 1962. In the spring of 1963, when children and adults marched for civil rights in Birmingham, Alabama, city police chief "Bull" Connor commanded police to unleash attack dogs and open powerful fire hoses on the marchers. Television broadcast these brutal scenes across the nation and the world. Gradually, the ordinary Americans who propelled the civil rights movement built the foundation for the elimination of Jim Crow. Public support for integrating public schools grew from thirty percent of Northern whites in 1942 to seventy-five percent in 1963, and among Southern whites, it grew from just two percent to thirty percent in the same period.[65] Southern support for legal segregation began to splinter, with some local governments acceding to change. These local victories in the South allowed civil rights activists to build on their successes and target the strongest bastions of segregation.[66]

The rising tide of civil rights finally washed away state segregation laws in the mid-1960s and laid down basic national rules for the inclusion of black citizens. President John F. Kennedy in 1963 sought Federal legislation to eliminate legal segregation in schools and public accommodations. After Kennedy's assassination, his successor, Lyndon Johnson, pressed for rapid passage of the proposal. Bipartisan support for this Civil Rights Act overcame the previously insurmountable roadblock of the Rules Committee in the House of Representatives, chaired by Virginia's Howard W. Smith, as well as a filibuster of the bill by Southern Senators. The 1964 Civil Rights Act banned segregation in schools, public accommodations, and the workplace. It outlawed discrimination in hiring, firing, training, or promoting employees because of their race, color, gender, or nationality, and established an Equal Employment Opportunity Commission (EEOC) to ensure compliance. The law also made illegal any discrimination in the use of Federal grant-in-aid funds by the state governments, local governments, and other grant recipients. The Voting Rights Act of 1965 outlawed literacy tests, allowed the Federal government to approve state election plans in advance, and permitted Federal supervision of voter registration and elections in several states, primarily in the South (after several extensions of this supervisory authority, it was renewed for another twenty-five years in 2006). The Twenty-Fourth Amendment, ratified in 1964, banned poll taxes as an obstacle to voting.[67]

It took considerable effort to implement these rules in the states that resisted them, but national law eventually prevailed.[68] The deep Southern states of Mississippi and Alabama, despite their resistance, were largely desegregated by the early 1970s. Mississippi disbanded its Sovereignty Commission in the late 1970s.[69]

The Continuing Racial Divide in American Politics

Civil rights leaders expanded the movement's agenda by tackling the consequences of racial exclusion throughout the country. These leaders focused on reducing "de facto" racial segregation, that is, segregation in housing, schools, and employment that existed without overt legal segregation. In Northern cities, real estate brokers, financial institutions, insurance companies, and others had long practiced "redlining," the practice of steering black (and other "undesirable" residents) together into aging areas of the city and allowing these areas to deteriorate. By the 1960s, such practices had produced stark segregation of whites and blacks in urban areas. Economic conditions were deteriorating in many areas of concentrated African American populations. High unemployment, a lack of investment, worn-out and dilapidated buildings, overcrowded schools, poor services, a lack of stores, and indifferent governments made the promise of desegregation ring hollow in these areas. Dr. Martin Luther King moved into the black ghetto in Chicago in 1966 and campaigned for effective fair housing laws in the North.[70]

This new civil rights frontier resulted in new—and often very controversial—efforts to alleviate de facto segregation and expand Federal civil rights activism. The NAACP "mirrored the federal structure of the American state—with local, state, and national branches," enabling these individual branches to tailor different strategies for compliance to different places.[71] Federal courts, Federal agencies, and the NAACP pressured state and local governments to equalize opportunities. The EEOC learned to work with the various state and local agencies around the country, gaining power from the alliances that federalism made possible.[72] Efforts to address past employment and college admissions discrimination resulted in affirmative action programs. These programs explicitly take race, gender, ethnicity, disability, military service, or the economic status of job or college applicants into account. They aim to ensure that employers hire and schools admit a sufficient number of minorities or women to guarantee diverse workforces and classes. In 1971, *Swann* v. *Charlotte-Mecklenburg Board of Education*, the Supreme Court upheld the use of busing of students to correct a racial imbalance among schools.[73] Several cities, including Boston, Los Angeles, and San Francisco, then were required to use busing to achieve mixed racial balance in elementary and secondary schools.

As the remedies for racial exclusion expanded, conflict over civil rights became emotional and divisive throughout the nation. Busing and affirmative action in employment and education sparked a strong backlash. Boston, a city that once had been a hotbed of abolition, exploded in violence between working class whites and African Americans over the busing issue in the 1970s.[74] A string of important Supreme Court cases trimmed back, but did not destroy, affirmative action in education and employment.[75] Opponents of affirmative action turned to the states to advance their cause. In 1996, California voters approved Proposition 209, which banned preferential treatment for "any individual or group on the basis of race, sex, color, ethnicity, or national origin in the operation of public employment, public education, or public contracting." Michigan voters approved a similar proposal in 2006.[76]

Racial differences increasingly defined the two political parties after the 1960s. African Americans voted overwhelmingly Democratic in elections after 1964, and the national Democratic Party more strongly embraced racial liberalism and expanded national protection of civil rights. Many white Southerners and some white Northern voters, however, became alienated from the Democratic Party. Some drifted to the third party candidacy of Alabama's segregationist governor, George Wallace, in 1968. Meanwhile, "the Republican Party, from political circumstances and deliberate choice," evolved from a party of racial liberalism and active national government in the 1860s into a party of racial and economic conservatism in the late twentieth century.[77] The Republican Party gained new strength among Southern voters by opposing Federal power and arguing for states' rights on economic and racial issues. Republican presidential nominee Barry Goldwater emphasized states' rights and opposition to national power in his 1964 campaign, and he won five Southern states. In 1968, Republican Richard Nixon and third party candidate Wallace won all the former Confederate states except President Lyndon Johnson's home state of Texas. No Democratic presidential candidate from 1968 through 2008 received a majority of the white popular vote in the United States, and only Jimmy Carter in 1976 received the electoral votes of a majority of the Southern states.

Ronald Reagan's administration opposed busing to remedy school segregation and affirmative action to remedy segregation in education and employment, and it did not hesitate to use national power to restrict state and local discretion in this area. The Reagan Justice Department challenged state and local affirmative action programs in Detroit, New Orleans, and Boston, and joined busing opponents who sought to stop judicially mandated busing programs in Norfolk, Virginia, Nashville, Tennessee, and Charleston, South Carolina.[78] It reduced the ability of the Federal government to enforce civil rights by cutting enforcement budgets and staff, and virtually stopped lawsuits on housing and employment discrimination. It used federalism skillfully, delegating some enforcement of civil rights to the state and local governments, and at the same time tried to void local employment agreements based on quotas and timetables. States generally relaxed antidiscrimination enforcement as the Reagan administration delegated them more control of grants-in-aid.

Race in American Political Development: Today's Inheritance

Federalism has shaped the treatment of race deeply and relentlessly in American history. Federalism helped entrench slavery, delay the incorporation of blacks on equal terms with whites, and fragment the efforts to extend that incorporation. Since the 1960s, states have continued to serve as a key battleground in struggles over the legacy of legalized and de facto racial discrimination.

The consequences of the long struggle over racial inclusion profoundly affect American life today. There is no doubt that African Americans are financially better off than they were in 1960, and that the black middle class is stronger. But decade after decade of unskilled low-wage labor, the lack of access to quality education, legal segregation in the South and de facto segregation in the North systematically deprived many African American families of the accumulated advantages that allowed many whites to vault readily into the middle class. Black Americans have confronted much greater obstacles than whites in building wealth over generations. The Federal Reserve Board pointed out in 2008 that for "every dollar of wealth held by the typical white family, the African American family has only one dime."[79] Segregation in neighborhoods remains a legacy of years of residential segregation practices. Schools are resegregating.[80] Tough state crime policies have produced more prisoners, and more than half of all prisoners were African Americans in the mid-2000s. There were more African American men in prison than in colleges and universities.[81]

While the election of Barack Obama to the presidency in 2008 signals that the United States has come a long way in dealing with its racial problems, public opinion indicates that race remains a deep fault line in American politics.[82] Perceptions and attitudes remain deeply divided by race. Thirty-seven percent of African Americans believe they have been stopped by the police because of their race; thirty-five percent say they have been denied a job because of their race, and twenty percent say they have been denied housing because of their race.[83] Whites see things very differently. Over eighty percent of whites believe that blacks have just as good a chance as whites to be hired for a job for which they are qualified, and that blacks are treated equally in housing and while shopping. Only thirty-eight percent of blacks believe that blacks have an equal chance at jobs, less than half believe that blacks are treated equally in housing or shopping.[84] Outright racial prejudice, while constantly shrinking, is still present in American life. In a 2001 referendum, for example, Alabama became the last state to repeal its law banning interracial marriages. However, in that vote, more than forty percent of the electorate voted to support laws that outlawed marriages between blacks and whites.[85]

The central role of federalism in America's racial dilemma cemented the power of states' rights as a strategic political weapon in American politics. In conflicts over the growth of the American economy, federalism played an equally important and enduring role.

5   Federalism, Capitalism, and Economic Growth

Capitalism has been the engine of American prosperity and the source of the most basic political conflicts that changed the course of the nation. Government supervision is an essential part of any capitalist economy for two reasons. Government administers the laws, institutions, and policies that foster the expansion of free markets. Government also receives demands for policies that mitigate the damaging effects of free markets on citizens, such as unemployment, poverty, and pollution. Because government must nurture free markets at the same time that it must mitigate their effects, conflicts over the way government should supervise capitalist development are persistent and intense in all capitalist democracies like the United States.

Federalism has helped make the American variety of capitalism different from that in other nations by allowing these economic conflicts to spill onto two battlefields. Americans have fought about not only how government should supervise market-driven economic development, but also over which level of government—the Federal government or the states—should supervise it. Because the Constitution gave the states the power to govern most aspects of American markets, states drove early American economic development by constructing the basic rules for market expansion. Even though the Federal government played a greater role in setting basic rules for free markets between the Civil War and the 1930s, the states actively managed the transition of the United States to a predominantly urban industrial economy. Federalism in this period helped distinguish American capitalism from that in other nations by fostering the large corporation, the policing of business behavior, and the fragmentation of business's political interests. Reformers in the New Deal, the 1960s, and the 1990s accepted corporate-driven, free market capitalism as an established fact, and policy-makers at both the national and state levels have worked to harness corporations as vehicles to cushion the impacts of dynamic markets on real people. Federalism generally has shored up the political influence of individual American businesses, while it also has contributed to confrontational regulations that foster exceptional antagonism between business and government.

Federalism is by no means the sole cause of the uniquely American path for governing the economy. Many other factors have contributed. American society often demands less of government because it is so wealthy, opportunities to advance seem abundant, immigrants have diversified the nation, and class conflict has been subdued. American core values are traditionally liberal, emphasizing freedom, free markets, self-reliance, and limited government, leaving relatively little space for socialism or conservative authoritarianism. The separation of legislative, executive, and judicial power encourages the separation of taxes and spending, undermining support for government action.[1] Federalism alone is not a sufficient explanation of American economic governance, but it is a pervasive factor that is necessary for understanding the path of economic governance in the United States.

Why Economic Development Matters

As political scientist Graham Wilson observed, the United States "has long had a reputation as the most capitalist of the advanced industrialized countries."[2] Free market capitalism transformed the United States from a scattered collection of frontier farming colonies into the world's leading economy, distinctive for its unsurpassed wealth, dynamic growth, and global corporations.[3]

Capitalist economies do not develop naturally; governments have nurtured them with laws protecting property and contracts, tax and tariff schemes that benefit business, and public infrastructure to encourage commerce. Historian Colleen Dunlavy described this public role in capitalist growth as government's "structuring presence."[4] Economist Karl Polanyi argued that governments created free markets by actively extending property rights, enforcing business agreements, and breaking down barriers to buying and selling. Governments used their power to turn land, labor, and capital into marketable commodities. Governments also encouraged commerce by fostering roads, canals, railroads, and air travel to extend commerce. Very often, private business sought and supported these government policies. Ambitious economic entrepreneurs themselves often have taken the lead in demanding government policies that make their efforts to build private enterprise more successful. As the economy became larger and more complicated, the task of maintaining and managing free markets became more complicated and has required ever more government involvement.[5] American state and national governments have been actively involved in nurturing the nation's economy in all these ways from the start.

But economic growth results in constant, often wrenching change in nations like the United States. Whole industries rise and fall as the economy churns, elevating new goods, technologies, businesses and jobs, while marginalizing or eradicating other industries, technologies, business firms, and jobs. Economist Joseph Schumpeter argued that this ongoing process of "creative destruction" was inherent in capitalist growth. Creative destruction allows the economy continually to reinvent itself and become more productive.[6] In a democracy, creative destruction that accompanies capitalist growth makes it likely that a large number of voters will reward government leaders who try to stop, slow, or mitigate those consequences of capitalist growth that harm or threaten them. While entrepreneurs seek a favorable and largely unfettered environment for investment, citizens who risk losing their jobs, or those who must survive without any income because of their age or disability, often demand government help. Moreover, businesses in vulnerable industries often seek government restrictions on markets to protect them from damaging competition.

Recognizing these cross pressures, Polanyi identified a *double movement* in capitalist development: pressure for unfettered markets on the one hand, and efforts to mitigate the effects of market-driven economic growth on the other. Governments nurture markets, but their success causes uncertainty and turmoil, sparking "a deep-seated movement ... to resist the pernicious effects of a market-controlled economy."[7] Government, then, is placed in the middle of this double movement, receiving demands that markets be left alone and that markets and capitalists be brought under more control. Nowhere was this "double movement" more conspicuous than in the United States, where democracy took root early and widely, and where political parties and interest groups mobilized to use democracy to both grow the economy and to mitigate its effects.

Governing capitalism, then, is central to the core questions of politics: who gets what, when, and how.[8] James Madison recognized the economic roots of politics in the *Federalist*, observing that the "most common and durable source of political factions

> has been the various and unequal distribution of property. Those who hold and those who are without property have ever formed distinct interests in society. Those who are creditors, and those who are debtors, fall under a like discrimination. A landed interest, a manufacturing interest, a mercantile interest, a moneyed interest, with many lesser interests, grow up of necessity in civilized nations, and divide them into different classes, actuated by different sentiments and views. The regulation of these various and interfering interests forms the principal task of modern legislation, and involves the spirit of party and faction in the necessary and ordinary operations of the government.[9]

Conflict over government's role in the economy has shaped more aspects of American political development than any other conflict. Struggles to change the advantages and disadvantages distributed by market-driven economic development have taken many specific forms. Taken together, these struggles have been passionate and unremitting. They emerge as clashes between labor and capital, between different regions of the country, between sectors of the economy and between industries.

In any democracy, successful economic development cannot simply be *economically* viable and efficient. To succeed, economic development must be *politically* viable and efficient as well. Successful economic development requires a workable balance of contending political forces pressing for market expansion and the mitigation of markets' unwelcome impacts.[10] Federalism has played a critical role in making the governance of the economy in the United States politically viable.

How Federalism Affected American Economic Development

In the United States, where these endless and ever-present conflicts played out on the double battleground of federalism, the division of national and state power favored the promotion of market expansion and inhibited efforts to mitigate the impact of those markets. Political fights over economic development were fought out, first, over the appropriate role of any government toward markets and business, and second, over whether the state or national governments should perform this role. As Chapter 2 discussed, the national government lacked the Constitutional tools of economic management, and could not generally police markets and safeguard citizens until the 1930s. The national government did have some important tools for encouraging market expansion, including the power to generate substantial revenues through tariffs, the ability to use tariffs to increase the cost of foreign goods and thus reduce foreign competition for U.S. manufacturers, and control of vast public lands. States had the authority to use the tools of economic management, but the states were exposed to substantial competition from other states, and could not effectively limit these interstate competitive pressures. State efforts to restrict business or redistribute profits created an unusually swift, strong, and harsh political backlash. The states' exposure to economic competition from other states, then, encouraged states to use these tools much more readily to aid business growth than to restrict it—although some states pioneered American efforts to regulate capitalism.

Federalism, then, had two effects on the management of American economic growth. First, it allowed those who opposed government efforts to restrict market expansion to dig in behind states' rights and oppose the expansion of national power to mitigate the effects. Federalism in the United States tended to be "market-preserving": it limited the ability of American public officials to restrict business and to redistribute wealth from those who profited from capitalism to others.[11] But, second, the very fact that federalism encouraged the growth of strong private enterprises also encouraged public policies that treated business as a hostile adversary.

Economic Development in the Early Republic

States managed most of the American economy before the Civil War, and the national government played a relatively small role. Some national leaders called for a much more active Federal role. The first U.S. Secretary of the Treasury, Alexander Hamilton, pressed for the national government to centralize the control of public credit, to establish a national bank, and to use a host of tools to encourage the expansion of American manufacturing.[12] The U.S. Supreme Court, guided by Chief Justice John Marshall, ruled that potential national power was broad, and it further narrowed all states' power to interfere in interstate commerce and corporate law.[13] Several congressional leaders advocated an active national government program for investing in internal improvements, such as canals and roads, to knit the economy together nationally. Representative Henry Clay of Kentucky advocated an "American System" that would maintain a national bank, impose high tariffs, and use the proceeds from the tariffs to build infrastructure.[14]

But political party competition helped put the brakes on the expansion of Federal authority.[15] Thomas Jefferson's Democratic-Republican Party and its successor, the Democratic Party rebuilt by Andrew Jackson, blocked an active Federal role in the economy. Instead, these national leaders reinforced the *state* management of economic growth. State control of economic development served the political needs of the Democrats because it allowed Southern and Northern states to develop slave and free economies, respectively, without fracturing the party's electoral coalition by nationalizing the slavery issue. Democratic-Republican presidents James Madison (1809–17) and James Monroe (1817–26), and Democrats Andrew Jackson (1829–37), James K. Polk (1845–49), Franklin Pierce (1853–57), and James Buchanan (1857–61) prominently vetoed important congressional bills authorizing Federal involvement in building and maintaining highways, canals, and colleges.[16] Jackson fiercely battled the Second Bank of the United States, refusing to extend its charter and distributing its assets to state banks.[17] By eliminating this bank, Jackson's Democratic Party allowed the states to regulate banks to suit the political needs of local politics and economic development.

This decentralized economic management put the Northern states in charge of guiding the early stages of American industrial growth. These states took command of market expansion in the early republic because most of economic growth occurred within areas that were small enough for states to control, because the states had enough authority and experience to govern growing economic activity, and because the national government found it politically expedient to let the states occupy the field.[18] Each state adopted different laws and rules for private enterprise, creating a somewhat different economic environment than that in neighboring states.[19] Each state implemented rules about products, packaging, urban markets, roadways, riverways, ports, gambling, liquor, and other activities. States licensed auctioneers, tavern keepers, and ferries as virtual agents of the state.[20]

While the states' policies differed, these states generally privileged the expansion of markets and fostered private entrepreneurship. Most important, states provided legal charters for corporations, documents that spelled out the legal rights and responsibilities of incorporated businesses and other organizations. These charters limited the corporations' liability to lawsuits and taxes. During these years, the states expanded the use of corporate charters, from banks, and canal, turnpike, and bridge companies, to manufacturing enterprises, utilities, and railroads. By the 1840s, states were beginning to enact general corporation laws to expand these benefits more widely.[21] For the states, corporations were vehicles of the public interest that would increase wealth within the state and provide other benefits as well. For example, Connecticut in 1819 required manufacturers to teach child-employees reading, writing, and arithmetic. State-chartered banks aimed to ensure private investment and stable currency and credit. Before 1863, these state banks provided most of the nation's currency.[22]

To make their state more attractive to business, states often gave away or subsidized water, land, timber, and minerals for private interests, and allowed private interests to use the power of eminent domain to obtain even more land.[23] States competed with neighboring states to attract investment and new enterprises to drive their economic growth. This competition encouraged states to subsidize or privilege private enterprise and to keep business regulation in check.[24]

States' governments also invested heavily in large infrastructure projects to foster economic growth. New York state's ambitious Erie Canal, approved just months after Madison's veto of national public works funding, became an enormously profitable state government initiative that aided New York producers at the expense of out-of-state interests. The canal dramatically strengthened the economic power of New York City and helped make Chicago the commercial hub of the Midwest.[25] Other states emulated New York with a wide range of ambitious canal, highway, and railroad projects. All these efforts required state government planning for economic growth and market expansion.[26] In the decades before the Civil War, American states acted more vigorously than the government of Prussia in funding—and even owning outright—major capital works such as canals and railroads.[27] The financial panic of 1837 caused many of these state projects to fail, forcing several states to default on the debts they incurred to build them. Exposed to intense interstate competition and under pressure from investors, many of the states (eventually all but one) imposed strict limits on their annual budget deficits and spending. At the same time, states also began to invest in higher education, motivated in part by the explicit desire to retain students and to develop the skills of their citizens.[28]

By 1860, Northern states were building a commercial and manufacturing economy distinct from the Southern plantation economy. Only forty percent of Northerners still worked in agriculture, compared to eighty-six percent of Southerners. Northern cities were growing rapidly, and investment in Northern manufacturing was outpacing the South.[29] Southern states lacked the investments in transportation and education that were helping drive Northern growth.[30] As civil war tore the nation apart, the Northern economy, guided by the state governments, was poised to grow explosively.

Federalism, Giant Corporations, and Antitrust, 1860–1900

Markets burst across state boundaries after the Civil War. Railroads crisscrossed state lines, visibly nationalizing American markets. Between 1860 and 1916, railroad mileage in the United States expanded from 30,000 miles (already half the railroad mileage in the world) to 250,000 miles. Railroads vastly expanded markets for American iron, steel, coal, wheat, corn, processed meat, and manufactured products, both within the United States and beyond it.[31] Because of the immense size of the market for American products, many other enterprises such as Standard Oil, International Harvester, General Electric, Carnegie Steel, and American Telephone and Telegraph expanded on a colossal scale.[32]

Political parties and courts both promoted national rules that encouraged this nationalization of markets and constrained the backlash against it. After winning the presidency and Congress in 1860, Republican Party leaders used the national government to build high tariff barriers to protect Northern industry, to enforce the controversial gold standard (fixing the value of American currency to gold, to attract investors and fuel capitalist growth), to distribute public lands to railroads and homesteaders (thus transferring millions of acres of public land into private markets), and to fill the national courts with judges usually opposed to restrictions on national markets.[33] Federal and state court decisions often favored the nationalization of markets and deflected state efforts to restrict the impact of market expansion. In cases such as *Santa Clara County* v. *Southern Pacific Railroad Company* (1886), the U.S. Supreme Court interpreted the Fourteenth Amendment as a guarantee of corporate rights (equating corporations with individuals) and limited public restrictions on individual businesses.[34] Both Republicans and Democrats supported such decisions.[35] These rulings "extended the formal authority of Congress at the expense of the states, despite the intense pressures from below."[36] The courts, in effect, were creating a "no man's land" in which neither the states nor the national government could interfere with the expanding free market.

Market expansion, in turn, made it increasingly difficult for states to contain the further expansion of markets, or balance the "double movement" of capitalist growth with policies that regulated economic change. While the states continued to promote private enterprise, many found that the growing presence of out-of-state enterprises, along with competition with other states, was limiting their latitude to regulate business. States continued to offer tax exemptions and subsidies to favor particular enterprises, and like the Federal government, they gave away substantial public land to the railroads. Coal increasingly fueled the nineteenth century American economy, and "each state had its own energy policy—which, taken together, created a highly fragmented and somewhat chaotic regulatory regime that encouraged the production and consumption of vast quantities of coal," according to historian Sean Patrick Adams.[37] Harry Scheiber concluded more generally that "highly important, localized activities such as mining or lumbering were placed in a position to virtually control political power," especially in the newer Western states.[38]

Railroads posed the greatest challenge to the states' economic authority and sparked new state experiments with economic regulation. With billions of dollars of capital and thousands of workers, railroad corporations were the first huge private enterprises that transcended state borders. The large railroad companies and the tycoons who ran them seemed to have limitless resources, boundless political influence, and few scruples. To reduce competition and increase their profits, some railroads created "pools," legal agreements to keep rates high. Angry farmers and citizens hurt by these practices demanded that state politicians use government power to stop them. The Granger and later the Populist movements put forward proposals to rein in the railroads.[39] These movements flared most intensely in the Midwestern, Southern, and Western states, on the edge of the nation's manufacturing core. Illinois and Minnesota initiated railroad commissions to set maximum railroad rates in their states. These commissions sought to reduce the railroads to another state constituent whose demands for profit could be balanced against the economic demands of other constituents.[40] Initially, the U.S. Supreme Court upheld Illinois' right to use their regulatory powers in this way.[41] Soon, however, the Court changed its interpretation of state laws and blocked their interference in the railroad market that was indispensable for the growing economy. In the case of *Wabash, St. Louis and Pacific Railway Company* v. *Illinois* (1886), the Supreme Court ruled that states could not interfere with interstate railroad rates and that "it is always in the power of congress to make such reasonable regulations as the interests of interstate commerce may demand, without denuding the states of their just powers over their own roads and their own corporations."[42]

As soon as the Court disarmed the states of their power to regulate these railroads, Representative John Reagan (D-TX) proposed a national law to police unfair railroad behavior. Congress quickly enacted the Interstate Commerce Act in 1887 to neutralize the economic weapons that railroads had used to escape state control. This law established the first national regulatory agency, the Interstate Commerce Commission (ICC), and gave it the authority to challenge the prices that interstate railroads set for freight. Separate Supreme Court decisions made it impossible for railroads to cooperate in setting minimum prices to guarantee profits.

In response, many railroads simply merged into corporations that were large enough to control their costs. These mergers, in turn, increased the burden on the ICC to keep rates reasonable. Thus, federalism and growing corporations set in motion a sequence of events that encouraged even larger, stronger corporations, and at the same time, encouraged the state and national governments to take a more adversarial role toward these corporations.[43]

The late-nineteenth century "double movement" now took the form of larger corporations and adversarial public regulation when it extended to all the notorious large private businesses, or the "trusts." At this time, European governments tolerated or even encouraged business cartels, which involved organized cooperation among businesses to control prices, production, and wages and maintain them at stable levels beneficial to all the participants in the cartel. Cartels allowed businesses in competitive industries such as machinery, coal, or textiles to remain independent and all the firms to enjoy increased profits.[44] But the rules of American federalism at this time prevented American firms from using government to enforce similar "pooling" agreements on prices and production. American state and Federal courts would not enforce such agreements. Even if states attempted to help enforce the agreements, they could not protect employers inside the state from predatory competitors beyond the state's boundaries. Federal courts usually struck down state efforts to use taxes and other policy tools to protect instate businesses, on the grounds that such laws interfered with interstate commerce.[45]

In response to these circumstances, American states pioneered antitrust policy. Instead of managing business collusion, as in Europe, states actively tried to stop the trusts from controlling prices and production. If federalism made it impossible to control collusion, they could instead prevent it, and try to force more market competition over which they *could* exercise some control. Twenty-one states enacted constitutional or statutory prohibitions on trusts by 1890. These state laws, in turn, made it obvious that some national law was required to police interstate trusts that lay beyond the power of the individual states. Congress addressed this gap with the Sherman Antitrust Act of 1890, declaring illegal "[e]very contract, combination in the form of trust or otherwise, or conspiracy, in restraint of trade or commerce *among* the several states ... " (emphasis added) The Sherman Act made it clear that states, not the national government, controlled corporate law.[46] While other countries allowed and even encouraged cartels, then, federalism steered the United States to try to outlaw the very behaviors that made cartels attractive to business.

Because states still controlled corporate law, however, any one state could gain a tremendous economic advantage over its neighbors simply by changing its laws to *encourage* trusts while the other states strengthened corporate regulations. A business-friendly corporate law would allow a trust to change itself from a loose, illegal agreement into a tightly controlled, unified corporation legally chartered by a single state. Such a large corporation would escape antitrust prosecution, while having the power to control prices and production even more effectively than a trust. New Jersey, close to New York City and Philadelphia, immediately took advantage of its strategic location by relaxing its corporate laws and enticing large firms to seek New Jersey charters. In 1895, the Supreme Court reinforced New Jersey's strategy, ruling that the Sherman Act could not be applied to manufacturers, even if their products were distributed across state lines.[47]

Public regulation of corporations now drained away through the gaps in state and national government authority. Twenty-nine competing industrial concerns consolidated from 1895 through 1898; sixty-three consolidated in 1899, and fifty-seven more between 1901 and 1903. Most of these newly consolidated corporations, and all the largest ones (including U.S. Steel, American Sugar Refining, and Standard Oil)—1100 corporations in all—incorporated in New Jersey.[48] New Jersey's success increased the competitive pressure on other states, such as New York, to relax their corporate laws as well.[49] Delaware eventually made its corporate law more attractive than that in New Jersey, and today remains the corporate home for tens of thousands of U.S. and offshore corporations.

American federalism, then, encouraged the paradoxical American response, Polanyi's "double movement" in U.S. capitalism. First, federalism advanced the expansion of the market economy and the construction of the American corporation, an institution which enjoyed more power than individual firms in Europe. Second, however, federalism and the rise of the corporation encouraged American governments to channel the backlash against market expansion into antitrust, an adversarial regulation of business behavior without parallel in comparable nations. American federalism, then, helps explain two distinctive features of American capitalism: the giant corporation and antitrust. These features framed the public supervision of the economy in the twentieth century.

The Progressive Era, 1900–33

The corporations that were emerging at the start of the twentieth century became vehicles for managing "double movement" in the United States. In the Progressive Era, Americans began to disagree strongly over the degree of corporate freedom necessary for driving economic growth. Republican President Theodore Roosevelt, the first president to take office after the great merger movement, explicitly advocated presidential power to negotiate this conflict. He sought a Bureau of Corporations that would provide more discretionary power for the executive branch to govern corporate behavior. But American corporations did not need or want the national government gaining such power over their future. Without business support within his own party, Roosevelt's proposals failed. Instead, a kind of political "natural selection" favored a more confrontational approach. Roosevelt's efforts to prosecute large corporations' behavior (followed by those of his hand-picked successor, William Howard Taft) seemed more acceptable and successful.[50]

Taft's successor, Democrat Woodrow Wilson, approached corporations from the perspective of the Southerners, Populist-inspired farmers, and union leaders that constituted his party's political coalition. Wilson's administration updated the party's strategic use of federalism: it provided an expedient political glue that held together an anti-corporate coalition in economically diverse states. Wilson moved to establish stronger national control of corporate conduct while reinforcing state-level business powers. At the national level, Wilson attempted to neutralize corporate advantages by enforcing market discipline. The Clayton Antitrust Act (1914) and the Federal Trade Commission Act (1914) aimed to broaden Federal power to police corporate behavior. The Federal Trade Commission Act, like the earlier Pure Food and Drug Act (1906), could protect consumers from interstate business predators that the states could not reach. For the Democrats, this strategy preserved decentralized economic power and potentially enabled the states to better control it. The Democrats complemented these reforms with the Federal Reserve Act (1913), establishing more government control of the financial system, but organized into decentralized regions to allow the regional Federal Reserve banks to tailor financial policy to the needs of different areas of the nation.[51]

Meanwhile, the states were expanding their capacity to regulate business. State financial laws aimed to help domestic state interests, and also to keep private finance dispersed and thus easier for state governments to manage. A number of states prohibited banks from establishing branches, thus fragmenting banking to the community level. State-chartered banks outnumbered national banks by two to one in the Progressive Era (though they had only one third of the deposits of the national banks). States deliberately set requirements for new banks lower than Federal requirements to induce new banks to seek state rather than Federal charters. On the Great Plains, states reinforced the decentralized banking system by implementing deposit insurance in the early 1900s, aiding the growth of small banks.

The states also exercised complete regulatory jurisdiction over the important insurance and securities industries. Many states either encouraged or required insurance companies to reinvest within the state those assets acquired from state policy-holders. Texas's 1907 "Robertson law," for example, offered lower tax rates to insurance companies that reinvested seventy-five percent of their reserves in the state of Texas. In the absence of any Federal rules for trading corporate stocks, almost all the states enacted "blue sky" laws between 1911 and 1931, establishing state regulation of stock and other securities offerings inside the state. "Blue sky" laws permitted state regulators to prohibit the sale of certain securities, thereby serving the interests of both state consumers and the small banks and securities firms in each state. To prevent out-of-state retailers from crowding in-state merchants, six states passed laws between 1929 and 1931 to prevent the incursion of out-of-state retail store chains on domestic stores.[52]

The states governed natural resources and energy in a way that balanced economic growth and the interests of state voters. Between 1907 and 1914, most states created public utility commissions (PUCs) to regulate electricity, gas, telephones, and urban rail transit.[53] These commissions balanced the interests of utility companies and state consumers in setting rates, customer service requirements, and corporate profit rules. During a 1919 Chicago streetcar strike, for example, the Illinois public utility commission granted workers a higher wage and permitted the lines to charge higher fares to cover the costs.[54] Texas expanded the jurisdiction of its Railroad Commission to include oil production and pipelines. The discovery of a massive East Texas oil field in 1930 stimulated too many wells and too much oil. Oil prices collapsed. In response, Texas gave its Railroad Commission the power to stabilize prices by setting production limits (called "prorating") for each oil well. The Commission's prorating rules served the interests of the many Texans who derived oil royalties from individual wells. Texas's regulations also raised oil prices nationwide.[55]

The New Deal, 1933–45

Catastrophic depression and the disintegration of American capitalism swept Franklin Roosevelt and large Democratic majorities into power in 1933.[56] The nation's economic product fell by almost half, and unemployment hit unprecedented levels. Business seemed caught in an unbreakable cycle of cost cuts and layoffs that seemed to be out of control. Heavily in debt because of the expansive construction of roads, schools, and other projects in the 1920s, the states slashed budgets for public works. The collapse of private and public construction swelled the ranks of the jobless.[57]

Initially, Roosevelt's New Deal program moved to stabilize economic sectors by authorizing the businesses in each major industry to regulate themselves, with national enforcement of their agreements. The National Industrial Recovery Act (NIRA) authorized national cartels in more than five hundred industries, from coal and steel to umbrellas and licorice. Each industry developed a code of fair competition aimed at limiting price, production, and wage cuts. But these efforts were failing by 1935. In that year the Supreme Court, specifically aiming to protect "the domain of state power," struck down the NIRA as an unwarranted interference with the states' regulatory authority.[58] Lower courts in the Federal judicial system had issued sixteen hundred orders by 1935 to prevent Federal officials from carrying out acts of Congress.[59]

After the collapse of its support for these business cartels, the New Deal returned to the Democratic formula of the Progressive Era: expanding national efforts to police business conduct while underwriting state regulatory prerogatives in key markets. By the late 1930s, Assistant Attorney General Thurman Arnold and the Justice Department revived antitrust prosecutions against corporations.

The Federal government issued regulations that ensured a substantial state role in managing the economy. According to historian William Childs, new Federal regulations "maintained regulatory authorities in the states *and* mandated cooperative action between state and national regulatory commissions."[60] The Public Utility Holding Company Act of 1935 broke apart the large interstate utility holding companies, enabling states to have more control over electricity and natural gas.[61] The Connally Hot Oil Act of 1935, written in response to death of the NIRA, supported the oil states' control of production by prohibiting interstate transport of oil produced in violation of state prorating quotas. This law allowed Texas, Oklahoma, and Louisiana to coordinate oil production among themselves, and to stabilize prices to benefit the oil industry within their own states.[62] The 1935 Motor Carriers Act extended Federal regulations from railroads to trucks and interstate buses, but also required the national government to preserve state regulation of motor vehicles as much as possible (a provision that also protected racial segregation in transportation in the South).[63] The Federal Communications Commission established national regulation of interstate and international telephone and telegraph transmission, but left intrastate phone regulation to the states. A Federal Civil Aeronautics Board regulated most of the airline industry, but allowed states to regulate the intrastate airline service (California later did so). The Robinson-Patman Act prohibited chain stores and large retail stores from extracting price concessions and using price discrimination against small businesses and suppliers, reinforcing the existing state anti-chain-store laws.[64] A new Federal Securities and Exchange Commission (SEC) supervised corporate securities and the stock exchanges, but state securities commissions would examine many stock issues before the SEC, influence SEC decisions, and participate in some investigations.[65]

While many New Deal rules depended on Federal–state cooperation, others nationalized the governance of parts of the American political economy. National deposit insurance indemnified depositors. The national government extended Federal charters to savings and loans. The Banking Act of 1935 centralized the Federal Reserve System and strengthened the independence and authority of its Board of Governors and its Chairman. The Glass-Steagall Act required commercial and investment banks to separate, and it prohibited commercial banks from underwriting most securities. Glass-Steagall also required state chartered banks to join the Federal Deposit Insurance Corporation as a condition of participating in the Federal Reserve System.[66] The New Deal established a more centralized governance of agriculture through price support measures and output controls linked to soil conservation programs. The Tennessee Valley Authority (TVA) aimed to use national power to develop electricity and modern farming in one of the nation's poorest regions.[67]

Even these nationalizing efforts left the states with continued responsibilities. The Glass-Steagall Act allowed commercial banks to continue underwriting securities issued by state and local governments. Federal law underwrote state financial regulation by subjecting national banks to the different rate ceilings imposed by the various states. The TVA relied heavily on existing state and local agencies to implement plans; in the South, this delegation of responsibility reinforced racial segregation. The insurance industry remained almost entirely subject to state supervision.

Liberal Supervision of Capitalism, 1945–81

After Franklin Roosevelt's death in 1945, liberal ideas about economic governance dominated national economic policy for over thirty years. Democrats controlled Congress for most of the thirty-five years after World War II, and held the presidency more often than Republicans. In the 1950s, moderate Republican President Dwight Eisenhower implicitly conceded that the Federal government would not shrink to its pre-New Deal size, and in the 1970s, President Richard Nixon promoted active public management of the economy.[68] Keynesian ideas of national economic management of the economy were widely accepted by the 1960s. As prescribed by the British economist John Maynard Keynes, more Federal spending and lower taxes could stimulate the economy, while lower spending and higher taxes could slow it.[69] Such a fiscal policy affected overall spending and taxes, but would not interfere with private decisions about how business would invest its money.[70]

Expanding notions of rights and risk after World War II increased popular support for more regulation of business. In every case, state governments initially grappled with these concerns (as in antidiscrimination laws in Chapter 4). For example, California passed the first statewide air pollution regulations in 1947. But interstate exposure to economic competition limited the scope and strength of such efforts across the states, leaving such regulation very uneven nationally. While most states had enacted air pollution legislation by 1963, for example, most state laws also aimed to protect the state's attractiveness to business. Pennsylvania's law, for example, provided that state clean air measures not "unreasonably obstruct the attraction, development, and expansion of business, industry, and commerce in the Commonwealth." Michigan, Wisconsin, and Missouri— three leading auto manufacturing states—lacked any air pollution laws at all.[71] Because the costs of specific environmental regulations often are narrow and potentially deep in particular states, it is not surprising that some states have pioneered environmental laws while many states neglect environmental enforcement.[72] Business sometimes took a lead in complaining about the resulting patchwork of state regulations and in demanding more uniform national standards. Automobile manufacturers, for example, voiced strong concerns about manufacturing different cars to meet different pollution requirements in each state, and pressed instead for a single set of national automobile pollution rules.

By the 1970s, the pressure for social regulation and frustration with states' efforts had resulted in a flood of new Federal business regulations. Congress enacted laws to eliminate discrimination, enhance occupational safety and health, protect employee retirement, reduce environmental hazards, and protect consumers. As political scientists Richard A. Harris and Sidney M. Milkis pointed out, these regulations explicitly aimed to restrict business discretionary behavior and to "minimize the prospects of business exercising undue influence in the administration of regulatory affairs."[73] These laws established many new Federal agencies, including the Environmental Protection Agency, the Consumer Product Safety Commission, the National Highway Traffic Safety Administration, and the Occupational Safety and Health Administration. These agencies affected the lives of most Americans, from the air they breathed to the water they drank, the cars they drove, the workplaces where they labored, and the items they purchased with their income.[74] These laws also multiplied adversarial confrontations between Federal regulators and business. Since the states already occupied many regulatory fields, many of these regulations delegated to the states a significant role in implementation.[75] For example, the Clean Air Act of 1970, usually viewed as a leading example of national command and control regulation, depended on State Implementation Plans (SIPs) to guide the regulation of power plants, factories, and other stationary sources of air pollution.[76] States adopted some uniform laws to guide the economy, most notably the Uniform Commercial Code, which is the basis for commercial contracts, payments, shipping, and warranties.[77]

Technological change and economic expansion were making it more difficult for states to continue to exercise state authority over many lines of business. Pressures mounted to loosen state-level financial regulations. Satellites and computers globalized and accelerated financial transactions, while they encouraged more complicated financial instruments. In the 1960s, Texas already had relaxed savings and loan regulations and allowed thrifts to invest in more speculative real estate ventures. By the late 1970s, rising prices were squeezing thrift institutions that found themselves burdened with long-term, low interest home loans. States reduced or eliminated prohibitions on branch banking, and eased other financial regulations. State and Federal regulators allowed thrifts to enter new but riskier loan markets. A 1978 U.S. Supreme Court decision made it impossible for states to prevent out-of-state credit card companies from soliciting business within their state, causing a repeat of the turn-of-the-century interstate race of regulatory laxity. South Dakota and Delaware deregulated interest rates and relaxed other banking rules. South Dakota enticed Citicorp to establish a national credit card center in Sioux Falls. Delaware's governor then traveled around the country to lure similar credit card operations to his state.[78] Credit card companies became the engine of Delaware's economy for the next two decades. By the mid-2000s, lending institutions in Delaware held forty-three percent of total credit card loans made by insured depository institutions.[79]

Conservative Supervision of Capitalism, 1981–2009

The expanding scope of national regulation provoked growing business opposition, and this business mobilization contributed to the success of Republican candidates beginning in the late 1970s.[80] Republicans held the White House for all but eight years from 1981 to 2009, and held a majority in at least one house of Congress during six of the eight years of Democrat Bill Clinton's presidency. Republican leaders aimed to reduce economic regulations (a process that began under Democrat Jimmy Carter in the late 1970s).[81] In practice, however, the Republican administration responded favorably to frequent business demands that the national government retain regulatory authority and preempt more restrictive state laws. Business preferred conservative national regulations to liberal state regulations, and to varied state laws. An industry official explained the preference for conservative national regulation: "I would rather deal with one [F]ederal gorilla than 50 state monkeys."[82]

Conservative nationalism flowered fully in the late 1990s and early 2000s. The Financial Services Modernization Act of 1999 (the Gramm-Leach-Bliley Act, named for its Republican sponsors) repealed New Deal era banking law and preempted states from prohibiting any of the banking activities allowed by Federal law. Gramm-Leach-Bliley also pressured states to relax regulations on insurance companies. In 1996, the Federal Energy Regulatory Commission's Order 888 forced more utilities to purchase wholesale power from independent providers, and placed substantial competitive pressures on the states to deregulate electricity. Pressured by this competition and lured by the hope of reducing consumer costs, more than a dozen states deregulated electrical utilities (although California's subsequent energy crisis slowed momentum for electricity deregulation). The Telecommunications Act of 1996 required state regulatory commissions to admit new entrants into local telephone services. The Public Company Accounting Reform and Investor Protection Act of 2002, enacted after the Enron scandal, expanded Federal control over corporate law.[83] The Energy Policy Act of 2005 transferred responsibility for electrical transmission and liquefied natural gas to the Federal government.

Despite four generations of policy nationalization, today the American states remain important managers of the American economy. States continue to regulate major parts of the economy, manage infrastructure, administer public education, and strive to attract business investment.[84] The states and, under state supervision, the local governments have developed creative fiscal instruments for encouraging economic development projects.[85] According to political scientist Kenneth Thomas, state and local governments spent forty-seven billion dollars in investment incentives in 2005.[86] State attorneys general, who are often upwardly mobile elected officials, very actively fight to control out-of-state firms that adversely affect in-state constituents. State attorneys general have pursued antitrust actions against Microsoft, pharmaceutical manufacturers, and recorded music distributors. Most notably, when state attorneys general in the 1990s sued tobacco companies for damages to citizens' health, they helped engineer a master national agreement to settle the case.[87] The antitrust lawsuit against Microsoft was joined by the attorneys general of twenty states, including major software and Internet centers California and Massachusetts (but notably not the Attorney General of Washington state, Microsoft's corporate home). At the same time, market nationalization and globalization has increased opportunities for business to shop among jurisdictions offering favorable business laws.[88]

The financial crisis of 2008 underscored the importance of the states in the American economy. The collapse of insurance giant AIG occurred against a backdrop of state, rather than national, regulation of the insurance industry. Representative Paul Kanjorski, chairman of a key oversight subcommittee in the House of Representatives, said that "The [F]ederal government really has no insight, no information, and no regulatory authority of any significance over insurance."[89] Instead, "States alone continue to have the primary authority to regulate insurance today. For that reason, Congress has historically only passed insurance legislation to respond to a crisis, address a market failure, or adopt narrowly-focused insurance reforms ... "[90] It is very revealing that the first important investigation of AIG was conducted by New York state Attorney General Andrew Cuomo.[91]

Federalism and the American Variety of Capitalism

Federalism helped guide the unique path of economic governance in the United States. Federalism is not the sole cause of the exceptional course of America's response to the "double movement" of capitalist growth and the mitigation of its consequences. It has been a necessary factor that has with others—such as traditional liberal ideology, social mobility, national affluence, and the separation of government powers—shaped the path of American economic policy.

Today, different capitalist nations supervise capitalism in different ways, and among these nations, the United States stands out for the latitude it allows business, and its confrontational and litigious approach when it does interact with business.[92] As political scientist David Vogel wrote in

1978, "[w]hen all the myriad instances of governmental support of business have been accounted for, the American state remains, by virtually every conceivable qualitative and quantitative criteria, the least interventionist in the advanced industrial world."

> The United States is virtually the only capitalist nation which engages neither in an incomes policy, wage-price controls, nor in national planning; and the degree of state participation in production is smaller in the United States than in virtually any other nation in the world—industrial or nonindustrial. To the extent that the United States has moved toward establishing institutions or mechanisms that make some sort of public economic policy possible, i.e. the enactment of the Federal Reserve System to supervise private banking or the establishment of the Council of Economic Advisors to legitimate fiscal policy—it has done so far later than any other industrial system. The American state still lacks essential information about the basic functioning of the economy and even if that information were available the fragmentation of authority and power within the [F]ederal bureaucracy would make any coordinated government policy extremely problematic.[93]

Many European nations have encouraged more business collaboration, leadership by peak organizations of business and labor, and national guidance of the economy. However, in the United States, business is more fragmented, pluralistic, and lacks central, powerful organization—that is, business is part of the American pluralist interest group system (Chapter 3). Paradoxically, however, while American businesses have had more freedom than counterparts abroad, American regulations often have been more rigid and confrontational than in comparable nations.[94]

The federal system, and the opportunities of a vast national market, encouraged the evolution of an exceptionally resilient form of business, one that became both a vehicle for balancing American capitalism and a target of adversarial regulation.[95] It also encouraged the states to experiment with regulations of business behavior, an approach to mitigating the consequence of markets that became institutionalized in Federal government policy. The Constitution's distribution of power created a double battleground for business supervision, a battleground that political parties and interest groups exploited in a way that encouraged the unique development of American capitalism. Federalism's role in shaping the path of modern government activism began to take clear shape during the Progressive Era.

Part III

The Construction of Active Government

6 Progressive Reform

Progressive reform swept the United States from the 1890s to World War I. The Progressive movement strengthened government at all levels, opening up politics and producing a host of innovative policies. The surge of support for the second part of Polanyi's "double movement"—mitigating the impact of capitalism on Americans—had never been stronger than it was in the years from 1890 to 1920. Stalwart labor unions and women's groups battled for new state and national policies aimed to mitigate the effects of industrialization on vulnerable Americans.[1]

Progressive efforts to make American government more active and professional had to overcome the hurdles of American federalism. Nineteenth-century federalism put formidable obstacles in the path of reform: state governments with limited powers and diverse interests, a national government with very limited authority to police behavior, a Supreme Court that protected market freedoms from national and state government interference, a Democratic Party that protected white supremacy in the South, and powerful economic interests with the motive and the means to use federalism to defend their prerogatives. But federalism also created many different sites for change, and progressives adapted to the constraints of federalism by using the states to construct a springboard for national reforms.

Progressives changed American federalism by increasing direct popular engagement in government, mitigating some of the problems of industrialization, and professionalizing governments at all levels. Progressives were particularly successful in their efforts to democratize government through primary elections, initiative and referendum, voting rights for women, and the direct popular election of U.S. Senators. Proponents of active government used federalism to win women's suffrage and enact prohibition. Reforms that tackled substantive problems of industrialization produced inconsistent results. Progressive success in some of the states, such as Wisconsin, Massachusetts, and California, turned these states into laboratories of policy innovation. But across the nation, interstate economic competition limited the scale and scope of these reforms. The case of child labor shows how efforts to strengthen national police powers were defeated on the battlefield of federalism. Because Federal government taxing power was established and broad Federal police powers were not, national reformers were more successful in tapping Federal revenues to fund grants to encourage state activism in narrow policy areas, such as highways and vocational education. These grant-in-aid programs produced coalitions of expert policy administrators in the Federal and state governments, establishing professional policy coalitions that added further complexity to the politics of federalism. The Progressive Era left a legacy of institutional innovations layered on top of an existing federal system that enhanced state power even as it enhanced national power.

The Progressive Impulse

Industrialization remade the American economy between the Civil War and the New Deal, and as it did, it caused a tidal wave of change throughout American society and politics. By the early twentieth century, the United States was an industrial behemoth with dynamic commercial cities and integrated national markets. Millions of new immigrants came to the United States, and these new residents came from Italy, Greece, Poland, Russia, and other regions of southern and eastern Europe. These immigrants injected new diversity and new challenges into American politics.[2] Fueled by high birthrates as well as immigration, the American population nearly doubled between 1890 and 1930. Most of this growth occurred in the cities; by 1920, a majority of American lived in urban areas. Technological changes, the spread of education, and better health substantially improved the quality of American life. Telephones, the rail network, and finally automobiles and trucks, nearly erased state barriers to information, travel, and commerce.[3] Muckraking newspapers and magazines had enormous national scope, broadcasting scandal, crime, and misery to audiences of unprecedented size.[4]

These economic and social changes swamped nineteenth century federalism, which depended heavily on courts and patronage parties. A host of new professional and policy organizations, such as the National Municipal League, the American Association for Labor Legislation, and the National Conference of State Boards of Health, sprang up between 1877 and 1920, all urging reform and government action at all levels. Organized labor grew more powerful in industrial and mining areas, and advanced a forceful policy agenda to further the interests of workers. Women's organizations fought for protections for children, widows, and working women. These organizations helped nationalize politics by sharing grievances, intelligence, and tactics across state, and even national boundaries.[5]

"Progressivism" was the name given to this collection of reform impulses of the early twentieth century. Historian Alonzo Hamby described Progressivism as an inherently *political movement* that addressed ideas, interests and issues stemming from the modernization of American society."[6] Armies of reform battled to make politics more democratic, government more professional, and capitalism more humane. With the expansion of the corporation and national markets firmly established, progressives insisted on a variety of responses to mitigate problems they identified, including poverty, unemployment, disease, the inability to work, and alcohol. Progressive reformers pressured all levels of government to respond to these problems.

The Expansion of Government and Democracy

State and local taxes, spending and employment far outpaced the Federal government in these years. Following the lead of Wisconsin in 1911, thirteen states implemented a workable income tax by 1922. State income taxes increased state revenue and strengthened state government authority. Between 1902 and 1932, Federal tax revenues per person, bolstered by a Federal income tax, doubled to $14.51. In the same period, state and local government revenues per capita increased almost five times, from $10.86 per person in 1902 to $49.33 in 1932. With more revenue, governments spent more. Federal direct spending per capita increased from $7.14 to $31.88 in this thirty-year period, and state and local government spending increased from $12.80 to $62.15. The number of Americans employed by government at all levels tripled to three million by 1928. Local governments employed about a million of these workers, and local public education employed another million. State employment increased to about 300,000 in 1928, and had grown faster in these years than Federal employment (561,000 in 1928).[7]

At all levels of government, power flowed to elected executives (the U.S. president, state governors, and city mayors). Progressive executives, such as U.S. Presidents Theodore Roosevelt and Woodrow Wilson, state governors Robert LaFollette of Wisconsin and Hiram Johnson of California, and city mayor Tom Johnson of Cleveland, galvanized support for an active policy agenda and built political coalitions to support it. Theodore Roosevelt, for example, boldly employed presidential power to protect millions of acres of the American land from mining and timber companies.[8] Public agencies, such as the U.S. Forest Service, the Bureau of Chemistry in the U.S. Department of Agriculture, the Wisconsin Industrial Commission, and the New York City Bureau of Municipal Research gained authority by infusing policy with expertise and energy.[9] Professionalized budget and legislative bill preparation at all levels enhanced the reform agenda. Improved non-partisan civil service administration laid the basis for better state government. The commission and city manager forms of government brought more efficiency into cities.[10]

As progressive reforms shifted power to executives and experts, they undermined the power of political parties and legislative bodies. Many reformers aimed to undercut the influence of these institutions because they seemed to promote blatant corruption and the nefarious monopolies.

The widespread use of the secret ballot made it harder for party bosses to control the outcome of elections.[11] Between 1899 and 1915, nearly all the states had implemented the direct primary election, forcing the parties to use more open election processes to nominate their candidates for state offices. Primaries opened the selection process to a much wider range of participants than a small group of party big shots, and helped mobilize voters to support party candidates.[12] Populists demanded that voters be given the power to make legislation directly through initiatives placed on the ballot by citizen petition, or referenda placed on the ballot by legislatures. A variety of groups that opposed entrenched interests, such as organized labor, supporters of prohibiting alcohol, advocates of professionalized government, and out-of-power political parties coalesced to authorize the initiative and referendum in about twenty states between 1898 and 1920.[13] By the early 1910s, thirty state legislatures had sent resolutions to Congress demanding a Constitutional amendment providing for direct, popular election of Senators rather than election by the state legislatures. These state actions made it possible to win rapid approval of the Seventeenth Amendment, establishing direct election of Senators in all the states.[14]

Political scientist Margaret Weir pointed out that these political reforms did not endow state governments with much more will to address the problems created by industrialization (the second part of Polanyi's "double movement") because they did nothing to correct the rural bias of the state legislatures. In the states where Progressivism had the most impact, the initiative, the referendum, and enhanced executive powers all bypassed and weakened legislatures. But legislatures still made law in these states. The apportionment of state legislative seats in all the states over-represented rural areas and underrepresented cities. Even though cities were rapidly adding population, there were no requirements for periodic redistricting to equalize the state legislative districts. The states with the two largest industrial cities, New York and Illinois, prohibited their large cities from gaining legislative majorities.[15] Most state legislatures also lacked much capacity to respond to an activist agenda. By 1900, only six states had legislatures that met every year. Most state legislatures met every other year, often for a constitutionally limited period (as short as forty days in Wyoming).[16] While political reforms made the states more open to reformers' ideas, then, the states' willingness to respond to the problems of industrialization remained uneven and limited.

State Policy Innovation and its Limits

Some states took the lead in coping with the new challenges of industrializing America. Wisconsin, for example, pioneered the state income tax, the industrial commission, and a workers' compensation system. New York's factory laws, Illinois' Anti-Sweatshop Act of 1893, Missouri and Illinois' mothers' aid laws of 1911, Massachusetts' 1912 minimum wage law for women, and Oregon's 1913 law limiting the regular working day to ten hours each marked an unprecedented state effort to regulate working conditions and the impact of industrial change on individuals. These kinds of laws inspired progressives such as Louis Brandeis to conclude that innovative states, including Massachusetts, New York, Wisconsin, and the Pacific coast states, served the nation as "social laboratories."[17]

But constrained state economic authority, along with economic competition among the states, limited the scale, scope, and impact of these state responses to industrialization. Opponents of state labor regulations and welfare policies constantly invoked the problem of interstate economic competition to slow and stop state innovation. Business foes of effective factory regulation and inspection, laws setting maximum hours and minimum wages, bans on child labor, and initiatives to provide state-managed workers compensation or health insurance constantly bludgeoned these proposals as threats to state industries and therefore state economic growth and prosperity.[18] The opposition succeeded much more often than it failed, leaving a patchwork of reform across the nation. States that resisted policies to mitigate industrialization attracted, tried to attract, or threatened to attract business away from states that went to the frontiers of regulating employers.

The wide disparity that separated the industrially advanced Northeastern and Midwestern states and relatively poor Southern states intensified the problem. Massachusetts was as industrialized as any region in Europe, while many Southern states remained agricultural and had a large pool of low-wage, unskilled workers. Southern leaders advertised their low wages and lack of regulation to attract Northern businesses. The president of the Georgia Industrial Association urged Northern manufacturers that "If things don't work out right in New England, come down where conditions are better! Try Georgia!"[19]

Interstate economic competition, in turn, deeply influenced the way policy experts designed American proposals to mitigate the impact of industrialization. Reformers abroad, such as Sir William Beveridge in Britain, proposed fully national policies for dealing with industrial problems like unemployment, because their governments had full authority over economic management. Their American counterparts, such as John R. Commons of the University of Wisconsin, had to design policies that the most progressive states could implement with a more limited set of tools, and without doing too much damage to their competitive position with respect to other states. Limitations on state powers and interstate competition foreclosed some of the options enjoyed by Beveridge, forcing the Americans to be much more responsive to the demands of in-state industries. These creative reformers invented programs to attract the "responsible" employers and punish only the most irresponsible businesses, thus dividing business interests.[20]

Commons and many other reformers therefore made a virtue of the necessity of federalism by turning the industrial corporation into a vehicle for mitigating the effects of industrialization. They made business incentives the preferred policy tool for encouraging private business to act responsibly. Such notable Progressive Era reformers began to envision a corporation-centered welfare state that could thrive under "American" circumstances. For example, they designed workers' compensation and unemployment insurance to favor employers who kept work injuries and layoffs to a minimum, while penalizing employers with high rates of work injuries and layoffs. These inventive policy designs, once made into laws, themselves became institutions that limited the future impact of national laws.

Organized Labor

Federalism influenced the strategies of trade unions and women, two of the most powerful forces for reform in the Progressive Era. In the United States, as in most of the industrializing nations, trade unions spearheaded the drive to mitigate the effects of industrial capitalism. Because states had authority to govern most of the nation's workplaces, state policymakers found themselves in the middle of politically explosive battles between employers who defended their prerogatives and workers who demanded shorter hours, better wages, and safer working conditions.

Unions sought government help reluctantly. By 1900, the leaders of the nation's leading labor organization, the American Federation of Labor (AFL), concluded that unions could not overcome the political obstacles presented by the lack of Federal authority, interstate economic competition, and resistance to effective labor laws in most states. Instead, the AFL's leaders dedicated themselves to a strategy of "voluntarism" based on the idea that unions had to win "pure and simple" material gains for workers by using their own economic power directly to wrest concessions from employers.

But despite their dedication to winning as many protections as possible without government help, trade unions lobbied for many new laws to shore up their economic power. Unions sought public regulations that established a floor of labor protections for children and women, who were difficult to enlist in unions. Unions also fought for laws that would protect their key organizing tools, such as the right to strike, and for bureaus of labor statistics and public employment offices to give unions more leverage with employers. Unions, as well as employers, supported laws establishing fixed compensation for workers injured on the job; by 1919, this formidable union–business alliance helped enact workers' compensation laws in all but one of the states outside the old Confederacy, as well as half of the ex-Confederate states.[21]

The AFL had to depend heavily on its state affiliates to pressure the states to provide more beneficial laws for unions. The Federal government lacked authority to legislate for any workers beyond Federal employees and those employees in the indisputably interstate occupations such as running the railroads. State labor federations and specific unions became the principal force for state laws setting maximum hours, effective factory inspection, and new labor policies. A few of the state federations advocated more far-reaching legislation, sometimes in defiance of the national AFL leaders. These federations lobbied for laws mandating the eight-hour day for male as well as female workers, and new government-run insurance plans for workplace injuries and health.[22] In more unionized states like Massachusetts, New York, and Illinois, with massive concentrations of industry, the influence of progressive reformers and organized labor made some labor laws politically irresistible. New York implemented far-reaching workplace regulations after 146 people died in the 1911 Triangle tenement factory fire.

But in other states, opponents of labor regulation invoked fears of interstate competition to defeat factory inspection laws, laws limiting the work day to eight hours, the regulation of convict labor, laws requiring one day's rest in seven, the regulation of child labor, and minimum wage laws. In many cases, states that enacted factory regulations provided little enforcement, in effect, allowing legislators to claim credit for responding to demands for labor protections without actually imposing costs on employers. The state of West Virginia actively used its power to help fight the unionization of its coal fields, ensuring that wages in state's mines would remain lower than those in other states, allowing West Virginia mine owners to sell coal at a lower price than unionized neighbors.[23]

As a result, American labor protections spread unevenly and state labor regulations became widely disparate, in turn undermining trade union power. The largest corporations could simply overwhelm unions with their unilateral control of jobs. U.S. Steel eviscerated unions by shifting production from a unionizing plant in one state to non-union plants in other states, giving the company an insurmountable advantage in the battle with unions.[24] The large corporations could also undermine unions by investing heavily in new mass production techniques, such as the assembly line, and in employee benefit programs that made the appeal of unions less urgent. At the same time, smaller employers often battled unionization with a ferocity unparalleled in Europe. American organized labor fragmented, maintaining strength where it retained the most economic power (such as the construction trades) but losing the organization of less skilled industrial workers in the growing steel and auto factories of the nation. Because so many of the great industrial plants lacked unions, and because these industrial unions were the strongest advocates of protective labor policy, advocacy for government labor protections was weaker in the United States than in comparable industrializing nations.[25] Even the most progressive states did not provide the labor protections for male workers that were being implemented in Europe and Australia.

Women

While AFL unions battled for an ever-narrowing policy agenda, women fought with more success to win the right to vote and establish protections for female workers, children, and the broader community. Trade unions were more concentrated in a smaller number of industrial states, forcing their leaders to limit their policy agenda, while women were able to exert more pressure across all the states because women populated all the nation's political jurisdictions.

By 1900, women, though still largely denied the vote, influenced reform by building organizations to pressure government.[26] Women reformers already had fought long, tough battles for equitable laws. In the early American republic, voting was an exclusively male domain and married women's political citizenship and property rights were hamstrung by coverture, a legal doctrine that allowed husbands to own property, make contracts, and sell property without any participation from their wives. In the nineteenth century, states began to liberalize these coverture laws, less for women's benefit than to free up dated constraints on the expansion of market and property transactions.[27] The National Women's Suffrage Association, enhanced by merger in 1890, became the central voice for the women's right to vote. A number of local, state, and national organizations took up the suffrage cause, and mastered both inside lobbying and marches and demonstrations to pressure their way to success.[28] The Women's Christian Temperance Union, the largest women's group in the 1880s, helped build women's lobbying skills on banishing alcohol and other issues.[29] The Women's Trade Union League, organized at the AFL convention of 1903, took a leadership role in organizing the heavily female garment-making industry. Local women's clubs sprang up in large cities, creating the foundation for a new national General Federation of Women's Clubs in 1890, and state federations a few years later. These clubs lobbied for better health, housing, and conditions for children in the industrial cities.[30] The National Consumer's League, founded by female reformers in 1899 and led by Florence Kelley for over thirty years, was a principal advocate of child labor laws. The National Congress of Mothers (later the National Congress of Parents and Teachers, or the PTA), pressed for more government attention to public education as well as marriage and family.[31] These temperance, suffrage, and women's club organizations were stronger and more interconnected nationally as the Progressive movement gathered strength.[32]

Women used federalism most skillfully to win the right to vote. From 1870 to 1910, most efforts to amend state constitutions to allow women to vote failed, but by the Progressive Era, nineteen states allowed women the vote in local municipal, school board, tax, or bond issue elections.[33] Congress admitted Wyoming in 1890 as the first state to allow a general right to vote for women, and Utah followed in 1896.[34] Then, in 1910, suffragist organizations won a galvanizing victory in Washington state, followed by California, Arizona, Kansas, and Oregon. Illinois granted women the vote in presidential and local elections in 1913, and several more states extended votes to women. As more states gave women the right to vote, the constituency for guaranteeing women's suffrage nationally grew larger. In 1918, President Wilson, who had not supported national women's suffrage, committed himself to a vote for a Constitutional amendment to guarantee suffrage. Southern members of Congress and members from many large industrial states fought against this amendment, but now found themselves outnumbered by members from states that already had extended suffrage. The proposed Nineteenth Amendment was submitted to the states in 1919 and took effect when Tennessee became the thirty-sixth state to ratify it the following year.[35]

Meanwhile, female-led reformers discovered that, by appealing to the exceptional needs and roles of women and children, they could persuade male policy-makers to enact protective labor legislation for these groups. The Supreme Court's decision in *Lochner* v. *New York* (1905) seemed to prohibit government regulation of hours in private employment, but three years later the Court made an exception for women in *Muller* v. *Oregon* (1908).[36] A majority of the Court accepted the argument that the states like Oregon could limit women's working hours because the female "is properly placed in a class by herself," and it emphasized the need to protect motherhood and female reproduction.[37] This decision moved coalitions of trade unions and progressive women's groups, notably the Consumers' Leagues and the General Federation of Women's Clubs, to pressure for women's hours laws in other states. Thirty-two states passed new laws regulating the employment of women and children immediately after *Muller*.[38] Virtually all the states had some restrictions on women's working hours by the mid-1920s, but seventeen states permitted women to work more than fifty-four hours a week (six states had no regulation of women's hours at all). The Consumers Leagues, the Women's Trade Union League, the American Association for Labor Legislation, some unions, and some progressive employers had very limited success in expanding this agenda to establish effective minimum wage laws for women.[39]

The plight of widows and their children also energized many female reformers to battle for state programs to ensure income for them. The loss of a male breadwinner threatened destitution for a mother and her children because no other income was available for the family. "Mothers' aid" or "widows' pension" programs emerged in Chicago and Kansas City, Missouri in the first decade of the twentieth century. Mothers' aid provided a family stipend so that fatherless families could stay together. A White House conference on the Care of Dependent Children in 1909, along with the publicity in such outlets as women's magazines, helped make "mothers' aid" a focus of reformers' attention. The General Federation of Women's Clubs, the National Consumer's League, and the National Congress of

Mothers all lobbied for the enactment of these laws within their states. Twenty states enacted mother's aid laws by 1913, and thirty-nine states had enacted such laws by the end of the decade. Through the 1920s, most states expanded eligibility and raised benefits for mother's aid, though eligibility remained very restrictive and the income assistance low.[40]

In the United States, laws that protected female workers and provided income for widows began to lay the foundation for what political scientist Theda Skocpol describes as a "maternalist welfare state." Maternalist policies were managed by agencies (often led by women) responsible for enforcing regulations and distributing benefits to soften the impact of industrialization on women and their children.[41] While some female reformers such as Florence Kelley believed that special protections for women would serve as an "entering wedge" that lay a foundation for broad, inclusive labor protections for men and women, experience dashed these hopes. The success of women's suffrage eliminated a common cause that united women politically.[42] Women remained outsiders in American government, without the full protection of citizenship promised to African Americans in the Fourteenth Amendment. Progressive state policies, in fact, reinforced women's role as outsiders by segregating the mitigation of industrialization by gender.[43]

Successful National Regulation: Prohibition

Like the women's suffrage movement, reformers who sought to banish the sale and consumption of alcohol used federalism successfully to build support for national change. Prohibitionists had success in banning alcohol in some places in the nineteenth century. But Federal control of interstate commerce made it impossible to stop alcohol from other states from being brought into "dry" states. The Federal government had little incentive to prohibit alcohol because Federal taxes on distilled liquor were a valuable source of revenue.[44] In 1887, the Supreme Court upheld the right of states to ban alcohol without compensating manufacturers for property losses, reinforcing the prohibitionists' state-by-state strategy of reform. However, the Court also ruled that states could not interfere with interstate commerce, a national responsibility, by banning alcohol manufactured in other states.[45] State bans on alcohol could not reach the hard liquor producers because distillers were concentrated in a few states whose governments resisted prohibition. By 1890, seven states banned alcohol (Maine, Vermont, New Hampshire, North Dakota, South Dakota, Kansas, and Iowa), and a new Federal law, the Wilson Act, empowered these states to enforce prohibition against liquor from other states.[46]

Stalled by 1900, prohibitionists began to pursue more pragmatic and localized approaches to reform. The Ohio Anti-Saloon League emphasized more effective monitoring and enforcement of liquor laws. The Anti-Saloon League reformers built from the ground up, seeking county or even local option laws that permitted alcohol bans within small geographical areas. The Anti-Saloon League approach spread to a majority of states, and a national Anti-Saloon League became a formidable lobbying presence in Washington, DC. Thirty-seven states enacted local option laws by 1900. These Leagues also used statewide initiatives and referenda to win moderate steps toward limiting alcohol within the states. As local alcohol bans increased, so did membership in the state anti-saloon leagues, and support for state and national prohibition. The League helped change Federal liquor tax enforcement into a tool that complemented prohibition in the states, and secured stronger interstate commerce limitations on the interstate shipment of liquor. These laws in turn enabled the states to expand prohibition further. Eighteen states had enacted laws banning even the personal use of alcohol by 1917.[47] In December 1917, Congress sent a Constitutional amendment banning alcohol to the states, and by mid-January, thirty-six states had ratified the Eighteenth Amendment. In 1919, Congress enacted the Volstead Act to implement national alcohol prohibition (which lasted until the repeal of the Eighteenth Amendment in 1933).[48]

Ironically, federalism helped produce three unanticipated consequences of national prohibition. First, the Volstead Act delegated enforcement to the states, and the states' enforcement varied drastically, with some states undermining the law by tolerating widespread drinking. Second, uneven enforcement gave local criminal organizations room to grow into interstate organized crime networks unprecedented in American history. Third, the battle against liquor and spreading crime gave entrepreneurial Federal officials—most notably J. Edgar Hoover, head of the agency that became the Federal Bureau of Investigation—an opportunity to expand the reach of national law enforcement and to build political alliances that substantially strengthened national power in this field.[49]

Federalism and the Limits of Reform: Child Labor

In some cases, federalism stymied reform despite broad public support.[50] Child labor is the best example. The plight of children working in factories was one of the most prominent issues of the Progressive Era. By 1900, over a quarter of a million children between the ages of ten and fifteen worked in textile mills, glass factories, and other manufacturing jobs, and many more worked in domestic and street trades. By 1902, Massachusetts, New York, Connecticut, Illinois, and Indiana had legally limited work to children aged fourteen, a limit comparable to that in Britain and Germany. Many other states resisted child labor laws, particularly in the Southeast where low-wage child labor gave the growing textile industry a big advantage over Northern factories. Most of the textile mills in Alabama, Georgia, North Carolina, and South Carolina in 1907 employed children under twelve, and some young as six.[51]

Florence Kelley and others organized the National Child Labor Committee (NCLC), the core of a broad coalition that pressed for stricter child labor standards nationwide. These reformers developed a model state law to restrict child labor and lobbied for its adoption by all the states. By 1912, only nine states had met the standards laid out in the NCLC's 1904 model state law, and state laws were becoming more varied.[52] The NCLC also helped develop a Federal child labor bill. When the U.S. House of Representatives' Labor Committee unanimously approved this bill, it expressed frustration with the state-by-state strategy.

> Session after session the friends of the children, approaching the legislatures of their respective States, have been met by the plea of the manufacturers that legislation State by State was unfair; that it was unjust to ask them to compete with other States of different standards; that if they must advance they should be permitted to advance in the company of their neighbors and competitors.[53]

U.S. Senator Paul Husting (D–WI) acknowledged that "some States have dealt" with the problem, but said that "in my State and in my legislature when the child-labor proposition was approached … it was held up to us that we were going to ruin our own manufacturers" by reducing the profits of businesses in the state while increasing those of neighboring states. Representative Augustus Gardner (R–MA) stated that "We prohibit child labor in Massachusetts and so it is clearly to our interest to prohibit child labor in States which compete with us."[54]

Congress enacted a Federal Child Labor Act in 1916, and when it did, its opponents seized on federalism to shield themselves from it. Opponents of the Federal law, led by the textile mill operators in the Southeast, quickly challenged its constitutionality in court. They brought the case in a sympathetic venue, the Federal District Court of Western North Carolina, which declared the Federal law unconstitutional.[55] The U.S. Supreme Court agreed, ruling in *Hammer* v. *Dagenhart* that if such Federal regulatory authority were to be accepted, "all freedom of commerce will be at an end, and the power of the States over local matters may be eliminated, and thus our system of government be practically destroyed."[56] Reformers adjusted and successfully lobbied for a new Federal law that taxed employers' net profits an additional ten percent each year that they failed to conform to the child labor standards. Once again, opponents arranged for a challenge to the law, and the Supreme Court struck down this child labor tax.[57] Chief Justice William Howard Taft wrote that if the Court upheld such Federal regulation, it would "break down all constitutional limitation of the powers of Congress and completely wipe out the sovereignty of the States."[58] Next, Congress sent the states a Constitutional amendment outlawing child labor. Opponents, strengthened and emboldened, successfully blocked its ratification and convinced thirty-five states to reject it by

1933.[59] Only the Fair Labor Standards Act of 1938 finally established lasting national regulation of child labor.

Uniform Laws

These cases all show how a wide variety of Progressive Era interests, including prohibitionists, child-labor reformers, the Federation of Women's Clubs, and the American Federation of Labor were casting about for ways to transcend state boundaries and establish national reform. At one time or another, many tried to lobby the states to enact uniform laws—such as the model child labor law—to make law identical across the states without Federal intervention.

The uniform law strategy began in the late nineteenth century, when differences in state commercial regulations were inhibiting commerce. The American Bar Association and New York state helped establish a National Conference of Commissioners on Uniform State Laws in 1892, creating an institutional base for spreading these uniform laws. But grueling state-by-state campaigns to pass these laws depleted reformers' resources and drained their energy. When such rules posed a threat to a strong state interest, the interest fought to prevent reform, often in the state where it was most needed. Reformers could not match the superior resources of the Southern textile industry, or other determined business interests in their uniform law campaigns. Because they had to show that such a law would *not* put the state at a disadvantage, those seeking uniform laws found it easier to enact laws promoting commerce than laws restricting it. Very few uniform laws, even for commercial transactions, ever were adopted by all the states.[60] It was Federal spending power that provided an alternative way to motivate states across the nation to take action.

Layering Change: Federal Grants

Crusades for national regulation smashed into the limits of Federal regulatory authority under the Constitution, a barrier surmounted by Constitutional amendment in the case of prohibition but not child labor. Federal revenue and spending were more firmly established than regulation, and the Sixteenth Amendment, which specifically authorized a Federal income tax, reinforced this Federal power. Strong interest groups in the states supported Federal aid for specific activities. These groups included organizations of reform-minded experts in different fields of public policy. These organized policy experts wanted the Federal government to take leadership in spurring all the state governments to take an active role in fields such as highway-building. For nationally-minded policy reformers, experts already located in the states could be brought into a network of experts bound by Federal grants that would transcend the geographical parochialism of the states and the state-based party system. Between the 1870s and 1929, observed political scientist Kimberley Johnson, dozens of new Federal policy initiatives "knit together legislators, bureaucrats, interest groups, reformers, and citizens into ever tighter bonds, and raised the bar of what it was possible for American government, whether at the national or state level, to do."[61] Federal cash would be the most effective, legitimate way to knit these policy networks together.

Federal grants-in-aid could put Federal revenue to work to bypass even moribund state governments in a specific field and establish a national fabric of specific state activities nourished by Federal money. Under a grant-in-aid program, the Federal government would send money in the form of grants to the states on the condition that they establish a specific kind of public agency or program and match Federal funds with some of their own funds. Because these grants could move poor states to undertake a policy by substantially reducing its cost, they enabled the national government to address a particular public problem nationally even if the states retained jurisdiction over that problem. Since grants-in-aid allowed the states to control important choices about the use of Federal funds (such as preserving racial segregation), the states and their congressional representatives found them ideal. These grants layered new policies atop the existing federal system they also tightened the political alliance of program experts across different levels of government.[62]

The most important Progressive Era grants fostered market-driven economic growth by providing funds for building roads, training the workforce, and improving the quality of agriculture. A broad coalition of interests, including state and national road improvement groups, highway building groups, the Grangers, and bicyclists lobbied for more funding for highways during the Progressive Era, when cars and trucks were transforming American transportation. As in other areas, states like New York led the nation by creating state highway departments. Other states did little. A Federal bureau (eventually the Bureau of Public Roads) promoted the goals of the road improvement movement by disseminating the nationwide need for better roads, providing a model state road bill, and building functional alliances with state highway departments and with other Federal agencies with an interest in highways, such as the Forest Service and the Post Office. The Federal Road Act of 1916 aimed to jumpstart all the states by providing five million dollars in Federal grants to fund the construction and improvement of rural roads. A state would have to match the Federal highway grant, dollar for dollar, to qualify. The law increased state government capacity by mandating state-created highway departments as a condition of receiving matching grants, and it also increased national policy authority because the states voluntarily acceded to some national rules in return for the grants. Five years later, over a million cars were registered in the United States, and, with the strong support of the automobile and highway construction industries, the law was broadened. These highway acts encouraged national standards by limiting expenditures to a system of national roads that would be linked at state boundaries, comprising about 200,000 miles, or one-tenth of American roads.[63] The functional Federal–state alliances in highway policy strengthened over time, and by the 1930s, according to historian Michael Fein, "state and [F]ederal road-building officials were enmeshed in a long-standing, interdependent relationship built around their shared commitment to a traffic-service vision of highway development."[64]

Vocational educators achieved similar results with Federal grants. By 1913, eight of the industrialized states established state-run or state-funded industrial education. A national group of educational leaders, businessmen, public officials, and social reformers created the National Society for the Promotion of Industrial Education (NSPIE), which became the preeminent lobbying group for Federal aid to vocational education. Although the American Federation of Labor and the National Association of Manufacturers both endorsed a plan for national grants to spur industrial education, state rivalry delayed its progress in Congress. Many Southern Members of Congress sought help for agricultural education and disputed aid for industrial education in the cities. After a national commission brought the sides together, Congress enacted the Smith-Hughes Vocational Education Act in 1917. The law provided over a million dollars in Federal matching grants to the states for teachers' salaries and training in the first year, increasing to seven million dollars by 1924. State boards of vocational education retained wide discretion in using the funds. Hundreds of thousands of teenagers received part-time schooling under the Act. Southern state vocational educators used Federal grants for agricultural rather than industrial training, and they channeled most of the money to white school districts, reinforcing African American disadvantages. Even with this grant program, seventeen states still provided no vocational instruction in 1930.[65]

Farmers also benefited from the Smith-Lever Act of 1914, which provided matching grants to the states to establish cooperative extension services, jointly supervised by the state land-grant colleges and the U.S. Department of Agriculture. The law aimed to establish, in each rural county, agents of this extension service who would provide hands-on instruction to county residents in scientific, up-to-date farming and home economics techniques. By World War I, there were 1,400 extension agents, including a number of African Americans.[66] Extension agents, in turn, organized rural farmers into local "farm bureaus." Beginning in Missouri in 1915, farm bureaus organized at the state level, and by 1920, the overarching American Farm Bureau Federation was formally established. The Farm Bureau almost immediately became the nation's most powerful farm lobby. In this way, the strategy of layering and bypassing helped agrarian politics mutate from populist insurgency in the late nineteenth century into pluralist politics in the early twentieth century.[67]

In the 1920s, road building and vocational education programs constituted over ninety percent of all Federal grant spending. Such Federal grants that encouraged economic growth were more politically popular than grants aimed at mitigating the problems of industrial society. The Shepard-Towner Maternity and Infancy Protection Act of 1921 was the exception that proved the rule. The U.S. Children's Bureau, established in 1912, proposed a system of grants-in–aid to encourage states to improve the health of mothers and babies. The bill had the support of the General Federation of Women's Clubs, the National Women's Trade Union League, the National Consumer's League, and the Women's Christian Temperance Union, among others. But the bill also generated strong opposition, especially from the medical associations that opposed any loss of doctor control. The Supreme Court upheld the law on the grounds that it did not "require the States to do or to yield anything. If Congress enacted it with the ulterior purpose of tempting them to yield, that purpose may be effectively frustrated by the simple expedient of not yielding."[68] The law was renewed for two years in 1927, but it was allowed to die in 1929.[69]

This emerging system of grants-in-aid proved to be the most successful way to overcome the obstacles to Federal policy leadership and to build a layer of broad national policy action in specific fields. It also served as a ready template for establishing new cooperative national–state policy activism in the New Deal and beyond.

Grants-in-aid established narrow, functional interest group alliances, dominated by policy experts across different levels of government and supported by formidable interest groups. For example, the Bureau of Public Roads helped create groups like the American Association for Highway Improvement, that lobbied state legislatures and Congress for more support for public roads. Commercial and construction interests joined in these focused lobbying campaigns.[70] The Department of Agriculture cultivated its connections with state officials who provided research and inspection services, and the Farm Bureau lent political support to these efforts.[71]

These policy-focused, intergovernmental alliances would strengthen and influence similar alliances in other policy areas in the coming decades. These new Federal–state–local alliances narrowed "the lines of authority, the concerns and interests, the flow of money, and the direction of programs" to specific areas, such as highways, vocational education, welfare, hospitals, and other areas. These lines of authority run "straight down," like the pickets running up and down in a picket fence.[72] These relationships stimulated a new politics based on shared professional interests and expertise. They also made it more difficult for elected state and local officials to control public policy.

The Progressive Legacy

Industrialization disrupted established relationships in the American federal system, and built pressures for government action. Progressive Era reformers changed American federalism to increase government leadership and establish more professional management of public programs. New institutions and reforms were layered on top of older ones. The fragmentation of power, the hardiness of the parochial party system, and an expanded policy agenda inspired a wide variety of special interests to mobilize for specific reforms, thus strengthening pressure groups in the United States.[73] These groups themselves were enlisted as an alternative to parties because they envisioned more modern and more national public policy.

American federalism helped ensure much more success for reforms that promoted market-driven economic growth than reforms that mitigated industrialization's consequences. The extraordinarily perceptive Florence Kelley wrote in 1905 that "When it is a question of the nation checking, even indirectly, their cruel robbery of the cradle," the industries that oppose child labor restrictions "urge that it is with West Virginia or with New Jersey that the friends of the children should deal, the state legislatures having been hitherto, on the whole, satisfactory to employers."[74] Kelley put a spotlight on the way New Jersey took advantage of federalism to shield the autonomy of large corporations, and the way states like West Virginia used it to shield a key state industry from government interference. By the time that the national government took a more active part in domestic affairs, the states occupied a broader domestic field of public policy. States had firmly entrenched programs involving long-established financial commitments and long-standing institutional ties. Thus, the states became the cornerstone for many of the national domestic initiatives that aimed to mitigate the nation's worst economic crisis, the Great Depression of the 1930s.

7   The New Deal

Growing urgency for government action swamped the nation's governments during the catastrophic Great Depression. Democratic President Franklin Roosevelt's "New Deal" triggered an energetic and far-reaching Federal response to the crisis.

But the Roosevelt administration inherited a system of federalism in which states had become more active in balancing market-driven economic growth and mitigating its consequences. The New Deal also inherited the decentralized Democratic Party, Southern segregation, and the business enterprises that dominated American capitalism. These legacies forced the New Deal to fight for national activism on two battlegrounds at once: first, to expand the scope of government, and second, to extend the scope of the national government relative to the states. The Roosevelt administration's strategy depended on enlisting all the states in helping to mitigate the nation's economic problems. Drawing on the model of durable Progressive Era grants programs, the New Deal designed most of its enduring national initiatives around grants and financial incentives for the states, layering new responsibilities on top of established ones. This politically expedient strategy allowed a few Northern states to pursue more active agendas for mitigating the economic crisis, while at the same time allowing the South to maintain low wages and legal segregation.

The New Deal changed federalism by elevating the Federal government to leadership in mitigating the problems of American industrial society. But while the New Deal energized the national government, it also energized and strengthened the states and intergovernmental networks of policy experts. Roosevelt's administration left a legacy of decentralized governance organized around crop production, highway construction, welfare administration, and other specialized programs. In agriculture, efforts to revitalize farm incomes came to depend heavily on the state agricultural extension services and the American Farm Bureau Federation. National relief and public works programs gave way to Federal grants-in-aid to the states, most notably for highway building. The Social Security Act of 1935 created a fully nationalized program only for old age insurance, and delegated considerable discretion to the states for providing unemployment insurance and helping the elderly, children, and the blind. Labor union rights were fully nationalized, but evolved in a way that permitted some of the fastest growing states to discourage union organizing. The New Deal, then, left a flourishing system of intergovernmental policy.

The Depression

The worst Depression in American history created irresistible pressures for government activism. After the 1929 stock market crash, the economy spiraled downward, damaging every American life in some way. Factories and stores shut by the tens of thousands. One American out of four was jobless by 1933, and many more endured pay cuts and severely shortened workweeks. The situation was worst in the large cities. In Chicago, manufacturing payrolls were cut in half between 1929 and 1933, and wages were cut by three-quarters. Two out of every five workers in the state of New York was jobless in 1933.[1] Thousands of banks failed, and with them millions of savings accounts simply vanished, wiping out many Americans' ability to weather the crisis.[2] Farmers faced drastically falling prices and, in the nation's midsection, devastating drought. An enormous tidal wave of human need swamped private charity, the first line of defense against need.[3]

The Depression quickly overwhelmed both local and state governments. Cities and towns depended on property taxes to fund welfare and all their other activities, but as property values fell and tax delinquencies multiplied, balanced budget requirements forced them to slash spending even as unemployment, homelessness, and hunger increased.[4] American cities' revenues fell by forty percent in these years, but state limits on municipal debt made it impossible for most cities to borrow the funds necessary to meet the rapidly mounting demands for help.[5] The states, too, faced declining revenues and increasing demands. The state legislatures, still amateur bodies dominated by rural interests and wary of their growing cities, often lacked not only the ability but will to respond to urban desperation. Half the state legislatures did not meet at all in 1932, as the Depression reached its worst point. Most state governors and legislators strongly resisted activist government.[6] States made the jobs crisis worse by cutting spending on public works. Facing popular outrage, at least sixteen states limited property taxes in the early 1930s.[7]

The states tried to respond to these growing problems. To make up for the lost revenues, many more states adopted income taxes. Two-thirds of the states taxed income by 1940. In 1932, Mississippi became the first state to enact a general sales tax, a source of state income so productive that fourteen states adopted a sales tax in 1933 alone. About half the states taxed sales by the end of the decade.[8] States increased their aid to localities, reducing local power and increasing the policy control of state officials. A few state legislatures established effective legislative councils to improve law-making expertise.[9]

In some of the most urbanized and progressive states, such as New York, Pennsylvania, Wisconsin, and Minnesota, state governments tried to battle the Depression more forcefully. In 1931, Governor Franklin D. Roosevelt of New York persuaded the state legislature to approve a fifty percent hike in the state income tax and create a Temporary Emergency Relief Administration (TERA). This agency, led by Harry Hopkins, provided local governments with twenty million dollars for relief by mid-1932. The needs were too enormous for even this unprecedented state aid to turn the tide, however. TERA funded relief for 160,000 New Yorkers in early 1932, but a million and a half were jobless. New York's efforts influenced other states. Between 1931 and 1935, forty-three states passed emergency unemployment relief laws, but only eight of these states provided any money for relief by 1933.[10] By then, eighteen states had enacted old-age relief programs, providing a small pension for elderly citizens who could no longer be expected to work. Wisconsin passed the first unemployment compensation law, although it was carefully tailored to protect Wisconsin employers from rivals in other states. The committee that developed the Wisconsin unemployment compensation law stated that "[o]bviously if Wisconsin is to pioneer in this field it must do so on a modest scale. The contributions required of employers must not be so great as to handicap them unduly in interstate competition."[11] With all these constraints on state and local government, demands for action inexorably focused on the national government.

The Transformation of Federalism

As the Depression deepened, President Herbert Hoover's cautious use of Federal power grew deeply unpopular. Hoover believed that the Federal government could do little to change the fundamental problems of the Depression, because "[e]conomic wounds must be healed by the action of the cells of the economic body—the producers and consumers themselves." Hoover believed that government should do no more than encourage "voluntary cooperation in the community." Almost three years after the stock market crash, the Hoover administration set up a Reconstruction Finance Corporation (RFC) charged with providing loans to businesses and to the states. The RFC required each state to deal with its own jobless and help its own needy citizens. Funds trickled out of the RFC very slowly, creating a flood of criticism as the Depression bottomed out during the winter of 1932–33.[12]

Frustration with Federal inaction swept Democratic candidates into Federal offices in the early 1930s. Outside the South, urban working class voters flocked to Franklin Roosevelt and congressional Democrats. Democratic candidates continued to dominate politics in the Southern states. Franklin Roosevelt rode this broad coalition to a landslide presidential victory in 1932, and won an even bigger landslide in 1936. Democrats won commanding majorities in the U.S. House and Senate.[13] Nationally, Democrats built a formidable coalition, one that won the allegiance of a plurality of voters for decades, and victory in eight out of ten presidential elections from 1932 through 1964.

Franklin Roosevelt campaigned on a promise to use national authority much more energetically, and he delivered on his promise. Late in the 1932 campaign, Roosevelt asserted that "The first obligation of government is the protection of the welfare and well-being, indeed the very existence, of its citizens ... " and that this "obligation extends beyond the states and to the Federal government itself, if and when it becomes apparent that states and communities are unable to take care of the necessary relief work ... "[14] In the first "Hundred Days" of the Roosevelt administration, the New Deal put in place fifteen major laws addressing banking, agriculture, industrial stabilization, relief and public works, home foreclosures, and the development of the Tennessee River valley.

The New Deal decisively and permanently transformed the relationships among governments in the United States, creating one of the most important and durable political changes in American history. Federal spending tripled from less than three billion dollars a year in 1930 to more than eight billion dollars in 1939.[15] Federal expenditures exceeded state and local spending for the first time, and this expenditure pattern has endured ever since (Figure 7.1). The Federal government took a permanent role as the principal fiscal engine of domestic policy in the United States.

Federal regulatory authority, previously constricted by a narrow interpretation of the Constitution, also grew enormously. During Roosevelt's first four years in office, the New Deal creatively used Federal taxing power

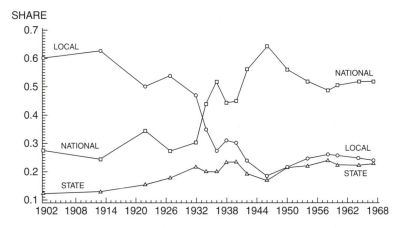

Figure 7.1 Federal, State, and Local Shares of All Non-Military Government Spending, 1902–1967

Source: John Joseph Wallis, "The Political Economy of New Deal Fiscal Federalism," *Economic Inquiry* 29 (July 3 1991), 510–52, Figure 1, page 511.

to institute agricultural reform and unemployment insurance. But Federal power to regulate the economy lagged far behind Federal taxing power. In 1935 and 1936, the Supreme Court struck down a number of New Deal laws on the grounds that they exceeded Constitutional authority, especially the authority to intervene in intrastate commerce. The most important case involved the Schechter Poultry Company of New York, charged with violating quality codes established under the National Industrial Recovery Act (NIRA) (see Chapter 5). The Supreme Court unanimously ruled against the NIRA, explaining that an economic crisis "may call for extraordinary remedies, but they cannot create or enlarge constitutional power." The NIRA violated the Constitution because of its broad delegation of power and, said the Court, "because it exceeds the power of Congress to regulate interstate commerce and invades the power reserved exclusively to the States."[16] An angry Roosevelt slammed the Schechter decision in a press conference. If the Federal government could not deal with the problems of construction, mining, and manufacturing, "they must be left wholly to the States, the Federal Government must abandon any legislation." National government in all other nations, Roosevelt argued, had the power to deal with national economic and social problems.[17] After his landslide reelection, Roosevelt proposed to break the Supreme Court bottleneck by "packing" the Supreme Court by appointing new justices. Although this plan failed, the Supreme Court in 1937 retreated from its narrow interpretation of the Constitution and upheld national power to regulate union organizing, even within a state. This much broader interpretation of the Commerce clause generally has been upheld ever since, and it has permitted the Federal government greatly to expand its tools for domestic policy management.[18]

The states also strengthened. Taken together, court decisions in this period freed *both* the Federal and the state governments to engage in a wider variety of public activities.[19] Although Federal spending grew enormously, the number of Federal employees never grew larger than the number of state and local employees.[20] The New Deal's strategy of adapting the Progressive Era to new purposes helps account for this gap between Federal spending and Federal employment.

Federalism and New Deal Politics

The political institutions that federalism had nurtured for decades posed formidable obstacles to the New Deal. The fragmented, state-based Democratic Party proved to be as much a roadblock as a vehicle for consolidating the administration's political strength. Many Democratic governors, state legislators, and mayors had built their own parochial coalitions independent of the national government. Most had the will and the ability to fight the loss of real power to national officials. State and local party leaders certainly welcomed new money and patronage jobs. As often as not, however, they tried to subvert the Federal conditions attached to the use of these resources.

According to James Patterson, these "governors and lawmakers naturally praised or obstructed the Roosevelt administration as political expedience seemed to dictate."[21]

The yawning gap between the Northern and Southern wings of the Democratic Party proved to be the most hazardous challenge for the New Deal. The Northern, urban wing of the party endorsed far-reaching national government activism to strengthen the position of workers and unions. Some Northern liberals grew more outspoken in support of protections for African Americans nationwide. Southern Democrats, in contrast, generally aimed to defend the now-entrenched social, economic, and political subordination of African Americans in their region. Unions made little headway in the South, a region that remained rural, severely underdeveloped, and desperately poor. The senior U.S. Representatives and Senators from the South who commanded the most important committees in Congress fiercely protected state control to shield racial segregation. In 1938, Roosevelt famously tried to replace conservative Southern Democrats in Congress who had opposed the New Deal. His "purge" failed spectacularly, strengthening his conservative opponents in his own party.[22]

The Democrats also encountered other political frustrations in the states. New Deal Democrats never had as much electoral success in most state legislative and executive elections as they had in national elections. Factionalism in state Democratic parties compounded the problem. Administration efforts to control the way fellow Democrats used Federal funds frequently proved time-consuming and sometimes futile. Even when Democrats succeeded in controlling Northern states, the disproportionate influence of rural legislators and the underrepresentation of the urban working class created resistance to the liberal Democrats, as it did in Michigan. State parties divided by factional disputes, weakened by Progressive Era reforms, and often led by individuals much more concerned with holding office than programmatic reform, made it impossible for a disciplined New Deal Democratic Party to penetrate Northern states successfully. The rise of labor unions in the Democratic Party created additional factional battles in some places. By 1938, Democratic political success was beginning to fade. Even in the most progressive states, leaders fought to retain their political independence of the New Deal.[23]

Northern factionalism and Southern conservatism were impediments to using the Democratic Party as a vehicle for developing fully national solutions to the Depression. The breach between the Roosevelt administration and state and local Democratic parties resulted in substantially slower and weaker efforts to mitigate economic problems in the states than in the national government.

Because of these obstacles, the New Deal "often found it less costly and hazardous to bypass rather than transform the Democratic Party," according to political scientist David Plotke.[24] The White House and executive branch agencies became more assertive in developing and controlling domestic policy.[25] The Roosevelt administration established new executive branch agencies led by experts and used these agencies to bypass Congress. Many of these agencies built coalitions directly with pressure groups (such as business, organized labor, or the Farm Bureau) or state and local experts (such as the highway and farm policy professionals) to bypass elected officials in the states. New Deal leaders believed that these interest groups could implement the Roosevelt administration's plans more faithfully than the state and local political parties.

Given the fragmentation and intransigence of state and local elements of the Democratic Party, professionally-minded interest groups seemed a particularly progressive and nationalizing force for improved policy, at least for tackling specific problems in their areas of expertise. Groups that represented interests with a stake in substantive policy improvements seemed a better bet to deliver active government than did recalcitrant, bickering political parties rooted in the era of a more passive government. Roosevelt already had advocated the construction of a "concert of interests" in his 1932 campaign and preparation for office.[26] The strategy of reinforcing Federal and interest group power laid the basis for the New Deal grants strategy.

The Grants Strategy and the Rise of Intergovernmental Relations

The hurdles of American federalism forced the New Deal to fight for broader Federal domestic authority, and at the same time to fight to overcome the resistance of the entrenched state institutions. Visionary ideas for national planning and policy prevailed in the early months of the New Deal and strongly influenced the design of the NIRA. But after its first year, enthusiasm for national power began to erode, and the Roosevelt administration began to adapt more pragmatically to the obstacles of federalism.[27]

Rather than mount a direct assault on state prerogatives, the pragmatic Roosevelt chose to try to adapt federalism to his activist national agenda. His own formative experiences, forged in the Progressive Era and the Depression in New York state, had taught him to deal with the tight constraints on national power as he struggled to extend state action. He knew well the Southern wing of the Democratic Party and its resistance to Federal control, and he had tried to bridge the gaps between the Northern and Southern wings. Roosevelt, then, tended to accept the view that states had to partner with the Federal government in most New Deal efforts, particularly after the initial flurry of Federal laws in 1933. While some of his advisers, such as Rexford Tugwell, pushed for much more nationally-directed policy, and others, such as Public Works Administration director Harold Ickes, tended to disdain local officials, many of the New Deal programs accommodated state variation and interests.[28]

The Federal grant-in-aid programs pioneered in the Progressive Era provided the most obvious, workable, and accepted tool for leveraging national activism while protecting the states' prerogatives. The national government would fund the programs and set some national rules for receiving grants, while states would share costs and determine eligibility and other important aspects of the programs. Grants-in-aid could channel national funds to the states and set national standards where the coalition agreed (on more money for construction projects and relief, for example), while at the same time permitting the states to control policy where the New Deal coalition was internally divided (as on racial segregation). This "cooperative" federalism through grants also served to blunt some of the opposition in Congress, where many members opposed uniform national programs or effective Federal oversight of program operations. Roosevelt hoped that innovative states would go beyond minimum requirements, as he had done as governor of New York.

The New Deal thus gravitated toward using Federal grants-in-aid to energize policy activism in all the states. Economic historian John Joseph Wallis described the growth of national grants-in-aid during the New Deal as "astounding." Federal grant spending exploded from $250 million in 1932 to $2.9 billion in 1934. Grants constituted thirty percent of all Federal spending in 1935.[29] Federal grants amounted to $4 billion in 1940, sixteen times higher than spending in 1932. In 1940, more than $2 billion of these grants were dedicated to relief and income support, while over $800 million went to agriculture, over $500 million to public works, and $171 million to highways.[30]

The narrowly defined purposes of these grants invited alliances with policy experts and interest groups in specific policy areas. Most of the new grants, like the Progressive Era grants, were *categorical* grants, that is, they were Federal funds given for specific, narrowly defined purposes like highway construction or aid to mothers with dependent children. In the long run, the Federal alliance with interest groups added a completely new dimension of complexity to the politics of federalism. Writing in the early 1950s, political scientist David Truman noted that "government functions that operate on a basis of grant-in-aid to the States find themselves in a web of relationships that resist change and disturbance. Because of the influence of federalism, these patterns are more complicated than those of activities directly administered by the Federal government."[31]

By the late 1930s, scholars were using a new concept—*intergovernmental relations*—to capture the new relationships spawned by the active collaboration of the national, state, and local policy-makers energized by the New Deal.[32] This term captures the transformation of American federalism during the crisis of the 1930s, and the inventive pragmatism of the Roosevelt administration in making use of the inherited institutions of American government. In this new, "cooperative" federalism, the Federal government emerged as an active, senior partner of the states, funding government action on a wide range of issues. The battlefield of federalism expanded into new areas, multiplying both the stakes and the conflicts over the use of public power in the United States. Nowhere is this pattern clearer than in agriculture.

Agriculture

The New Deal employed federalism to address the nation's severe agricultural crisis, and in the process strengthened state agricultural agencies and the Farm Bureau. Thirty million Americans lived on farms during the Depression, and collapsing prices for their crops devastated many of them. Agricultural groups and farm supporters had pressured the national government to limit the supply of key crops to the domestic market in the 1920s, aiming to stabilize prices at a level that could sustain farmers. The Agricultural Adjustment Act (AAA) of 1933 aimed to reduce crop production, thus boosting the prices of widely grown commodities like wheat, corn, cotton, rice, and tobacco. The AAA placed a new tax on food processors, and the U.S. Department of Agriculture used the revenues to pay farmers to bring fewer crops to market. For example, the Agriculture Department signed a million contracts with individual cotton-growers, who agreed to grow cotton on only two-thirds of the land used previously. In return, the Department paid each farmer for a Federal lease on the remaining land, and cotton was not grown on that land.[33]

Instead of delegating the responsibility for implementing the AAA to state governors, Secretary of Agriculture Henry Wallace bypassed them and placed the chief responsibility for administering this plan in the hands of the county extension agents created under the Smith-Lever Act of 1914. State extension service directors headed state AAA efforts. In effect, Wallace turned the program over to local expert professionals, strengthening their position relative to the elected officials in the state legislatures. The county extension agents in the states, in turn, organized local farmers in individual counties. The Farm Bureau seized on this opportunity to build its membership, persuading farmers that joining the Farm Bureau would bring them government payments. These tactics consolidated the political position of the AAA. The Farm Bureau's influence grew, even as its membership tilted toward more affluent farmers and against poorer farmers, particularly tenant farmers in the South.[34] New Deal advocates of the needy launched smaller programs designed to help these tenant farmers and the rural poor, and these efforts evolved into the Farm Security Administration (FSA). But the FSA's efforts threatened the county Extension Services and the more affluent, white landowners represented by the Farm Bureau. Political controversy resulted in substantial cuts in FSA authority later in the New Deal, and its transformation into a smaller agency, the Farmers' Home Administration, aimed at helping farmers purchase land.[35]

The political support for the AAA helped Federal farm programs survive the Supreme Court's 1936 decision that the AAA unconstitutionally interfered with the states' authority over agriculture. Quickly, the Federal government enacted the Soil Conservation and Domestic Allotment Act of 1936 to pay farmers for substituting soil conserving crops (such as grasses) for crops that led to soil erosion (such as corn, wheat, and cotton).[36] The Agricultural Adjustment Act of 1938 required the Federal government to set mandatory price supports for corn, cotton, and wheat, and to set mandatory production quotas for these and other commodities. The Supreme Court upheld this new AAA.

After World War II, American agricultural policy was dominated by alliances of farm interest groups, key congressional committees, and bureaucratic agencies that together managed separate commodities in a kind of specialized "subgovernment." In this way, farm policy became a model for interest group pluralism in the 1950s (see Chapter 3). Instead of fracturing across the geographical divisions of the federal system, Federal agricultural policy fractured into specialized, functional management of specific crops.[37]

Relief and Public Works

The states, which had shouldered responsibility for public welfare, were the fastest way to channel financial help to the victims of the Depression. Even before Roosevelt took office, Congress authorized the Reconstruction Finance Corporation to loan $300 million to the state governments to provide direct relief to needy Americans—if the states could prove that they had exhausted their own resources.[38] By the spring of 1933, however, this fund already was exhausted. On the same day he signed the AAA, Roosevelt also signed the Federal Emergency Relief Act, authorizing a new Federal Emergency Relief Administration (FERA) to distribute $500 million in grants-in-aid (not loans) to the states. Half this $500 million would require state and local governments to spend three dollars on relief for every dollar of Federal money they received. Harry Hopkins, now the head of FERA, had the authority to distribute the rest of the Federal money to address specific needs across the country. Hopkins required the states to establish state emergency relief agencies along the lines of the New York state agency he had managed, thus compelling the states to become more professional and build their capacity to help the needy. Between 1933 and 1940, the Federal relief programs administered by FERA, the Works Progress Administration, and the Social Security Act programs spent about $2 billion a year.[39] The New Deal provided relief through public employment projects such as the Civilian Conservation Corps (the CCC, 1933–42), the Public Works Administration (the PWA, 1933–38), the Civil Works Administration (the CWA, 1934–35), and the Works Progress Administration (the WPA, 1935–43).[40] These programs helped millions of needy Americans make it through the Depression.

While the Federal government directly ran many of these temporary work relief programs, it permanently increased state government effort in public welfare through FERA matching grants, WPA grants, and finally the permanent grant-in-aid programs established in 1935. This delegation of power to the states created severe problems for Hopkins and other administrators during the early New Deal. Some states, such as Utah, Minnesota, and Indiana, were very cooperative. But in other states, obstinate conservative Democrats or warring Democratic factions frustrated implementation. In some (but not all) states where they retained power, Republican leaders opposed these Roosevelt administration initiatives. In some cases, ambitious state leaders of both parties sought to turn these Federal funds to their personal political advantage. Ultimately, such conflicts resulted in the Federal takeover of programs in Georgia, Louisiana, Ohio, and Oklahoma.[41]

Federal–state highway construction proved to be the most lasting of these Federal–state initiatives, and one of the most important for the growth of intergovernmental relations until the 1960s. Falling public revenues during the Depression forced states to cut back their aggressive highway-building of the 1920s, and these cuts made the unemployment problem worse. The Hoover administration offered loans to the states to continue building highways. The National Industrial Recovery Act of 1933 provided $400 million in grants for road construction. Later, the Public Works Administration spent $1 billion on highways, and the Works Progress Administration spent $3.7 billion. Of all Federal workers on relief, an estimated thirty-five to forty-five percent were engaged in road building. In 1939, more than half of the states' total spending on roads came from the Federal government. The New Deal made two lasting changes in highway construction policy. First, Federal funds could now be used to construct urban, and not just rural highways, thus expanding the constituency for road-building grants-in-aid. Second, just as the Federal agriculture programs increased the influence of state and local experts and interest groups, so did highway grants-in-aid. State highway departments and highway engineers rose to preeminence in Federal–state highway collaboration, hemming in the role of state legislatures in these programs.[42] After World War II, Federal–state highway grants grew into another textbook example of a subgovernment dominated by experts and interests.

In 1935, the Roosevelt administration phased out FERA's work-relief responsibilities and delegated them to the nationally-run Works Progress Administration. The WPA employed over three million workers at its peak, and expended $13 billion before it ended in 1943. The Federally-run WPA funded highways, public buildings, water works, recreational facilities, and other public investments that did not compete with private businesses.[43] FERA turned over the responsibility for relief to the states. While some states stepped up and filled the gap left by the loss of FERA relief funds, some of the states hit hardest by the Depression, such as Illinois and Ohio, substantially reduced support for the needy.[44] At the same time, the Social Security Act of 1935 began to help many of the needy poor who could not work.

Social Security

In June, 1934, Roosevelt announced his intention to undertake "the great task of furthering the security of the citizen and his family through social insurance." He asserted that "three great objectives—the security of the home, the security of livelihood, and the security of social insurance" together "constitute a right which belongs to every individual and every family willing to work." States would play an essential role in implementing this national ideal. Roosevelt promised "a maximum of cooperation between States and the Federal Government." In his view, "the several States should meet at least a large portion of the cost of management, leaving to the Federal Government the responsibility of investing, maintaining and safeguarding the funds constituting the necessary insurance reserves."[45] A year later, large majorities in Congress approved the Social Security Act.

In the year between Roosevelt's 1934 speech and final congressional approval, policy designers had ensured that states would play a prominent role in nearly all the Social Security Act programs. Roosevelt charged a special Committee on Economic Security to develop the proposal in 1934, and he personally emphasized the importance of relying on the states "as much as possible." This committee was led by professional experts who had nurtured social insurance programs in states like New York and Wisconsin, and they shared Roosevelt's commitment to ensuring a major role for the states. Secretary of Labor Frances Perkins, who chaired the Committee, had served as New York State Industrial Commissioner under Roosevelt and had been developing an unemployment insurance plan for the state. Edwin Witte, an economist at the University of Wisconsin, who had collaborated in the development of the pioneering Wisconsin unemployment insurance program, served as executive director. These leaders favored substantial state responsibility for welfare, not only because they believed in state responsibility, but also because delegation of responsibility to the states was politically expedient. State control could allow conservative Southern Democrats to support such a bill, because it would allow Southern states to maintain the balance of racial power in their region. Since these Democrats had the seniority to block the bill in key committees, their support was critically important. State control also could reduce opposition of state and local officials outside the South, who were very wary of the controversies and conflicts that accompanied previous New Deal relief programs. Finally, the U.S. Supreme Court was more likely to uphold a program if it delegated authority to the states.[46]

Alone among the provisions of the Social Security Act, the Federal government would directly manage old-age insurance for retired workers.

Employers and workers in long-term, full-time jobs would make mandatory contributions to a Federally-run trust fund. This part of the Act became synonymous with the term "Social Security." Although the national design of this part of retirement pensions raised objections from Perkins and Witte, it was supported by key elements of business and labor.[47] There were five reasons that the Roosevelt administration proposed, and Congress approved, a fully national old-age insurance program rather than a program partially controlled by the states. First, one of the most meteoric social movements in American history was pressuring Washington in 1934 to levy a national sales tax and provide cash payments to every American over the age of sixty. This Townsend movement (inspired by retired Dr. Francis Townsend) attracted national attention, thousands of followers, and a reputation for substantial political clout.[48] Roosevelt acknowledged that "Congress can't stand the pressure of the Townsend plan unless we have a real old-age insurance system ... "[49] Second, unlike old-age pensions, widows' pension, and unemployment compensation, no state had created a government-sponsored old-age insurance program, so that no state occupied the field of this policy innovation, and none would dig in to oppose Federal interference with an existing program. Third, Federal policy-makers believed that nationally-run social insurance for the elderly would cost less than Federal–state grants for old-age pensions.[50] Fourth, the fact that American workers frequently moved across state lines made it difficult to design a state-based system for old-age insurance; a national plan allowed workers to build up their funds by working in one state, and then to retire and draw funds in another. Fifth, the program excluded domestic workers and agricultural workers, and for that reason, left much of the labor market in the South—particularly its racial composition—undisturbed.

Unlike old-age insurance for workers, unemployment insurance (Title III)—the section that its own authors believed to be the most important part of Social Security—was designed to be administered by the states. The experts disagreed about whether the program should be fully national or a shared Federal–state responsibility, but President Roosevelt's own preference for state-run systems bolstered the latter position. To help the law survive a test in the Supreme Court, it allowed states to implement different kinds of plans, including Wisconsin's plan to tax employers based on their record of joblessness, or a plan like Ohio's fully public plan. In the end, the Social Security Act allowed the states broad discretion over who would be eligible for unemployment compensation, how long a jobless person had to wait to draw benefits, how much they could receive in benefits and for how long, and how the program would be funded. All the states established unemployment compensation programs by the end of 1937. Business successfully lobbied most states to establish programs more like that in Wisconsin, because its program, based on the ideas of John R. Commons, was more favorable to business and made the states more sensitive to interstate competition. Ever since, the states and their congressional representatives have fought off efforts to nationalize the unemployment insurance system.[51]

The Social Security Act also established major Federal–state grant program categories for other needy Americans, strictly separating benefit programs for those who were not expected to work from those who were. Thirty states already provided some income assistance to the elderly by 1935. These state programs provided very limited help; only three percent of the elderly were receiving benefits, and the average benefit was sixty-five cents a day. In 1931, nearly all the states provided support for widowed mothers and children, but the programs were severely underfunded and limited in scope. Twenty-six states had laws providing financial support for needy blind people. The authors of the Social Security Act used grants to induce all the states to establish such programs. Title I created a matching grant program to encourage all states to administer old-age assistance programs for the aged poor. Title IV established Federal–state grants to encourage all the states "to furnish financial assistance, as far as practicable under the conditions in such State, to needy dependent children." Title X provided a Federal grant program for the blind.[52]

Congress guaranteed that these Social Security grant-in-aid programs protected the states' policy independence and discretion in implementing welfare policy. Most important, states had much discretion to define "need" and set benefit levels. Predictably, state definitions of need and benefit levels soon varied widely. In 1942, California provided average monthly payments of $36.91 for Old Age Assistance, $57.48 per family for Aid to Dependent Children, and $46.95 for Aid to the Blind. In the same year, average monthly payments in Mississippi were $9.05 for Old Age Assistance, $20.17 per family for Aid to Dependent Children, and $10.63 for Aid to the Blind.[53] The Social Security Act left intact the states' general relief programs, which predated the Depression, were entirely run by each state, and still served a substantial clientele after the 1930s.[54]

The Committee on Economic Security considered adding a program for national health insurance to the Social Security bill. Committee members believed that such a program would cost less than other program titles, particularly if combined with the program of services for the unemployed, mothers, and children. But the Roosevelt administration refused to support health insurance. Many supporters of Social Security believed that the addition of health insurance would generate enough opposition to sink the entire plan. Instead, the Social Security Act included Title V for maternal and child health care services, enlarging on the now-defunct Sheppard-Towner grants.[55] Although the Roosevelt Administration created a committee to study the issue of health insurance further, it never proposed a plan. When members of Congress in the 1940s pressed for a system of grants to the states to set up health insurance, the proposal died because of the opposition of a powerful coalition of interest groups, led by the American Medical Association and including the U.S. Chamber of Commerce, the American

Farm Bureau Federation, and others. Instead of a comprehensive health insurance plan as an addition to the Social Security Act, Congress expanded Veterans' hospitals (a fully nationalized system) and passed a grant-in-aid program, the Hospital Survey and Construction Act (the Hill-Burton Act) of 1946, that encouraged states to plan and aid hospital construction.[56]

The Social Security Act's grant-in-aid programs did inject some national priorities into state policy. All the states enacted and administered unemployment compensation and aid programs for the needy. As in the highway and agricultural initiatives, these programs compelled the states to build new public bureaus, because the Social Security Act required that a single state agency had to take responsibility for administering each program in the state. At the insistence of Congress, however, the Social Security Act allowed states to make their own personnel decisions, thus permitting states to perpetuate and extend patronage arrangements (as Kentucky Representative Fred Vinson explained, "No damned social workers are going to come into my State to tell our people whom they shall hire").[57] This template was applied to health grants. By 1936, all the states had created maternal and child health care divisions, and the law helped create state public health departments, state public health laboratories, and it funded public health education in state universities.[58]

Although the Social Security Act formally ignored gender and race distinctions, the law in practice strongly favored white males and provided fewer benefit opportunities for working women and minorities. As political scientist Suzanne Mettler pointed out, the Old Age Insurance program was designed for primary bread-winners, that is, males who headed households. Most women did not work, and when they did, they tended to work intermittently. The fact that agricultural and domestic workers (such as maids) were excluded from social insurance eliminated two-thirds of blacks and many women from benefits. At the same time, states used their discretion to design unemployment compensation programs to exclude most women.[59] The New Deal's support for trade unions also heavily benefited men.

Organized Labor

The New Deal fostered the growth of trade unions, expanding an important political constituency and a counterweight to business in many states. Unions would complement the Social Security Act by negotiating better wages, benefits, and working conditions for their members. Although the National Industrial Recovery Act of 1933 had specified that workers had the right to organize in unions, employers often undermined the spirit of this law by setting up "company" unions that they fully controlled. The National Labor Relations Act of 1935 protected unions organized independently of employers, and transferred much union regulation away from the courts to a new National Labor Relations Board. Union organization expanded dramatically, and by 1947, a third of the non-agricultural labor force was unionized.[60] The Fair Labor Standards Act of 1938 effectively shored up unions by setting a national wage floor under manufacturing wages and a national upper limit on daily working hours. These wage and hour regulations allowed unions to negotiate for more favorable wages, hours, working conditions, and benefits.[61] Some states also passed laws that benefited unions, and established minimum wage and working standards higher than those set by the Federal government.

In the 1940s, Republicans artfully used federalism to try to limit the advances of unions. The Taft-Hartley Act of 1947, passed by a Republican Congress over President Truman's veto, allowed states to prohibit the union shop (that is, workplaces that require union membership as a condition of employment). All the former Confederate States, and twenty-two states in all, subsequently enacted these laws, commonly termed "right to work" laws. These laws utilized the natural competitiveness of the American states to blunt the expansion of trade unions. State "right-to-work" laws severely impeded the ability of unions to organize and sustain themselves in the South and West, the nation's fastest growing area in the second half of the twentieth century.[62]

The New Deal Legacy

The New Deal changed the United States, vaulting the national government into a lasting preeminence in American domestic policy. While the Roosevelt Administration greatly increased national government revenue and administrative capacity, it constructed a cooperative partnership with the states. Federalism and the institutions it had shaped for a century and a half—decentralized political parties and interest groups, white dominance in Southern law, the ascendance of large corporations, and the cooperative Federal–state innovations of the Progressive Era—profoundly shaped the *way* the New Deal implemented national action.

The Roosevelt administration deliberately channeled many of its initiatives through experts and interest groups, aiming to infuse more professionalism and responsiveness to national goals into state and local policy. As political scientist Theodore Lowi explained, this strategy "helped flank the constitutional problems of federalism."[63] The New Deal's politically expedient layering and bypassing strategies avoided a direct, brutal, and costly confrontation with deeply rooted political institutions nursed along by decades of decentralized evolution. But the strategy had three high costs of its own. First, it added more fragmentation to public policy by planting the seeds for strong, separate, autonomous policy communities dedicated to specific crops, welfare programs, highway building projects, or other narrowly focused policy agendas. These narrow policy communities had considerable resilience and political strength, and often made it more difficult to address new public policy problems. Second, grants and contracts among governments established a new arena of political conflict, one that was almost invisible to the public. Extensive new intergovernmental relationships created thousands of potential disputes in the policy process, each with the potential to undermine national purposes and bend them to parochial desires. While grants opened new opportunities for the poor and the powerless, they also created new sources of delay, obstruction, and frustration. Third, Federal policies delivered through states made many policies vulnerable to interstate rivalry and competition. These factors continued to constrain states' ability to pursue innovative and potentially expensive policy experiments.

The same diversity that hemmed in the New Deal would complicate future efforts to achieve far-reaching national policy change. The inherent conflicts in this new system became clearer when a later generation of liberals tried to expand the scope of government to extend government activism a generation after the Depression.

8   Liberal Activism and Intergovernmental Relations

During the prosperous decades of the mid-twentieth century, liberal reformers used Federal power to address discrimination, poverty, illness, educational inequity, pollution, and urban decline. These liberals inherited the intergovernmental activism of the New Deal and sought to build on it to expand rights and broaden opportunity. Liberals in the 1960s changed federalism by adding more Federal rules and grants programs, and by shifting grants to new recipients. Rather than reverse all these liberal efforts, Republican President Richard Nixon used federalism to shift as much control over Federally-funded programs as possible to state and local governments. Both Democrats and Republicans, then, expanded the Federal role, employing federalism as a selective political tool to achieve their larger goals.

Liberal policy injected the Federal government into most of the important policies that state and local governments had previously monopolized: public education, health, criminal justice, and environmental protection. State and local governments were engaged as agents of Federal purpose, and intergovernmental relations fully flowered. This system fragmented the political battlefield of federalism into many smaller conflicts over the state and local use of Federal dollars, and the constituencies that Federal rules and grants would affect.

Nationalization and New Political Demands

Major changes weakened the decentralized scaffolding of the United States in the decades after World War II. First, geographical distinctions began to erode as American life nationalized. A few national media networks dominated television, which quickly became the predominant source of news and entertainment across America. The Cold War focused more attention on national security and the Federal government. Suburbs across the nation fostered a similar suburban lifestyle, dominated by single family housing developments, shopping malls, and restaurant chains. By 1980, forty percent of the American population lived in suburbs, a larger share than lived in the central cities in metropolitan areas (twenty-eight percent) or in rural areas (thirty-two percent).[1]

The long-established economic gap between the South and the rest of the nation almost disappeared. In 1930, the South was a poor, rural agricultural economy with very limited industry, its wealth lagging far behind the Northeast and Midwest. The average person living in the Southeastern states in 1930 still had only half the income of the average American. But because of economic development efforts, wartime industrial production, the decline of agriculture, and the growth of cities, the income of the average person in the Southeast was nearly ninety percent of the average American income by 1960.

Second, demands for national action and national rules increased as the population increased and grew more affluent. The U.S. population grew over seventy percent from 1940 to 1980, driven by a post-war "baby boom" and medical advances that allowed the average American to live years longer. Overall, jobs were relatively plentiful, workers' paychecks increased, and many enjoyed more leisure time. Women's role in American society was transforming rapidly, changing perspectives on social needs. By the 1980s, two-thirds of women were in the labor force, a large majority in the expanding service sector.[2] As Americans grew more secure financially, more placed a higher priority on "post-material" values such as the quality of life, participation, civil rights and liberties, the environment, and safer products.[3]

The U.S. Supreme Court added fuel to the nationalizing impulse by issuing many rulings that limited state and local government discretion. Under Chief Justice Earl Warren (1954–69), the Court imposed new Federal rules to protect minorities, to ensure fair criminal procedures, to equalize the population of state-drawn electoral districts, to protect free speech, and to limit the role of government in religious practice. These rulings expanded the reach of the Federal judiciary in defining the boundaries of state and national authority. In these cases, the Court used judicial review "to bring the states into line with the nationally dominant constitutional vision," targeting states that resisted national trends.[4] Political scientist Martha Derthick observed that, after Warren left the Court, "[F]ederal judges repeatedly ordered state and local governments to do quite specific things in regard to prisons, mental hospitals, police behavior, and much else" in the 1970s. In her view, "[a] whole new perception of the state governments as subordinates of the national government, properly subject to command, had taken root, laying the basis for the regulation that spread like a vine through the garden of American federalism in the 1970s."[5]

These changes helped drive another wave of national reform. The civil rights movement inspired growing demands for equal treatment of women, Latinos, the disabled, and gays. Demands also grew for more opportunity, participation, open government, and public transparency.[6]

Liberal Democrats, Grants Activism, and Intergovernmental Relations

The states provided a political launch pad for post-war liberals who spearheaded the political response to these demands. A new generation of younger liberal Democrats built careers by expanding the political agenda and revitalizing the Democratic Party in their states. These Democrats sought more universal protections for the rights of minorities, women, and the poor, and more national action to address "post-material" concerns. Minnesota's Hubert Humphrey fought for civil rights, for example, and Wisconsin's Gaylord Nelson and Maine's Edmund Muskie championed environmental protection. The 1972 presidential campaign of Senator George McGovern of South Dakota brought together many of these themes. These Democrats helped rejuvenate their political party in more than a dozen Northern and Western states, contributing to substantial Democratic influence in the states and majorities in Congress through the 1970s. They strongly influenced the presidential administrations of John F. Kennedy (1961–63) and Lyndon Johnson (1963–69). Johnson ambitiously fought to extend Federal action to the unfinished agenda of the Roosevelt-Truman years, and also to address civil rights, equal opportunity, and a host of other newer concerns.[7]

Liberal Democrats inherited and built upon the New Deal's grants activism. During the height of liberal influence in the 1960s, Democrats envisioned grants-in-aid as a catalyst that would steer state governments, local governments, and private institutions to tackle their national priorities. These Democrats greatly expanded the range and funding of grant programs. At the same time, they frequently bypassed state governments by channeling money directly to cities and their preferred interests, and they layered many new national rules and requirements on top of the Federal grants system.

Johnson's landslide 1964 election victory, combined with huge majorities in Congress, opened a window of opportunity for an enormous expansion of grants. During Johnson's presidency, two hundred and ten new grant programs were enacted—more grant-in-aid programs than had been created in all the previous years of American history.[8] Federal spending on grants-in-aid doubled to twenty billion dollars between 1964 and 1968. The Federal government dramatically expanded grants for assistance and services for the poor. Federal grants for education and policing made the Federal government a presence in fields that state and local governments had monopolized since the nation's founding. Nelson Rockefeller, New York's Republican governor, described this emerging new system as "creative federalism," and the Johnson administration enthusiastically embraced this language.[9]

"Creative federalism" in the 1960s differed from the New Deal grants strategy in four important ways. First, the new grant spending of the

1960s addressed the new priorities of the time: poverty, racial exclusion, and equal opportunity for all citizens. Table 8.1 shows that Federal grants for highway and transportation constituted over forty percent of Federal grant spending in 1960. By 1970, transportation grants were less than twenty percent of grant spending (though they were larger in terms of absolute value). Grants for health and income support together constituted more than two out of every five Federal grant dollars in 1970. By the 2000s, grants for health care alone would be almost half of Federal grant spending.

Second, many Federal grants in this period conspicuously bypassed the state governments and directed money to cities, counties, and private businesses and not-for-profit groups. The War on Poverty and the Model Cities program provided grants directly to community-based organizations to increase the influence of lower-income residents and remove the programs from the direct control of mayors, city councils, and other local power-brokers. Democrats also shifted grants toward cities and metropolitan areas, which received seventy percent of grant dollars by 1968.[10] These grants drew new recipients into the intergovernmental system and expanded the constituency for grants activism.

Third, the Federal government layered more regulations on grant recipients to leverage more control over them. One type of regulation was the *crosscutting* requirement that mandated all Federal grant recipients to obey a particular regulation, regardless of the purpose of the grant. The 1964 Civil Rights Act prohibited "discrimination under any program or activity receiving Federal financial assistance" and authorized Federal officials to withdraw grants from state governments, local governments, and other organizations that practiced discrimination. The narrower *crossover* requirement provided that recipients of specific types of grant could be penalized if they did not meet the requirement of a new law. The Highway Beautification Act of 1965, for example, allowed Federal officials to penalize state highways departments ten percent of their grants if they did not comply with new Federal rules regulating billboards. *Partial preemption* established national responsibility for managing a program, but delegated implementation to the states and local governments *if* they met standards specified by the Federal government. For example, the Water Quality Act gave each state a year to develop its standards for the quality of water in its lakes, rivers, and other bodies of water inside its boundaries. If a state failed to do so, the Federal government could establish and enforce its standards within that state.[11] Combined with requirements for specific grant programs, the number of Federal requirements for Federal grants increased from 4 in 1960 to 1,034 in 1978.[12]

Fourth, with the major exception of Medicaid, most of the new liberal grant programs were *project* grants, which required grant applicants to propose a project (such as a specific job training program) to a Federal agency. Federal administrators, rather than Congress, then authorized to

Table 8.1 Grants to State and Local Governments by Function, 1960–2010 (in Millions of Dollars)

Function and Fund Group	1960 Amount (millions)	1960 Percent of All Grants	1970 Amount (millions)	1970 Percent of All Grants	1980 Amount (millions)	1980 Percent of All Grants	1990 Amount (millions)	1990 Percent of All Grants	2000 Amount (millions)	2000 Percent of All Grants	2010 estimate Amount (millions)	2010 estimate Percent of All Grants
National defense	5	0.1%	37	0.2%	93	0.1%	241	0.2%	2	0.0%	82	0.0%
Energy	6	0.1%	25	0.1%	499	0.5%	461	0.3%	433	0.2%	5,927	0.9%
Natural resources and environment	108	1.5%	411	1.7%	5,363	5.9%	3,745	2.8%	4,595	1.6%	8,836	1.4%
Agriculture	243	3.5%	604	2.5%	569	0.6%	1,285	0.9%	724	0.3%	1,231	0.2%
Commerce and housing credit	2	0.0%	4	0.0%	3	0.0%	....	....	1,218	0.4%	2,125	0.3%
Transportation	2,999	42.7%	4,599	19.1%	13,022	14.2%	19,174	14.2%	32,222	11.3%	72,249	11.1%
Community and regional development	109	1.6%	1,780	7.4%	6,486	7.1%	4,965	3.7%	8,665	3.0%	21,221	3.2%
Education, training, employment, and social services	525	7.5%	6,417	26.7%	21,862	23.9%	21,780	16.1%	36,672	12.8%	111,715	17.1%
Health	214	3.0%	3,849	16.0%	15,758	17.2%	43,890	32.4%	124,843	43.7%	294,613	45.1%
Income security	2,635	37.5%	5,795	24.1%	18,495	20.2%	36,768	27.2%	68,653	24.0%	121,818	18.6%
Social security	8	0.1%	18	0.1%	90	0.1%	....	....	6	0.0%	26	0.0%
Veterans' benefits and services	....	....	....	....	....	....	134	0.1%	434	0.2%	935	0.1%
Administration of justice	....	....	42	0.2%	529	0.6%	574	0.4%	5,263	1.8%	5,783	0.9%
General government	165	2.4%	479	2.0%	8,616	9.4%	2,309	1.7%	2,144	0.7%	7,104	1.1%
Total outlays for grants to State and local governments	7,019		24,065		91,385		135,325		285,874		653,665	

Source: U.S. Office of Management and Budget, President's Budget, 2010, Historical Tables, Table 12.2, http://www.whitehouse.gov/omb/budget/historicals/ (accessed January 17, 2011).

grant funds for that purpose. Until the 1960s, most grants were *formula* grants, that is, they distributed funds based on a formula established by Congress. The formula grants entitled state governments and other recipients to Federal money, limiting Federal administrative control. Project grants, in contrast, enhanced the Federal executive branch by forcing recipients to compete to satisfy more Federal agency requirements and priorities tailored to each grant. Four out of five grant programs added between 1962 and 1966 were project grants, and project grants accounted for half of grant spending in 1969 (up from a quarter in 1964).[13]

By 1969, this new Federal grants system was growing stronger politically. Specific grant programs nurtured specific "benefits coalitions," that is, political alliances of government officials, interest groups, and experts across the Federal, state, and local levels who benefited from the grants. For example, such a benefits coalition organized around Federal grants for job training, and included governors, mayors, county leaders, U.S. Department of Labor officials, community organizations, trade unions, and the National Alliance of Business.[14]

Coalitions of intergovernmental policy specialists, initiated in the Progressive Era and extended by the New Deal, broadened much further and grew more resilient. Governor Terry Sanford of North Carolina described the intergovernmental relations that resulted as "picket-fence" federalism: specialists at the different levels of government together exercise much control over specific functional programs—such as public housing, education, health and hospitals, like—all arranged like the pickets in a picket fence, nailed onto the three supportive "horizontal rails" of the national, state, and local levels of government.[15] In addition, interest groups representing governments, including cities (the United States Conference of Mayors and the National League of Cities), the National Association of Counties, and the National Governors Association all influenced the growth of intergovernmental grants more generally.[16] These interest organizations were gaining influence at the expense of local political parties that steadily were weakening.[17]

Increased Federal grants funding raised the political stakes and made grants more contentious. Conflicts often broke out over who would receive money, for what purpose, and with what strings attached. City mayors and minority groups, as a natural part of the Democratic coalition, favored grants formulae based on need, as well as a direct connection to Federal grants agencies, thus bypassing the states. Counties, especially the large and rapidly growing suburban counties outside city limits, were much more Republican than the cities; these counties and the states favored fewer strings and formulae based on population rather than need. U.S. Senators and Representatives tried to maximize Federal benefits for their states and districts, while also maximizing local control over the way the grant programs were run. Grant programs that emerged from Congress, then, tended to be distributed widely and evenly across states and House districts, regardless of need. Not surprisingly, Congress usually passed such grant programs with large, bipartisan majorities.[18]

Grants Activism and the Republicans

The popularity of grants convinced Republican presidents in these years to accept grants activism and to try to shift grants toward their own state and local allies. Republican power to redirect grants was limited, however. During most of Dwight Eisenhower's administration (1953–61) and all of the administrations of Richard Nixon (1969–74) and Gerald Ford (1974–77), Republican presidents had to share power with a Democratic majority in both the U.S. House and Senate (1955–81). Eisenhower established a Commission on Intergovernmental Relations (the Kestenbaum Commission, 1953), charged with identifying Federal activities that could be turned over to the states. The Commission had very little impact, however. Instead, Eisenhower seized on grants for highway construction as a way to pursue policy activism while promoting economic development and increasing state responsibility. The National Interstate and Defense Highways Act created the largest public works project in American history, routing $25 billion in Federal grants to the states to establish a 41,000-mile network of controlled-access expressways. The Federal government would provide ninety percent of the cost of building the system, and lay down national engineering rules for consistency. State transportation departments would build the roads. This highways act further strengthened the alliance of Federal and state highway engineers.[19]

   Richard Nixon, who inherited the Great Society's grant expansion when he took office in 1969, aimed to use "*block*" grants to redirect grants more broadly (and away from the beneficiaries the Democrats had targeted). Nixon announced "a New Federalism in which power, funds and respon-sibility will flow from Washington to the States and the people." Nixon's "New Federalism" would group together several similar categorical grant programs, and turn over to the states the money and responsibility for this single block of formerly separate programs. These block grants would shift money to the state level, allowing the states more discretion in managing the services funded. Nixon also supported *general revenue sharing*, embodied in the State and Local Fiscal Assistance Act of 1972. General revenue sharing provided Federal grants for *any* purpose the state or local government chose. Funds were distributed by a set formula. State governments directly received one-third of these general revenue-sharing funds, and the rest went to general purpose local governments such as counties, cities, and towns. This plan had strong, bipartisan support from governors, mayors, state and local admin-istrators, and the intergovernmental groups that represented them.[20] In contrast to the Federal controls that accompanied the Johnson administration's project grants, general revenue sharing had minimal Federal requirements, and helped the states and suburbs, no matter how wealthy or poor.[21]

The Nixon Administration proposed to convert 129 categorical grants into six *"block"* grants for urban community development, job training, law enforcement, education, transportation, and rural community development. One such block grant, the Comprehensive Employment and Training Act of 1973, combined seventeen job training grant programs into a single program. The Community Development Block Grant (CDBG) of 1974 combined urban renewal, Model Cities, and five other programs. But Congress refused to approve the four other block grants that Nixon initially proposed. Congress also included more Federal requirements and regulations than Nixon wanted.[22] During Nixon's administration, the National Environmental Policy Act of 1969, the Educational Rights and Privacy Act of 1974, and several laws prohibiting discrimination on the basis of sex, age, and disability added new crosscutting requirements to all Federal grants.[23]

Nixon's "New Federalism" increased grant spending, but it also shifted grants-in-aid away from the Democrats' central city constituency and toward the growing Republican constituency in suburban and rural areas and in Sunbelt states.[24] With Federal spending and budget deficits coming under increasing criticism in the late 1970s, Democratic President Jimmy Carter began to cut away at grants. Like his Republican predecessor Gerald Ford, Carter reduced revenue sharing. Carter also added some new restrictions and regulations to grant programs, and "targeted" them to more specific groups. In effect, the Carter targeting strategy shifted grants back toward urban Democratic constituencies in the aging cities of the Midwest and Northeast.

Activism by Proxy

By 1980, the grant system had grown enormously. Both Democratic and Republican presidential administrations had increased grant spending steadily. At their peak in 1978, grants constituted seventeen percent of total Federal spending, a percentage not exceeded again until the administration of George W. Bush (Figures 8.1 and 8.2).

By the end of the 1970s, Federal policy activism had left a legacy of activism through agents outside the Federal government, or activism "by proxy." During both Democratic and Republican presidential administrations after World War II, the Federal government had fueled policy activism by providing conditional funds to a wide variety of public, non-profit, and private organizations. A study in the late 1970s made this pattern clear: *"considerably less than one-tenth of the {F}ederal budget is allotted to domestic activities that the {F}ederal government performs itself"* (emphasis added).[25] In effect, the Federal government was writing checks that state and local governments and other organizations cashed and spent, particularly on the problems of poverty, health, education, and cities.

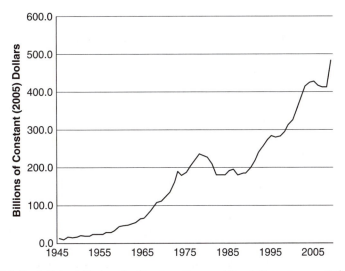

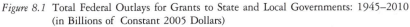

Figure 8.1 Total Federal Outlays for Grants to State and Local Governments: 1945–2010 (in Billions of Constant 2005 Dollars)
Source: U.S. Office of Management and Budget, *President's Budget, Historical Tables*, Table 12.1, http://www.whitehouse.gov/omb/budget/historicals (accessed July 5, 2010).

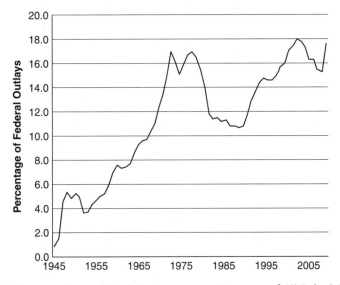

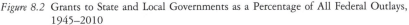

Figure 8.2 Grants to State and Local Governments as a Percentage of All Federal Outlays, 1945–2010
Source: U.S. Office of Management and Budget, *President's Budget, Historical Tables*, Table 12.1, http://www.whitehouse.gov/omb/budget/historicals (accessed July 5, 2010).

Poverty

Those who sought to reduce American poverty in the 1960s inherited a system divided between the Federal and state governments. The nationally run Social Security old-age insurance program was popular and entrenched. Social Security became a very effective anti-poverty program that served thirty-five million people and substantially reduced poverty among the elderly.[26] But the state-managed Aid to Dependent Children program (Title IV of the Social Security Act) was increasingly criticized and associated with the scornful term, "welfare." The number of recipients of Aid to Dependent Children (changed in 1962 to "Aid to Families with Dependent Children," or AFDC) doubled between 1955 and 1965, and exceeded ten million by the early 1970s.[27]

The mounting cost of AFDC drew more criticism at all levels. Connecticut Governor Abraham Ribicoff, a liberal Democrat, complained that "few state problems were as frustrating and as bothersome as the whole problem of welfare costs." State and local governments began to try to limit access to the program. Some states disqualified those who had migrated from other states. Several states required a "suitable home" to qualify for assistance, and others established "man-in-the-house" rules that disqualified any household with a resident male. Newburgh, New York announced that able-bodied men who refused city work would lose their benefits, that unmarried mothers would lose benefits if they had an additional child, and that all recipients, except the aged and disabled, were entitled to only three months of assistance per calendar year. Meanwhile, some cities and counties instituted job training and placement programs to help recipients become more "self-sufficient."[28]

The Kennedy Administration built bipartisan support for more Federal assistance to the states to help reduce their welfare costs. The Public Welfare Amendments of 1962 increased grants for social services, aiming to encourage all the states to help the poor become self-sufficient. States were reluctant to take up the opportunity to provide these services. Eventually, however, California and Illinois discovered that their states could use these social services grants to "purchase" services from other state agencies, which allowed these states to fund ongoing state expenditures with Federal grants intended for the poor.[29]

The Johnson administration added a new Federal antipoverty strategy: it would bypass the state and local governments entirely, creating and funding new organizations to concentrate and coordinate help for the poor. The Economic Opportunity Act—the "War on Poverty"—authorized $315 million for "Community Action Programs" to pull together several kinds of services (such as day care, literacy education, job training, and employment counseling) in the areas of greatest need. It promised the poor "maximum feasible participation" in determining how this money would be spent. The ambitions of the War on Poverty never were matched by adequate resources, however. The program never came close to spending as much as the Federal–state AFDC system, and Community Action Agencies did not control most of the funding for the poor that Congress appropriated. Moreover, War on Poverty funding was not sustained for enough years to allow it to correct its problems. The Johnson Administration championed the War on Poverty in part because it believed that the initiative would reduce the growth of welfare expenditures.[30] While the War on Poverty withered, Supreme Court decisions in the 1960s and 1970s loosened restrictions on AFDC eligibility, opening the program to even more recipients.[31]

Other Federal grant programs, such as Food Stamps, expanded the states' role in mitigating poverty. The food stamp program, funded by the Federal government, supplemented the income of the poor with a voucher to purchase groceries. State and county governments administered the program in conjunction with AFDC. Food stamps were popular politically because the program benefited farmers as well as the urban poor. This political marriage of agricultural and urban interests has been an important and enduring part of the U.S. welfare system ever since.[32]

By the end of the 1960s, the fragmented American welfare system seemed beyond control. In 1969, the President's Commission on Income Maintenance Programs concluded that there existed "over 300 separate programs of cash Public Assistance receiving Federal funds, covering different categories of the population under widely varying standards" and that Federal officials did not have "[c]omplete and accurate knowledge of the actual operations of state and local programs ... The multiplicity of governments involved has made effective policy coordinating nearly impossible."[33] State governors and other leaders of both parties pressured Richard Nixon for welfare reform before he took office. Republican governors in large states demanded financial relief and uniform welfare standards.[34]

Both Richard Nixon and Jimmy Carter proposed to simplify the system by nationalizing income support for the poor, but both found it impossible to build a sufficient consensus to do so. Nixon proposed a "Family Assistance Plan" as a way to strengthen state and local governments by reducing the financial pressure of increasing welfare costs.[35] Nixon's plan would provide uniform national benefits to welfare recipients regardless of their state of residence. Conservatives objected to the cost of the plan, Southern Democrats opposed the loss of their states' control over benefit levels, and Northern liberals criticized the proposal because its benefit levels seemed too low. This broad opposition sank Nixon's proposal.[36] In 1977, President Jimmy Carter proposed a "Program for Better Jobs and Income" that resembled Nixon's Family Assistance plan. This proposal aimed to consolidate existing programs, setting national benefit levels and eliminating food stamps. Although a coalition of governors, mayors, and county leaders rallied on behalf of Carter's idea, political opponents from the right and left again killed the proposal.[37] Congress did nationalize the categorical, Federal–state aid programs for the elderly, blind and disabled established in the Social Security Act. This Supplemental Security Income (SSI) program reduced benefit differences among the states and separated these groups of needy Americans from "welfare." By 1980, the American welfare system was more generous and more controversial than it had been in 1960.

Health

Health care for the elderly and the poor was an increasingly pressing problem in the 1950s. Aging Americans experienced widely publicized problems such as heart disease, strokes, and cancer. As early as 1947, New York state established a legislative committee on all the problems of aging. Organized labor, now more politically influential than ever, made health benefits for the elderly its top legislative priority. The health needs of elderly and retired workers seemed to be the most pressing gap in worker protection.[38] In the 1950s, the newly merged AFL-CIO developed a proposal to provide insurance for surgery, hospitalization, and nursing home care for Social Security retirees.[39]

Southern Democrats and Republicans in Congress initially were cool to the idea of Federal help for health costs, and at most were willing to provide help only to those elderly who were in poverty. Some states already were using Federal grant authority to pay for some health services for the poor. In 1960, Eisenhower's Secretary of Health, Education and Welfare, Arthur Fleming, announced a plan he called "Medicare." This grant-in-aid program would pay states to manage health services for the elderly poor. Southern Democrats, who had few unionized workers but many aging poor, found this proposal more congenial than the more ambitious plan of the AFL-CIO. Democratic Representative Wilbur Mills of Arkansas, the powerful chair of the House Ways and Means Committee, developed a new proposal to establish a category of public assistance: the medically indigent individual over the age of sixty-five. Under Mills' plan states could use their public assistance funds to cover some medical bills for these individuals. This plan passed overwhelmingly as the Kerr-Mills Act of 1960.[40]

Once Democrats returned to the White House in 1961, they embraced the AFL-CIO's broader insurance plan.[41] Lyndon Johnson made Federal health insurance his top priority after his 1964 landslide victory. With large Democratic majorities in Congress, enactment of a Federal health program became all but inevitable. Representative Mills adjusted to this political reality by broadening his bill, providing sections for recipients of the Social Security old-age insurance program that would cover hospital insurance ("Medicare Part A," that would benefit an estimated nineteen million people) and offer a voluntary Federal insurance plan to cover the costs of physicians and surgery ("Medicare Part B"). In addition, a new title XIX of the Social Security Act broadened the Kerr-Mills program into "Medicaid," a program of Federal–state grants to provide health coverage to all the poor under existing Federal–state income assistance programs. Federal cost-sharing was based on state's per capita income, benefiting poorer states like Arkansas. The bill passed Congress by huge margins.[42] The Johnson administration also initiated or expanded grants for community health and mental health centers, medical libraries, and regional cooperation in addressing the problems of heart disease, cancer, and strokes.[43]

Medicare and Medicaid were layered atop the original Social Security Act, and they reinforced that law's distinction between benefits based on entitlement and benefits based on need. Working Americans would receive health care benefits as a Federal entitlement along with Social Security retirement and disability insurance. Needy welfare recipients would receive health care benefits through the states, if they could show need and the lack of means to secure health care on their own. Unlike Medicare, Medicaid benefits and services would vary across the nation.

New health policy problems emerged after 1965. The number of working-age Americans who had no employer health insurance, but who were neither elderly nor impoverished, grew over the following years. The costs of health care continued to rise. Soon, liberals like Senator Edward Kennedy (D-MA) and Representative Martha W. Griffiths (D-MI) proposed a comprehensive national health insurance plan. In 1971, President Richard Nixon also announced a proposal for a comprehensive national health insurance program. Nixon's plan would require employers to provide health insurance and would replace Medicaid with an all-Federal plan. But comprehensive health care plans proposed by Nixon (and later by Jimmy Carter) died in Congress.[44]

Education

Before the 1950s, state and local governments controlled public education with virtually no Federal influence. A few New Deal programs provided some education, and its public works projects included school buildings. The National Educational Association (NEA), a coalition of state educational associations, resisted any additional Federal interference in education, and it defended state educational autonomy, including racial segregation.[45] The GI Bill of 1944 influenced the states only indirectly, by providing veterans with more access to higher education, heavily supplied by state governments.[46] In the early 1950s, the most important Federal rules affecting state and local education were Supreme Court decisions banning racial segregation.

Republican President Eisenhower was the first to enlarge the Federal role in education. The post-World War II baby boom, along with the construction of new suburban neighborhoods, created mounting pressures for new public schools and more teachers. Presidential candidate Eisenhower in 1952 promised to help the states build classrooms, and a 1955 White House conference on education increased support for Federal aid to public schools. Two specific controversies, however, made it hard to design a Federal bill that could muster sufficient support in Congress: first, Southern states insisted on maintaining racial segregation while Northern liberals increasingly challenged it, and second, the Catholic

Church insisted on Federal funds to help Catholic schools, while critics stoutly opposed allocating Federal money to parochial schools.[47] In October of 1957, the Soviet Union transformed the debate when it launched Sputnik I, the first successful orbiting satellite, thus beating the United States into outer space. Sputnik helped propel the National Defense Education Act (NDEA) of 1958 through Congress. The NDEA provided grants to the states for testing, guidance, and counseling in secondary schools, and Federal funds for hiring science teachers, for equipment and materials for math, science, and foreign modern language instruction, and for assistance to graduate students who sought to teach at college level.

By the early 1960s, the National Education Association cast its lot with the Democrats and pressed President Kennedy to support one billion dollars of Federal aid for school construction and teachers' salaries. Kennedy supported the NEA's plan in his presidential campaign. In 1963, Kennedy proposed a billion and a half dollars for teacher salary increases and school construction, but his proposal limited the aid to schools in needy areas. Lyndon Johnson moved forward with a proposal to spend a billion dollars a year on "the special education needs of educationally deprived children," distributed to all areas, based on the proportion of children living in poverty in each area. Because this plan distributed funds to a wider range of recipients than the Kennedy proposal, it enjoyed broader political support. With larger Democratic majorities in 1965, and a more conciliatory attitude in the NEA and the Catholic Church, Congress enacted this Elementary and Secondary Education Act (ESEA) by large margins. One title provided Federal aid for school libraries, textbooks, and other teaching materials, aid that could flow to parochial as well as public schools. Another section of the bill granted money to the states to strengthen their departments of education. This provision aimed "to allay fears about [F]ederal control of education," while it centralized more state control over education in state government and tightened the bonds between Federal, state, and local education policy experts.[48]

The ESEA established a lasting Federal role in elementary and secondary education. The War on Poverty of 1964 complemented the ESEA, bypassing the states to provide poverty areas with the Head Start program to provide preschool education and the Job Corps to fund urban employment training centers.[49] Federal spending on education multiplied tenfold between 1958 and 1968, and the Federal share of all education expenditures increased from less than three percent to ten percent.[50]

Johnson's Republican successors, Presidents Nixon and Ford, fought to reduce Federal education spending and to expand state discretion over expenditures. The states received somewhat more discretion over some education programs, but not the education "revenue sharing" that Republicans preferred.[51] Federal regulations of education increased tenfold from 1965 to 1977.

Liberal reforms strengthened the network of Federal, state, and local education professionals. The National Education Association became a solid, influential part of the Democratic coalition.[52] By 1980, the Federal government had established a separate Federal Department of Education, further strengthening the link between the Federal government, the NEA, and the state and local education establishment.

Crime Control

Criminal justice also underscored the expansion of Federal policy influence. State and local governments practically monopolized criminal justice before the 1960s. In that decade, as the Supreme Court began to nationalize some criminal rights, ruling that states had to provide lawyers to an indigent accused of a felony, and that police explicitly had to instruct a suspect in a felony case about his/her right against self-incrimination and his/her right to a lawyer. Opponents of the Supreme Court decisions proposed to remove the court's power to review state criminal rulings, but they failed. Instead, they strengthened police powers by allowing some wiretapping, more eye-witness testimony, and more of the confessions of those accused of a crime.[53] The Nixon administration influenced the Supreme Court's long-term perspective on criminal rights by appointing Federal judges with a more conservative interpretation of the Constitution.[54]

During the 1960s, increasing urban crime rates increased demands for more Federal effort to cut crime.[55] The Johnson administration established a Federal Law Enforcement Assistance Administration (LEAA) in 1965 and a small pilot program for law enforcement training. Johnson then proposed to expand this effort into a larger national program of grants to state and local governments to upgrade law enforcement and criminal justice. Congress passed the block grant for law enforcement in the Safe Streets Act of 1968. The Nixon administration enlarged these Law Enforcement Assistance grants, and expanded Federal authority over drug offenses and organized crime. Even though Gerald Ford's Attorney General, William Saxbe, termed LEAA a "dismal failure," the program continued through the Carter administration.[56]

Federal Regulation: Environmental Policy

Federal rule-making also expanded into areas traditionally controlled by the states during the 1960s and early 1970s. Civil rights protections were the most obvious example, but there were many others. The states had regulated workplace safety for more than a century when Congress passed the Federal Occupational Safety and Health Act of 1970, which addressed any "employment performed in a workplace" in the United States. The Consumer Product Safety Act of 1972 authorized the Federal government to regulate, or even ban, any consumer product that posed a danger. Of these laws, the most far-reaching and often controversial were laws establishing Federal responsibility for environmental protection, laws that affected the air Americans breathed and the water vital for agriculture, industry, energy, and everyday life.

Federal environmental regulations enlisted the states as partners. Some cities and states had initiated serious antipollution efforts well before the Federal government became involved. Cities with serious pollution problems, such as Los Angeles, Pittsburgh, and St. Louis, tried to restrict air pollution before the end of World War II. Thirty-three states and territories had enacted air pollution laws by 1963. Yet these efforts produced uneven results. Some of the large industrial states with the worst problem, such as Michigan, Wisconsin, and Missouri, had taken no action on air pollution. No more than five states had established programs to reduce water pollution.[57]

The Federal government moved cautiously to help the states deal with pollution problems. The bipartisan Water Pollution Control Act of 1948 established Federal loans to state and local governments to build waste treatment facilities. The program was converted to Federal grants-in-aid in 1956. The Eisenhower administration agreed to the Clean Air Act of 1955, a small program establishing Federal research on air pollution, but refused to support Federal involvement in abating the problem.[58]

Federal support for state environmental efforts increased in the 1960s, while antipollution efforts in many states slowly dragged along. The Clean Air Act of 1963 authorized the Federal government to help states enforce their own environmental standards. The Air Quality Act of 1967 required states to set criteria for air quality from stationary pollution sources (like power plants and factories), authorizing the national government to act if a state failed to do so. With California and more than a dozen other states imposing new vehicle emissions regulations, the Federal government set national standards for motor vehicle emissions—an action sought by automakers worried about the costs of complying with different state laws.[59] By 1970, however, the states had failed to meet all the requirements of the 1967 law.[60]

Republican Richard Nixon proposed national rules for air quality and stronger Federal enforcement. The Democrats in Congress proposed an even stronger Clean Air Act than Nixon proposed, and the bill became even more stringent as party leaders competed to make it stronger. The final Clean Air Act of 1970 required states to prepare explicit state implementation plans (SIPs) that detailed the regulations that the states would impose on polluters within their borders. In this way, congressional leaders hoped, the law would result in national clean air standards, but also preserve states' authority to tailor plans for meeting these rules to their own circumstances. Instead, the result was a spectacular series of bitter conflicts between local, state, and Federal administrators over the implementation of the law in different areas.[61]

Water pollution policy developed in a very similar way. The Water Quality Act of 1965 authorized the Federal government to set standards "for the quality of interstate waters" and established a new Federal enforcement agency. The law set a two-year deadline for the states to set standards for waters inside their borders, while it increased water quality grants. Opponents tried to fight the proposal on the battlefield of federalism; House Republicans agreed that water quality standards were necessary, but argued that these standards "should be established by the state and local agencies which are most familiar with all aspects of the matter in a given locality ... "[62] By 1971, four years after the deadline set in the 1965 Act, fewer than thirty states had formulated plans aimed at meeting Federal standards, and several plans did not provide for sufficient enforcement. Federal efforts to force action culminated in the Water Pollution Control Act of 1972. This law aimed to eliminate "the discharge of pollutants into the navigable waters" in the United States by 1985. The law mandated that industries install the best "practicable" technology by 1977 and the best "available" technology by 1983. It also authorized over $24 billion for grants for local waste treatment. Nixon vetoed the law, but Congress overrode the veto.[63]

Federal environmental regulations imposed limits on the states, but they also reinforced state authority because they allowed states to exercise new authority in implementing the law. The struggle between state discretion and the control of states' actions produced intense conflicts and legal challenges. According to R. Daniel Kelemen, an environmental scholar who compared environmental policy in the European Union and the United States,

> the development of environmental regulation in the United States demonstrates that the combination of fragmentation of power at the [F]ederal level with federalism has had intended and counterintuitive consequences. As in other federal systems in this study, the U.S. [F]ederal government has taken on a powerful role in environmental policymaking, while delegating most policy implementation to state governments. At the same time, however, it has placed greater constraints on the discretion of state governments than have other federal governments. The fragmentation of power in the U.S. [F]ederal government has encouraged the enactment of detailed, inflexible regulations, the emergence of active judicial review of administrative action, and, ultimately, the development of an adversarial, litigious approach to enforcement that severely constrains state government discretion in implementing [F]ederal laws.[64]

Shared Federal–state regulatory power, then, opened up a new, even more complex front in the ongoing battle over federalism: conflict over the states' varied implementation of Federal rules and regulations.

Intergovernmental Politics

By the end of the 1970s, federalism was as important to American political development as ever. But the battlefield of federalism had shattered into many more fronts. The Federal government was involved in areas of state and local governance in which it had never been prominently involved before—including education, health, criminal justice, workplace safety, and environmental protection. The term "intergovernmental relations" captured a new reality: the states seemed principally to serve as agents of the purposes of national government.

Martha Derthick believed that "The change in American federalism that took place in the 1960s was more profound than any that occurred in the New Deal."[65] In Derthick's view,

> What was distinctive about the 1960s was that, for the first time in a century, changing federalism became an end in itself, consciously pursued by numerous holders of national power who were trying to reconstruct American society and politics. It was not just an incidental by-product of war or modernization. With a view invariably to southern racism, which tainted states and localities as a class, Supreme Court majorities repeatedly rendered decisions that were more than indifferent to federalism—they were inimical. And when the Court's actions were complemented by the aggressively liberal, nationalizing Congress of the Great Society, in which northern liberals successfully challenged southern conservatives' control of the Democratic party in the Senate, the result was a profound and permanent change in the relations among governments in the federal system.[66]

Republicans and Democrats both expanded Federal activism through grants in this period. The partisan contest turned on who would receive Federal funds, and how the Federal government would restrict their discretion.

The Republican and Democratic struggles to expand grants and shift benefits to their constituencies made Federal policy more fragmented and more complicated. Federal officials faced the impossible task of managing billions of dollars by proxy. In perhaps the most widely discussed case study of this implementation problem, the U.S. Economic Development Administration provided millions of dollars in project grants to develop job opportunities for minorities in cities like Oakland, California. But after years of effort, these grants produced only a handful of permanent jobs for Oakland's minorities—literally, a textbook example of the difficulties of making the grants-in-aid effective, and of good intentions gone awry.[67] Local responsibility also produced drastically different results in different programs in different places. In the Comprehensive Employment and Training Act and other programs, the worst local abuses and mistakes were publicized nationally, and the publicity tarred the entire effort nationwide.

All these problems consumed vast amounts of time and money, strengthened critics of the Federal government, and undermined Federal legitimacy. The backlash against liberal activism helped usher conservatives into power in the 1980s.

9   Federalism and Conservative Governance after 1980

Liberal activism triggered growing opposition in the 1970s, and conservative Republicans rode this backlash into the White House in 1981. These conservatives inherited an active intergovernmental system of services and regulations led by the Federal government. Republican leaders like Ronald Reagan and his successors endorsed federalism in principal, but used both decentralization and centralized Federal government power strategically to turn this system toward their principal goals, to promote market-driven economic growth and traditional social values. In many ways, conservatives expanded Federal power and hemmed in the states.

This period of conservative dominance encouraged a resurgence of state policy leadership and policy innovation. States initiated major changes in anti-poverty, health, education, and environmental policy. The presidential administrations of Bill Clinton and George W. Bush sometimes used "waivers" to encourage state experiments that would produce outcomes they favored. These state innovations allowed both liberals and conservatives to advance their goals, and in turn allowed state interests to influence major changes in Federal policy.

The Backlash against Liberalism and the Rise of Conservatism

Americans lost confidence in government activism in the 1970s as the economy stagnated, manufacturing jobs eroded, the Watergate scandal undermined trust, and Vietnam raised doubts about American foreign policy.[1] Businesses complained that a thickening blanket of national environmental, workplace, and other regulations was smothering economic growth and damaging prosperity. Conservatives mounted increasingly aggressive efforts to diminish these restraints on business autonomy.[2] Meanwhile, controversies about morality and freedom fostered the rise of populist conservatism, dedicated to protecting traditional values against the nationalization of abortion and other rights.[3] These various streams of opposition began to flow together, raising support for a rollback of Federal activism.

Federalism served the purposes of this growing conservative opposition. Conservative political leaders such as Senator Barry Goldwater and California Governor Ronald Reagan (1967–75) defended state authority as a weapon for fighting national liberalism.[4] Conservatives built national "think tanks" to provide intellectual arguments for free-market and decentralized policy.[5] State and local officials added substance to these criticisms when they complained about excessive Federal interference. The mayor of New York complained that states and cities chafed "under the guns of dozens of Federal laws imposing increasingly draconian mandates."[6]

The political successes of conservatism at the state level reinforced conservatives' interest in decentralizing power. Californian voters overwhelmingly approved Proposition 13 in 1978, a conservative measure which lowered property taxes and made it more difficult for government to raise revenues. New tax restrictions spread to other states, including Massachusetts.[7] Conservative Republicans won prominent victories in races for the U.S. Senate and governorships in 1978, accelerating conservatives' political momentum.[8]

Two years later, the culturally conservative Southern states, once a bastion of Democratic strength, began to realign behind Republican presidential candidate Reagan. In 1980, the Republican ticket won all the Southern states except for Georgia (home of incumbent Jimmy Carter), and all voted for Reagan in 1984, George H.W. Bush in 1988, and George W. Bush in 2000 and 2004. Republicans built up a vast majority of Southern seats in the U.S. Senate and a majority of Southern seats in the House of Representatives.[9] Its strength in the South, along with strong support in the intermountain and plains states and in rural areas across the nation, provided a strong electoral base for the Republican Party into the twenty-first century.

Federalism and the Reagan Administration

Ronald Reagan's rhetoric championed federalism during his presidency (1981–89). The Federal government, said Reagan, "takes too much taxes from the people, too much authority from the States, too much liberty with the Constitution." Reagan said that the Federal government had become "overloaded, muscle-bound, if you will" because it had taken on too many responsibilities.[10] The Federal government should allow state and local governments to keep more of the revenue collected from their citizens.[11] While other presidents since the New Deal had viewed the Federal and state governments as partners, the Reagan administration viewed them as *competing* sovereigns.[12] In his first months in office, Reagan created an advisory committee on federalism to help "restore a proper constitutional relationship between the Federal, State, and local governments."[13] By 1987, Reagan codified his views of federalism in a directive to guide Federal officials. Executive Order 12612 stated that "In most areas of governmental concern, the States uniquely possess the constitutional authority, the resources, and the competence to discern the sentiments of the people and to govern accordingly." States should be encouraged to "develop their own policies to achieve program objectives" and Federal officials should "[r]efrain, to the maximum extent possible, from establishing uniform, national standards for programs and, when possible, defer to the States to establish standards."[14]

Reagan's administration used federalism to pull the national government back from liberal policies. The Reagan administration sought to convert categorical grants to block grants and cut funding for them. Federal tax cuts and the initially deep cuts in Federal domestic spending (the Omnibus Budget Reconciliation Act, or OBRA, of 1981) aimed to cut the Federal government's ability to fund domestic programs, including all grants-in-aid. Ultimately, OBRA eliminated 140 grant programs and reduced Federal spending on grants by $6 billion from the previous budget. The law consolidated seventy-seven categorical grants into nine block grants covering health, social services, education, and community development, and cut Federal funding for these activities. Reagan in 1982 proposed—unsuccessfully—to turn over Aid to Families with Dependent Children (AFDC) and Food Stamps to the states, while nationalizing the Medicaid program, a swap of responsibilities that would "in a single stroke" accomplish "a realignment that will end cumbersome administration and spiraling costs at the Federal level."[15] In 1986, the Federal government ended general revenue sharing.

During Reagan's presidency, Federal grant-in-aid spending dropped for the first time since World War II. Federal spending on grants, adjusting for inflation, remained below the levels of the Carter administration (Figures 8.1 and 8.2).[16] The Reagan administration infused conservative provisions into the remaining grants programs and the intergovernmental system. For example, grant recipients were required to pay a larger share of the cost of many grants, in the hope that a higher matching requirement would reduce state and local government activism that had been heavily subsidized by the national government.[17]

Federalism after Reagan

The Reagan administration's cuts in grants programs were not durable. Overall, grant spending increased from eleven percent of Federal spending in 1990 to fifteen percent in 2009. By the time Reagan left office in 1989, the number of grant programs already had increased to 492, from 400 in 1982. In 1987, Democrats regained a majority in the U.S. Senate, and Congress soon expanded grants for water quality and transportation, overriding Reagan's veto. By 1990, Federal grants in inflation-adjusted dollars had returned to 1981 levels. Republican President George H.W. Bush (1989–93) proposed several block grant and decentralization plans, but had very limited success. The number of grant programs had grown to 593 at the end of Bush's presidency.[18] Funding for Federal grants grew steadily after Reagan left office, driven by spending mandated by Federal law (such as Medicaid) and by new Federal initiatives. Spending on grants-in-aid has increased in each Federal budget since the end of the 1980s.

President Bill Clinton (1993–2001), the first Democrat in the White House in a dozen years, emphasized many of the ideas about federalism articulated by Reagan: leaving authority to the states, consolidating categorical grants into block grants, and reducing unfunded requirements on state and local governments (a priority of the Republican Congress).[19] Grant spending increased about seventy percent during the Clinton administration.

The Clinton administration also used federalism more actively as a tool of presidential power. Clinton exploited "executive" federalism; the use of presidential tools to influence state and local governments to pursue the president's priorities.[20] *Waivers* were the most important of these tools. A waiver is a Federal permission to a state to deliberately avoid compliance with a Federal grant requirement so that the state can offer different kinds of services, provide services to different kinds of people, or control spending on services. Waivers were initiated in 1962 under Section 1115 of the Social Security Act, but were used very sparingly until the Reagan administration. These waivers are the result of bargaining between the president, Federal administrators, and state administrators. Waivers allow a president to pursue his priorities without involving Congress or the state legislatures, and they allow him to build alliances with individual governors. Clinton's administration made it easier for states to receive waivers, and awarded them much more freely than Reagan or Bush. The Clinton administration especially granted waivers to expand welfare services and Medicaid coverage.[21]

Republican President George W. Bush (2001–8) seemed to return to Reagan's conservative approach to federalism. Initially, Bush proposed to decentralize some powers to the states, arguing that the Constitution's framers "limited and enumerated the Federal Government's powers and reserved the remaining functions of government to the States."[22] But in sharp contrast to the Reagan administration, grant spending increased almost twice as much during the Bush administration than during the Clinton presidency.[23] Despite Bush's rhetorical commitment to Reagan's view of federalism and support for block grants, his administration did more to centralize policy than to decentralize it.

Conservative Nationalism

Conservative presidents since 1980 decentralized power *when and if* decentralization was likely to produce conservative results, but they expanded Federal power where state and local discretion would undercut their more important priorities, such as reducing business regulation. For example, the Reagan administration gave the states more power to implement clean air laws, aware that many states would relax the enforcement of these regulations on businesses within the state. At the same time, the Reagan administration sought to preempt states from regulating the transportation, communications, and banking industries to protect these sectors from state restrictions. The Bus Regulatory Reform Act of 1982 eliminated state and local power to regulate interstate bus transportation. The Surface Transportation Assistance Act of 1982 prohibited the states from regulating truck weights and lengths (forcing states to accept large, double-bottomed trucks). The Cable Communications Policy Act of 1984 made it difficult for state and local governments to deny cable TV a license renewal even if it sharply increased fees.[24] Reagan signed a law requiring states to crack down on drunk driving (or risk losing Federal grants). The Reagan administration also accepted national requirements on the states in areas like nuclear waste disposal and family support, where Democrats and Republicans agreed to impose partial national rules.

During Reagan's presidency alone, the Federal government preempted state authority in ten civil rights laws, thirty-one commercial and business laws, seventeen environmental laws, four financial laws, eleven health laws, two immigration laws, and seventeen safety laws. Reagan vetoed only two of these laws. Changes in the Federal tax code nationalized some rules for state and local bonds, a critically important government tool. Political scientist Joseph Zimmerman concluded that while Reagan's rhetoric advocated the decentralization of power to the states, in reality the administration "encouraged additional centralization of political power in several functional areas and prohibited state economic regulation of certain industries." The increased use of Federal preemption centralized American governance even while the states received new discretion to implement specific jobs, welfare, and urban development programs—with reduced Federal financial assistance. Zimmerman concluded that "At the close of the Reagan administration, intergovernmental relations were more coercive compared to 1980 as the result of the expanded use of crossover sanctions and preemption powers by the Congress."[25] Many of these regulations imposed new spending obligations on the state and local governments. The Safe Water Drinking Act Amendments of 1986 imposed an estimated \$2–3 billion annually on public water suppliers, and the Asbestos Hazard Emergency Response Act of 1986 required public school systems to spend an estimated \$3 billion over thirty years to remove hazardous asbestos from schools.[26]

After Reagan left office, conservative Republicans continued to use Federal power to advance their economic and political goals whether or not it limited the powers of the states. As Chapter 5 pointed out, conservative Republicans successfully added Federal laws to insulate markets against state interference, including the Telecommunications Act of 1996, the Financial Services Modernization Act of 1999, the Public Company Accounting Reform and Investor Protection Act of 2002, and the Energy Policy Act of 2005. President George H.W. Bush signed new laws that added important Federal mandates affecting state and local governments. The Clean Air Act Amendments of 1990 imposed stronger penalties on states that failed to meet Federal implementation timetables and benchmarks. States were required to expand Medicaid to all children in poverty up to the age of eighteen. The Americans with Disabilities Act of 1990 required state and local public agencies to spend millions of dollars to make public transportation and government structures accessible to disabled citizens.[27] The Clinton administration used the brief, two-year Democratic majority in Congress to add to new mandates in the Family and Medical Leave Act, Motor Voter Act, and the Brady Handgun Violence Prevention Act. In 1995, the new Republican majority in Congress enacted, and the president signed, the Unfunded Mandates Reform Act, requiring that the cost of Federal mandates for state and local legislation be made explicit in proposed legislation. But this law did not prohibit such mandates, and allowed a number of loopholes (for example, mandates added as conditions of receiving grants were not included).

The administration of George W. Bush further nationalized public policy to achieve conservative ends. According to federalism scholars Timothy Conlan and John Dinan, Bush lacked "any philosophical commitment to federalism."[28] The No Child Left Behind Act (NCLB) imposed more Federal control over elementary and secondary education. The Help America Vote Act of 2002 placed new requirements on state election procedures. The Real ID Act of 2005 required state-issued drivers' licenses and other identification documents to meet Federal standards.[29] Tax law changes and court decisions hemmed in state revenue options even more.

The Conservative Turn in the Federal Courts

Conservative Republicans also have made a strong effort to add like-minded jurists to the national court system. The Reagan Justice Department cultivated a network of conservative lawyers and judges.[30] Like elected conservatives, these judges had a mixed record of support for federalism.

Under Chief Justice William Rehnquist (1986–2005), the U.S. Supreme Court used federalism to undermine some Federal government powers, rather than to strengthen state prerogatives.[31] Before he became Chief Justice, Rehnquist dissented in the case of *Garcia* v. *San Antonio Metropolitan Transit Authority* (1985), in which a majority ruled that the legal boundary between Federal and state power was too unclear to be protected by a court, and that political safeguards adequately could protect state sovereignty. Rehnquist, citing the Tenth amendment, asserted that it was important for Federal courts to defend federalism. With Rehnquist elevated to Chief Justice in 1986, the court invalidated portions of several notable Federal laws, in part because they intruded on the states. These laws included the Indian Gaming Regulatory Act, the Violence against Women Act, the Americans with Disabilities Act (ADA), the Age Discrimination in

Employment Act, the Religious Freedom Restoration Act, the Brady Bill, and the Gun-Free School Zones Act. The Court, however, did not reject the broad grant of Federal power to regulate interstate commerce that its predecessors established in the late 1930s.[32] Rehnquist's successor as Chief Justice, John Roberts, had not established a clear record on federalism issues by the end of 2010.[33]

In the 2000s, federalism has reemerged as a spectacular ideological flashpoint on the Supreme Court. According to Linda Greenhouse, a respected journalist who covers the judicial system, "These days, federalism means war."[34] That war, in part, was being fueled by a new spirit of state activism.

The Resurgence of the States

When conservatives redirected policy discretion to the states, they were inviting much more capable states to take the initiative. Long before Reagan's inauguration, the states were greatly strengthening their governments. After 1960, most states reworked their constitutions to improve governance. States typically extended their governors' term of office from two years to four, and expanded gubernatorial powers and staff. Many states centralized public finance and strengthened policy supervision. State legislatures bolstered staff and established annual meetings. To meet Supreme Court requirements, states established equitable apportionment of legislative districts. State courts were reformed. States increased their budgets by increasing a wide variety of taxes and borrowing more money.[35]

The Federal retreat energized many states to take a more direct role in solving their problems.[36] Like their Progressive Era predecessors, liberal reformers who served as governors and state legislators in this period advanced innovative policies and resisted the conservative turn in national policy. States juggled their own budgets to smooth the impact of the 1981 Federal budget cuts, and asserted a new aggressive role in consumer protection, environmental regulation, and antitrust.[37] Many states absorbed some of the deep cuts in grants for welfare programs.[38] Wisconsin and other states developed innovative welfare policies and new economic development programs that encouraged venture capital, high-technology investment, and foreign trade, and regulated the closing of factories.[39] By the end of the Reagan administration, policy activists again were touting the states as "laboratories of democracy."[40]

State innovations have thrived since the 1980s. Some states addressed climate change, raised the minimum wage, strengthened anti-discrimination laws, and provided access to higher education for undocumented residents.[41] The National Conference of State Legislatures, the Council of State Governments, and other more narrowly focused organizations disseminated information on these state innovations and "best practices" to facilitate the diffusion of ideas to other states.

Equally important, many states have collaborated with others to increase their collective capacity to attack public problems. State governors became a powerful influence in designing key Federal laws through the National Governors Association (NGA). Other public sector organizations, including the National Conference of State Legislatures, the National League of Cities, the U.S. Conference of Mayors, the International City-County Management Association (city managers), and the National Association of Counties also provided a clearinghouse for policy information and pressed their interests in Washington.[42] The National Association of Attorneys General has been a very influential force in specific policy areas by brokering multistate legal action. State attorneys general directly challenged the power of tobacco companies, Wall Street firms, and other bastions of corporate power.[43]

States constructed more durable regional agreements to address problems that transcend their individual boundaries, such as water quality, homeland security, and access to prescription drugs.[44] States' regional agreements to deal with global warming are path-breaking examples of states' response to a problem that stymied the Federal government.[45] The National Conference of Commissioners of State Uniform Laws still develops model laws for the states, and encourages the states to adopt comparable laws. These model statutes address common civil and criminal legal issues, such as commercial transactions, real estate, marriage and child custody, inheritance, controlled substances, and child abduction.[46]

Richard Nathan used the phrase "the paradox of devolution" to describe the way the conservative ascendance in Federal policy has sparked so much state activism.[47] In his view,

> In periods when support for governmental activism was on the wane in Washington and in the country as a whole, the existence of a state-level counterforce kept the pressure on for public sector growth. Innovations, particularly those of progressive states, have been tested, refined, debugged, and often diffused across the country. In some cases, they have been morphed into national policies and programs ... In liberal periods, liberal activists are likely to view the center as their best bet for getting things done—as do conservative groups in conservative time. It is not federalism that these coalitions care about. It is advancing their interests.[48]

Conservatives, of course, also have used state innovations to advance their agenda. Besides tax limitations, which now exist in thirty states, a conservative-led movement to limit the terms of state legislators aimed to check legislative professionalism and state government capacity. Fifteen states have enacted term limits for state legislators.[49] Between 1981 and 1991, thirty-eight states passed enterprise zone legislation, reducing taxes and regulation in specific areas to encourage rapid development.[50] In the twenty-first century, social conservatives have successfully advanced stricter criminal sentences, restrictions on abortion, and bans on affirmative action and on gay marriage in a number of states.

Federalism and Public Policy in the Conservative Era

In addressing poverty, health, education, and the environment—the major policy areas that liberal reform era remade—the conservative era showed how conservatives as well as liberals continue to use federalism as a political weapon to achieve political goals. These policy areas also demonstrate the states' innovations and influence on Federal policy.

Poverty

Conservatives were determined to use federalism to transform Aid to Families with Dependent Children, the principal Federal–state income program for the poor. Conservatives criticized Aid to Families with Dependent Children (AFDC) for trapping welfare recipients in a culture of welfare dependence that held them back from work and self-reliance; they insisted that any support for the poor should require recipients to work. As more women joined the workforce, reluctance to require mothers to work for benefits began to fade.[51] The Reagan administration in 1981 encouraged states to experiment with income support programs that moved more welfare recipients into jobs. Wisconsin took the most advantage of the opportunity to experiment, implementing new work requirements for welfare recipients and stricter enforcement of child support payments. Beginning in 1987, Republican Governor Tommy Thompson of Wisconsin negotiated waivers with the Reagan administration to implement a number of additional welfare policy experiments to channel AFDC recipients into jobs. These experiments generated national publicity because they seemed to reduce welfare costs without increasing need.[52]

State officials played a key role in changing the national AFDC program at the end of Reagan's presidency. The National Governors Association, and especially Arkansas Governor Bill Clinton, helped craft the reforms in the Federal Family Support Act of 1988. This law expanded child-support enforcement requirements nationally, and strengthened rules requiring welfare recipients to search for work or participate in education and training. States would be required to provide child care for working parents, transportation, and health care for female welfare recipients who took jobs.[53]

As a presidential candidate, Clinton promised to "end welfare as we know it." Once in office, Clinton's administration used Section 1115 waivers much more aggressively than its predecessors to allow the states more latitude for income support experiments. By 1996, thirty-seven states were operating welfare waiver programs.[54] After taking control of the U.S. House of Representatives in 1995, Republicans, working with Republican governors, developed a restrictive national welfare reform proposal that turned AFDC into a block grant, set a time limit on eligibility, and imposed much stricter work requirements. After Clinton and the Republican majority in Congress reached an impasse on welfare reform in 1995, the NGA offered a revised bipartisan proposal. This plan laid the foundation for the Personal Responsibility and Work Opportunity Reconciliation Act of 1996, a compromise block grant that replaced ADFC with Temporary Assistance for Needy Families (TANF). The law set a five-year lifetime time limit on Federal income support, and strengthened work and child support requirements. When Republicans controlled Congress and the White House in 2005, they further tightened the work requirements and Federal restrictions on the states' use of TANF funds.[55]

Since the 1996 welfare reform, states have implemented both liberal and conservative versions of TANF. Many states expanded funding for a broad range of supportive activities, such as providing help with utility bills and expanding early childhood education for the poor. Vermont and Michigan used state funds to provide assistance beyond the five-year Federal limit. By 2009, twenty-three states supplemented their welfare programs with a state Earned Income Tax Credit. Conservative states used their discretion to tighten welfare restrictions further. While many states routinely increased welfare payments to a family as it added children, twenty state governments refused to provide additional welfare benefits to a family that added children.[56] Generally, the states were spending more on TANF and related services in 2004 than they were in 1995, and few states implemented plans that were exceptionally generous or tough. However, the value of TANF cash payments has continued to decline because very few states have increased their payments to take inflation into account. State welfare payment disparities persist; these disparities are much greater than cost of living differences among the states.[57] Many of those who left welfare for work remained in poverty, and a smaller percentage of children in poor families were receiving cash assistance.[58]

These reforms have produced an anti-poverty system that is more centralized than it was in 1960 or 1980, but in which outcomes remain widely varied. The states provide different levels of benefits and set different requirements for receiving these benefits. It also is an anti-poverty system that leaves large gaps. Nationally, child poverty increased during the 2000s, and by 2009, one child in five was living in poverty.[59]

Health

Government health care policy expanded significantly during the three decades after 1980. State health policy innovations and executive federalism built the framework for much of this expansion. In contrast to anti-poverty programs, the Reagan administration made few changes in Medicare, the fully Federal insurance program for elderly retirees. Medicaid, the largest Federal grant-in-aid program in 1981, did not suffer the cutbacks that AFDC and other grants programs experienced in the early 1980s. Medicaid had more influential political support in the states than welfare, because it funds hospitals, nursing homes, and doctors, and because many Medicaid recipients are elderly and disabled persons who are more likely to vote than are AFDC recipients. The 1981 OBRA slowed the increase in grants for Medicaid but did not cut them. Instead, the National Governors Association successfully lobbied for more state flexibility to control costs.[60]

States protected Medicaid funding in the 1980s, and some expanded the program.[61] A few states began to push for broader health care coverage, in part to cover children, in part to take up the slack as employers cut private health care coverage.[62] Six states enacted major health care reforms in the late 1980s and early 1990s. Here, the opportunistic use of federalism is especially clear. Massachusetts sought a Medicaid waiver as part of its ambitious Massachusetts Health Security Act of 1988, and Oregon sought a waiver in the Oregon Health Plan of 1989. The Republican George H.W. Bush administration initially denied the waivers to Massachusetts and Oregon. But the Democratic Clinton administration approved these waivers as a step toward developing liberal models for expanding health care coverage. While these states used waivers to expand health care, Florida used a waiver to control costs and apply more free market competition in health care.[63]

The failure of Clinton's national health care proposals in 1994 spurred states to further innovations, often with Federal support.[64] The Clinton administration secured a State Children's Health Insurance Program (later termed CHIP) in the 1997 Federal budget. This new grant-in-aid encouraged states to provide insurance coverage to children in families who lack health insurance but whose income was too high for Medicaid eligibility. The Bush administration announced a Health Insurance Flexibility and Accountability (HIFA) initiative in 2001, providing Section 1115 waivers to the states to use CHIP and Medicaid to provide insurance for the low-income uninsured. In 2005, Massachusetts received a waiver to create a "Safety Net Care Pool," the funding source for the pioneering Commonwealth Care program that provided government-managed insurance for low- and moderate-income state residents.[65]

The Obama administration used federalism to expand access to health care. Obama approved an expansion of CHIP in his first month in office.[66] The Federal government provided an additional $87 billion in grants to the states for health care as part of the 2009 stimulus package, and some states enacted benefit enhancements. Among its many provisions, the Patient Protection and Affordable Care Act of 2010 required states to set up insurance exchanges (institutions inspired by the Massachusetts reform and others) to provide insurance to those not covered by other forms of health insurance. The 2010 health care law also expanded Medicaid coverage to persons with incomes up to 133 percent of the poverty level. Opponents of the law turned to the states to fight it. In 2010, eight states passed measures barring state government involvement in individual or employer insurance mandates, and twenty state attorneys general challenged the law in court.[67]

Fiscal stress and balanced budget requirements, however, caused state cutbacks in health care during economic downturns. In the recession of the early 2000s, many states were using waivers primarily to control costs. States like Tennessee and Oregon, that had used waivers to make major expansions in health care coverage, were forced to cut back coverage and benefits. Twenty states cut Medicaid benefits, in fiscal 2010.[68]

Education

State experiences largely drove the educational reform agenda that culminated in the Federal No Child Left Behind law of 2001. Conservatives seized on education as a powerful example of the shortcomings of liberalism and the need for more decentralization, choice, and accountability. Conservatives emphasized vouchers as a tool for improving schools; under this plan, parents would receive government certificates for education, and could use these vouchers to pay for the public or private school of their choice.[69]

By 1981, states already were enacting new policy innovations to expand opportunity, increase performance accountability, and enable more parental choice. In the 1970s, Minnesota, Missouri, and other states initiated pre-kindergarten programs in public schools, and now a large majority of states fund prekindergarten programs.[70] In the 1970s and 1980s, state governors (especially in the South, where teachers' unions were relatively weak) initiated efforts to increase public schools' performance and results.[71] Minnesota in 1987 allowed parents to choose to send students to schools in neighboring districts, and in 1991 enacted an innovative program for "charter schools." These charter schools, funded at least in part by government, operate under less restrictive rules and regulations than regular local public schools, but are held accountable for results and for complying with their initial charter for operation. Charter schools proved very popular. President Clinton and some liberals embraced the idea. By 2005, forty states had enacted charter school legislation; 3,400 charter schools were in operation, serving about a million students. Milwaukee, Wisconsin initiated an experimental program of vouchers in 1990. Conservatives seized on the Milwaukee experiment to advocate vouchers in other parts of the nation, redefining vouchers as a tool to improve education for minorities and the poor. The voucher idea was implemented in Florida, Cleveland, and the District of Columbia.[72]

Performance standards for schools became an increasingly prominent part of school reform after a national report, *A Nation at Risk*, recommended new school curriculum standards, performance benchmarks, and accountability requirements.[73] The National Governors Association made education a top priority, pressing for clearer state-level goals and assessments. In 1990, President George H.W. Bush announced six nonbinding education goals that included competency testing in basic subjects in the fourth, eighth, and twelth grades. These broad goals were put into law in the Education 2000 Act of 1994. The NGA endorsed the goals and added more.[74] Democratic governors in Colorado and Oregon embraced the NGA standards, giving performance standards more credibility among liberals. By 2000, nearly all the states had established standards for English, mathematics, science, and social studies, assessed performance in eighth grade, and reported on district level achievement. Governor George W. Bush, for example, had implemented standards and assessment in Texas.

These state innovations laid the foundation for No Child Left Behind. Bush, now president, proposed NCLB and won the support of liberal Senator Edward Kennedy (D-MA). To continue to receive Federal funding, states had to conduct annual assessments in mathematics and reading, to measure the yearly progress of students, and to take steps to close the racial achievement gap. States, not the Federal government, set the standards and the tests. Schools that did not meet state standards would continue to receive assistance, but after four years they would be subject to extensive restructuring. NCLB also required states to provide teacher certification standards and more choice options for parents.[75] States were authorized to use funds for private, even for-profit entities.

According to federalism scholar Paul Posner, NCLB "marked a turning point in the centralization of our federal system."[76] Nine states rebelled against the NCLB, including conservative states like Texas and Utah, and liberal states like Connecticut. State opposition forced the U.S. Department of Education to introduce more flexibility in enforcing the law.[77]

Environmental Protection

Since 1980, conservatives have used federalism to free business from the fetters of environmental regulation, while liberals, often at the state level, have used federalism to cope with emerging environmental threats like climate change. The Reagan administration severely cut funding, personnel, the research budget, and the enforcement capacity of the U.S. Environmental Protection Agency (EPA). The Interior Department quickly approved the plans of the leading coal-producing states to regulate their strip-mining operations. EPA Director Anne Gorsuch Burford, a loyal Reagan supporter, routinely granted the states more freedom to enforce air quality, hazardous waste, and other environmental regulations as they saw fit. As a conservative strategy for reducing environmental regulation, federalism proved effective during the Reagan years. Only a small number of states replaced reductions in Federal antipollution funds. Between fiscal years 1979 and 1984, state, local, and other funding for air pollution decreased by six percent. Environmental deregulation at the national level exposed states to interstate competition, putting more pressure on them to relax their environmental rules.[78]

But as the Federal government disengaged from environmental regulation, some states pursued new environmental initiatives. California already led the nation with strict automobile pollution laws, far-reaching land use controls, and pioneering Coastal Commissions. California enacted a safe water act in 1986 that required public notice of exposure to carcinogenic or toxic chemicals. Minnesota's 1990 Toxic Pollution Prevention Act required hundreds of private companies to develop toxic pollution prevention plans and to meet state timelines for cutting pollutants. Oregon banned waste tires in 1987 and imposed a recycling fee on the purchase of new tires. Twenty-nine states developed hazardous waste disposal and cleanup programs. Ten required deposits on returnable beverage containers.[79]

Federal environmental regulation strengthened under George H.W. Bush and Bill Clinton. As it had in poverty and health care policy, the Clinton administration used executive federalism, delegating more authority to the states to grant permits and enforce environmental law. Meanwhile, the Environmental Council of the States (ECOS) was established in 1993 to advocate for state interests in environmental policy and to serve as a clearinghouse for state environmental policy information.[80] But as environmental rules expanded again, the states' enforcement burden grew. States were given little funding to implement the additional rules. Federal funds covered about seventy percent of the cost of the states' environmental protection activities in the early 1980s, but only covered thirty percent by 2001.[81]

George W. Bush began to use the states as Reagan had, delegating some authority for hazardous waste cleanup to the states while cutting for funds to carry out the tasks. But compared to Reagan, George W. Bush used Federal power much more aggressively to implement a conservative environmental agenda across the entire nation. The Energy Policy Act of 2005, for example, included almost a dozen provisions that preempted or limited state environmental and energy policy authority, and it exempted energy industries from a number of Federal–state environmental regulations. The Bush administration also preempted state regulations of mercury emissions, imposing less restrictive standards than those established in more than twenty states. The Bush administration strongly resisted pressure from states to take the lead in regulating climate change gases.[82]

Despite the resistance of the Bush administration, states took the lead in attacking the problem of climate change. California, Massachusetts, and other states enacted innovative policies to reduce greenhouse gas emissions and encourage the use of renewable energy. By 2010, twenty-three states had set targets for reducing greenhouse gas emissions; thirty-six states imposed requirements on electrical utilities specifying that a certain amount of electricity must come from renewable or alternative energy sources; thirty-four states set a minimum level of energy efficiency for commercial buildings; sixteen states set some kind of limit on carbon dioxide (CO_2) emissions from power plants.[83] Some states constructed regional agreements to limit carbon emissions, in an effort to broaden policy in an area larger than a single state, despite the absence of Federal involvement. The Regional Greenhouse Gas Initiative (RGGI) is an agreement of ten Northeastern and Mid-Atlantic states to establish a mandatory limit on their collective CO_2 emissions, and a "carbon market" for trading emissions permissions. RGGI aimed to cut CO_2 emissions from power plants by ten percent by 2018.[84]

According to political scientist Barry Rabe, the more liberal states probed "for areas to pursue innovative opportunities at the same time that they challenge[d] any instances of [F]ederal overreach or disengagement that they deem[ed] problematic. The result has been a steady increase in intergovernmental conflict from the previous decade."[85] Twelve states joined several cities and environmental groups in a lawsuit to force the EPA to regulate carbon dioxide as a pollutant; ten other states joined the defense of the Bush administration's refusal to regulate CO_2. In *Massachusetts* v. *EPA* (2007), a narrow Supreme Court majority ruled in favor of the states. Justice Stevens, writing for the majority, observed that Massachusetts was suing "for an injury to it in its capacity of quasi-sovereign. In that capacity the State has an interest independent of and behind the titles of its citizens, in all the earth and air within its domain. It has the last word as to whether its mountains shall be stripped of their forests and its inhabitants shall breathe pure air."[86]

Meanwhile, other states were using their authority to encourage the development of their petroleum, natural gas, timber, and other natural resources. Midwestern states encouraged the production of corn-based fuel, a product with ambiguous consequences for the environment, but positive benefits for their farmers. Once President Obama took office, his EPA Director declared CO_2 a pollutant. A dozen states filed suit to stop the EPA from issuing regulations to limit CO_2. Texas refused to comply with any new CO_2 rules, challenging the Federal government to take over environmental enforcement in the state.[87]

Culture War

Federalism has been a principal battleground in the cultural conflicts over abortion, gay rights, and other social issues of the conservative era.[88] Supreme Court decisions in the 1960s and 1970s laid down controversial national rules on emotionally-loaded areas governed by the states, such as prayer in public schools (*Engel* v. *Vitale*, 1962) and abortion law (*Roe* v. *Wade*, 1973).[89] Opposition to these rules helped mobilize evangelicals as a crucial part of the Republican political coalition. The Reagan administration, however, did not push hard for such conservative demands as a Constitutional amendment to ban abortion nationally. Even with additional Reagan appointees, the Supreme Court did not reverse *Roe* v. *Wade*.[90]

Frustrated by the failure to win a decisive Federal ban on abortion, its opponents took their fight to the states. Conservative governors, attorneys general and legislators used their authority to advocate and enact innovative laws tightening access to abortions. By 2010, thirty-eight states prohibited abortions after a specified point in the pregnancy, except when necessary to protect the woman's life or health. Twenty-four states required that a woman who was seeking an abortion must wait for a specified time (often 24 hours) after medical counseling. Four states restricted coverage of abortion in private insurance plans to cases in which the woman's life would be endangered if the pregnancy were carried to term. Alabama, Louisiana, Mississippi, and Oklahoma required abortion providers to offer the patient the opportunity to view an ultrasound of the fetus in the womb.[91]

Cultural liberals also have used federalism to advance their objectives. Twenty states by 1990 required businesses to guarantee their employees the right to return to their jobs after taking family or medical leave. These state laws paved the way for the 1993 Federal Family and Medical Leave Act. California and New Jersey later provided payments for family and medical leave.[92] Oregon and Washington enacted laws allowing euthanasia. Fifteen states had legalized medical marijuana by 2011.[93] California, Connecticut, Illinois, Iowa, Maryland, Massachusetts, New Jersey, and New York encouraged research using embryonic stem cells (a type of scientific research often opposed by abortion foes).[94]

Marriage rights for gays provide the best example of the way federalism has offered both liberals and conservatives a battlefield for winning the struggles of the culture war.[95] When the state of Hawaii seemed to be on the verge of legalizing gay marriage in 1996, Congress passed the Defense of Marriage Act (DOMA) by large, bipartisan margins, and President Clinton signed it. DOMA legally limited the term "marriage" in Federal law to "a legal union between one man and one woman as husband and wife," excluding same-sex partners. DOMA specified that states did not need to consider a same-sex marriage a legal marriage even if another state considered the marriage legal. Culturally conservative states such as Utah and Mississippi built on DOMA, tightening their own restrictions on gay couples; both these states prohibited same-sex couples from adopting children, for example. By 2009, twenty-nine states had amended their state constitutions to restrict marriage to one man and one woman, and another dozen states have laws that make the same restriction.

But culturally liberal states such as Massachusetts and Vermont protected gay marriage despite DOMA. These two states, along with Connecticut, New Hampshire, and Iowa, issued marriage licenses to same-sex couples by 2010. An additional half dozen states recognize spousal legal rights. Liberals have successfully expanded gay rights at the state level in many other ways. A dozen states explicitly prohibit discrimination based on sexual orientation and gender identity, thirteen prohibit housing discrimination against gays, fourteen address discrimination or harassment of gay students, ten legally allow gays to visit their partners in hospital, and thirty-one states include sexual orientation in laws against hate or bias crimes.[96]

The Strategic Use of Fragmentation

Like liberals before them, contemporary conservatives have used federalism strategically to implement government actions they desire. Conservatives like Ronald Reagan inherited the institutions and policies of intergovernmental activism that liberals had constructed, and tried to turn this intergovernmental system toward the benefit of business, market-driven economic growth, and moral traditionalism. In office, conservatives decentralized some policies and nationalized others to achieve these goals.

In this period, as in the Progressive Era, states became critical for both liberal and conservative innovations. More capable of actively solving problems than ever, states developed innovative approaches to poverty, education, health and environmental protection policy. Presidents encouraged some of these innovations, and state-level policy innovations in turn influenced such major Federal initiatives as the Personal Responsibility and Work Opportunity Reconciliation Act of 1996, the No Child Left Behind Act of 2001, and the Patient Protection and Affordable Care Act of 2010. As the twenty-first century unfolds, a new generation of policy-makers will inherit the system of American federalism that helped shape these results.

10 American Federalism in the Twenty-First Century

Federalism is deeply embedded in the genetic code of the American nation. Federalism has had an enduring impact on the way Americans have organized their political conflicts, contested race and economic growth, and enlarged government responsibilities. This book has emphasized three key themes in American federalism. First, federalism is a basic and enduring factor in the making of America because it always has been a pervasive force in the struggle to win and keep political, economic, and social power. Since the beginning of the American Republic, federalism has been a principal battlefield for the most divisive and durable conflicts that shaped the nation. Second, federalism has had a cumulative impact on American politics, policy, and life. The results of the battles over federalism are alive today, in American politics, law, and public policy, in the structure of American national governing institutions, and in the spectacle of American politics. Third, for the last century, government activism was built on top of nineteenth-century federalism and profoundly shaped the nature of active government in America. Federalism is deeply injected into the politics of every aspect of government activism today.

Federalism's impacts could have turned out differently. Political leaders chose to use federalism to take the United States on new paths; those choices, and many of the unique events surrounding them, could have been different. For example, if President George Washington had supported Jefferson's agricultural vision instead of Hamilton's, and Washington had put the nation's power behind commodity exports, then Jefferson's faction would have had little need to enlist "states' rights" in their defense, and Hamilton might have chosen other grounds than states' rights to battle Jefferson. If President Abraham Lincoln had survived his assassination attempt, or had been succeeded by a president who made the strength of the Republican Party his chief priority (instead of the Democrat Andrew Johnson), national power might have expanded more decisively earlier in the nation's history, creating a more activist national economic policy before industrialization, and perhaps a more durable set of effective civil rights protections for Southern blacks. And if the more nationalistic views of Theodore Roosevelt had had more far-reaching impact in Congress and in the Supreme Court during the Progressive Era, states might have played a less important role in government activism. But none of these things actually happened.

The double battleground established by the Constitution's framers continues to shape our politics and public policy now, and it will do so in the future. Even though the scope and power of the national government has expanded to levels inconceivable two centuries ago, states will continue to play an important role as administrators, as innovators, as microcosms of political development, and as potential roadblocks to centralized power. Federalism does not endure because the Constitution's parchment barriers are effective. It endures because the states always have served the purposes of powerful political interests, and when it is selectively used, federalism often brings these interests positive returns on their political investments.

The Book's Argument

The authors of the U.S. Constitution produced an unfinished framework for American federalism because they could not agree on the balance of national and state authority. Some of the delegates to the Constitutional Convention supported a very strong national government, and they hoped to place the states in an inferior role, mainly as instruments of national power. Others supported a national government with narrow and limited powers, one that would supplement and reinforce the existing states. These antagonists could only cement the structure of American government with the political mortar of compromise. Those who advocated broad national powers ensured that the new national government would have strong military, commercial, and taxing powers as well as elastic authority that could be stretched in the future. Those who advocated narrow national powers ensured that the states would retain most of their domestic authority and would influence national policy-making. The final Constitution authorized the national government to use the tools of national sovereignty, but the complex design of the national policy-making process made it difficult for the national government to use this authority easily. The Constitution authorized the states to govern everyday American life, but amputated the states' authority to deal with domestic problems with all the powers exercised by a sovereign state. An uncertain, gray area separated national and state authority, inviting political adversaries to use federalism as a weapon to gain advantage in American politics.

Political parties and interest groups brought this framework of federalism to life through an ongoing series of battles to control the indistinct frontiers of state and national authority. Federalism fragmented public offices and public policy, the chief prizes of politics. Political organizations that pursued these prizes adapted to American federalism by fragmenting themselves. Political parties grew strongest at the state and local level, while the national parties became inclusive tents that contained sprawling, diverse, internally divided allies who were unified by office-seeking and a few policy goals. For more than a century, the Democratic Party defended state prerogatives because states' rights allowed it a measure of unity and strength. Meanwhile, state government control of domestic policy encouraged interest groups that sought relatively narrow policy goals. American federalism, along with the separation of national powers, nurtured pluralism, a system in which many interest groups with limited objectives influence many discrete fragments of public policy.

U.S. federalism established a political battleground that has shaped fights over race and economic development, the two most fundamental, long-term conflicts in American politics. Southern states insisted on safeguarding slavery until its abolition, and on legally protecting white supremacy for more than eighty years after Reconstruction. Northern states constructed opposition to slavery in state "personal liberty" laws, and in laws striking at racial discrimination after World War II. These divergent state approaches to African American citizenship fueled a gruesome war between the states in the 1860s, and angry Southern state resistance to desegregation in the 1950s and 1960s. National civil rights laws in the 1960s ended legal segregation throughout the United States, but the African Americans' long struggle for equal citizenship still haunts American life today. While the national government now takes an active role in citizenship rights, states still serve as an alternative for addressing current civil rights issues.

Throughout American history, federalism has shaped political conflicts over market-driven economic growth, the most basic political struggle in all industrialized nations. Because the states supervised much of American capitalist development and also the mitigation of its effects, Americans have fought over capitalism on two battlefields: first, over the way government should regulate capitalism, and second, over the relative authority of the Federal government and the states to regulate it. Federalism encouraged the rise of large private corporations, the policing of corporate behavior, and the political fragmentation of business. Federalism generally has helped strengthen the political influence of American private enterprises, but at the same time is has helped make relations between government and business exceptionally antagonistic.

Since the last decades of the nineteenth century, American federalism has adapted to wrenching change as the nation grew, industrialized, nationalized, urbanized, and became more culturally diverse. From the 1890s to World War I, the Progressive Era strengthened government and enlarged its role, particularly in mitigating the effects of market-driven economic growth. Federalism obstructed some paths of progressive reform, such as the effort to ban child labor nationally, while it encouraged others, such as prohibition. Progressives successfully expanded democracy by establishing state primary elections, initiatives, and referenda, and expanding the franchise to women. While progressives used some state governments actively to mitigate the consequences of industrial capitalism, interstate economic competition dampened the spread of these reforms. The Progressive Era left a legacy of institutional innovations and public activism layered on top of the nineteenth-century federal system.

The Great Depression of the 1930s brought unprecedented change in American federalism. The New Deal fought to expand the scope of government responsibility while it broadened the scope of *national* government responsibility relative to the states. To allay resistance to national activism, the Roosevelt administration often enlisted the states as active partners in public policy. Many of the New Deal's lasting domestic policy initiatives depended on grants-in-aid and other incentives for the states. This strategy allowed liberals in the North to expand social welfare, while it allowed the Southern states to continue to supervise racial segregation. New Deal activism, then, strengthened *both* the national and the state governments.

In the decades after World War II, liberals expanded Federal responsibility for alleviating discrimination, poverty, pollution, and inequality of opportunity. These liberal reformers layered more new national rules and programs atop intergovernmental policies established in the Progressive Era and the New Deal. Much more than the New Deal, the national government expanded the scope of grants-in-aid designed to stimulate activism in states, local governments, and interest groups. New civil rights, environmental and workplace regulations also imposed national rules on every important economic interest in American society. Liberal reforms, then, produced a far-reaching, complex, and expensive system of intergovernmental relations. Republican President Richard Nixon employed federalism to redirect power to the state and local governments and away from Democratic grass roots constituencies. Many of the subsequent conflicts over domestic policy became displaced by disagreements about the relative authority of the national government and the states, often obscuring the political stakes involved in conflicts over the scope of public authority.

After 1980, conservatives used the battlefield of federalism selectively and surgically to reduce business regulation and cut social welfare. The Reagan administration turned over more authority to the states for the liberal programs championed by their predecessors, while they reduced Federal funding for these programs. From the 1980s through the early 2000s, conservatives established national economic regulations more friendly to business, and often preempted the states from implementing more restrictive regulations. Even in this conservative period, however, the scope, complexity, and cost of the intergovernmental policy system increased. Liberals and conservatives both turned to the states for policy innovation. Federal government power increased—and so did both the liberal and conservative use of state power to achieve political goals.

Federalism, then, has been and remains a crucial contributing factor to American political development. But federalism is only one of many factors. American culture, ideology, resources, other structures and organizations, and the contingencies of history also contributed to the making of America. Of all these factors, federalism has been among the least well understood, because of its impact on the conduct of American political conflict.

Federalism as an Expedient Political Battlefield

The political battlefield of federalism has served as the site for conflicts over the deep, continuing political disputes of American life: the scope of government power, the limits of markets, and the diversity of the nation. But for both conservatives and liberals, Republicans and Democrats, and pressure groups with narrow interests as well as those with broad aspirations, federalism is chiefly instrumental, a weapon for political combat.

Conservatives

Conservatives have a deep rhetorical commitment to federalism. After 2008, conservatives were particularly intent on brandishing federalism to counter the nationalizing features of the agenda advanced by President Obama and liberal Democrats. Republican Governor Rick Perry of Texas made "states' rights" a centerpiece of his wide-ranging criticism of Federal policy from the very start of the Obama administration.[1] Conservative Tea Party activists enthusiastically embraced politicians who insisted on defending states' prerogatives in opposing the Federal health care reform, or endorsing Arizona's controversial law to control undocumented immigrants. In 2010, for example, Virginia Attorney General Attorney General Ken Cuccinelli brought a Tea Party crowd to a standing ovation by defending the states, saying that the case against the health care bill "is not about health care. That case is about liberty," and "If we lose that case, state sovereignty has been whittled to nothing and federalism is dead."[2] According to political scientist Dennis J. Goldford, the Tea Parties put forward a populist, anti-Federal government interpretation of federalism that invokes arguments made before the New Deal.[3] Beyond the Tea Party insurgents, conservative policy research and advocacy organizations champion competitive federalism and provide intellectual ammunition for the critique of government power.[4] The Republican Study Committee, a caucus of conservative Republicans in the U.S. House of Representatives, established a "10th Amendment Task Force" to advocate their conservative interpretation of federalism (but the House Republicans' 2010 campaign document, the "Pledge to America," was virtually silent on the issue of federalism).[5] Some conservatives have expressed support for repealing the Seventeenth Amendment, providing for the direct election of Senators, arguing that if state legislatures select U.S. Senators, the Senators will be more faithful to the states' rights.[6]

Conservatives today, however, show little appreciation for the way conservative defenders of property rights and free markets always have depended on national restrictions of state autonomy, restrictions conservatives have very strongly encouraged throughout American history. "Market-preserving" federalism has never been market-preserving enough for those who wanted to ride American capitalism unbridled. These restrictions on state autonomy began with the amputation of state powers intentionally written into the U.S. Constitution. The key Supreme Court rulings that nationalized markets in the nineteenth century strongly asserted limits on the states. Recent conservative policy initiatives commonly restrict state economic regulation.

Conservatives, then, must better appreciate three things about American federalism. First, historically, conservatives are just as responsible for the expansion of national power as are liberals. Second, states will not produce reliably conservative policies. States' rights alone were never sufficient to sustain unrestricted business behavior. Third, most conservatives turn a blind eye to the national security state. A strong Federal military establishment has and must undermine federalism—as the Constitution's framers fully recognized.

Liberals

Liberals actively have used American federalism and states' authority throughout American history, though they rarely appreciate that they have done so. The ascendance of every period of reform has been rooted in a few states, with Massachusetts, New York, California, and Wisconsin routinely in the forefront. As Richard Nathan has pointed out, during periods of conservative ascendance in the national government, liberals have pursued their agenda at the state level and, in the states, begun to lay many of the elements of later national action.[7] State governments constructed pioneering initiatives in the hotly contested fields of labor policy, environmental policy, and health care policy prior to Federal action. In the twenty-first century, liberals have used the states energetically. During the administration of President George W. Bush, some state governments resisted controversial aspects of Bush education, homeland security, and national security policies.[8] California's 2006 Global Warming Solutions Act, and the ten-state Regional Greenhouse Gas Initiative (RGGI), are influential initiatives that already have shaped the future path of Federal climate change policy. In 2010, California's climate law easily survived a serious political challenge backed by oil companies and conservatives.[9] At the start of his administration, Democratic President Barack Obama provided financial support to the financially hard-pressed states. The Obama administration reduced some Bush regulations that constrained state discretion to experiment with liberal policy.[10] State attorneys general continue to use their offices to crusade against corporate misbehavior.[11]

Liberals, then, must consider the possibility that the states' liberal policy innovations have been a *political* prerequisite for constructing a viable coalition for expanding liberal activism nationally. Even in racial policy— the policy area that gave the term "states' rights" its most reprehensible connotation—state level liberalizing innovations consistently preceded national breakthroughs. In the early American republic, Northern states phased slavery out long before national emancipation. From the Northern "personal liberty" laws of the 1850s, to fair housing and employment laws beginning in the mid-1940s, and racial profiling and gay rights laws today, states have laid the basis for the national expansion of rights for minorities. I do not claim these laws fully achieved racial justice, certainly not nationally, or that they were as effective as supporters hoped. I only claim that the *political* construction of these kinds of rights began in states, and that the construction of national political support for these rights seemed to begin with the construction of concrete, supportive, and legitimating policy initiatives in important states.

Liberals and conservatives strongly prefer national standards for all issues they consider truly important. This preference is understandable. An effective national law or rule is simply the easiest, most decisive way to achieve enduring national policy success. The chief battles over federalism in building active government over the last century have turned on the struggle between national standards and state discretion, with liberals seeking national rules to protect vulnerable people, and conservatives seeking national rules to protect market-driven economic development. It was pragmatic for civil rights leaders to press for national rules to override the states, so that they would not have to battle on a state-by-state basis. It is just as pragmatic for conservatives to seek national preemption of state business regulation.

Federalism is principally a means to larger ends.[12] Political antagonists strongly support federalism and state's prerogatives—but only in areas that are unimportant or politically difficult for them. Truly disinterested advocates of federalism, for its own sake, are extremely rare in American public life. Federalism may still be the most widely evoked institution in American political fights that has no *natural* constituency. But how well does federalism provide the benefits its advocates say that it does?

Federalism's Virtues Revisited

How does the historical record of American federalism reflect on the arguments for federalism described in Chapter 1? Proponents have suggested that federalism supports rights and democracy, that it makes government more responsive, that it fosters innovation, that it promotes efficiency, and that it nurtures economic prosperity. The historical record is mixed.

Rights and Democracy

Though it is common to assert that, in general, federalism provides for the protection of rights, the record of American political development casts severe doubt on this claim. Rights are a bundle of different protections, and when people talk about rights in general terms, they often mean different things. Some people place a higher priority on some rights than others. For many people, especially for conservatives, property and economic rights take precedence, and for them, the record of U.S. federalism is reasonably good. For millions of Americans with direct, living, and vivid family memories, the most salient rights have involved racial exclusion in voting, accommodations, education, and employment. For those who give precedence to these rights, federalism and "states' rights" appear to have been a giant, immovable obstacle used to shield the subordination of racial minorities.

Moreover, for anyone who places precedence on any particular rights, those rights should hold for all Americans, not just for some. This belief that a particular right—whether to be free of environmental rules or to marry a gay partner—trumps the value of federalism. The precedence of favored rights over federalism holds as strongly for conservatives as it does for liberals. I conclude that it is very hard to generalize that American federalism has a record of preserving rights, taken collectively.[13] Indeed, Americans have not agreed on the rights all should enjoy.

While federalism has an ambiguous record in preserving *rights*, American federalism clearly is important to American *democracy*, in the sense that it provides an institutional base for a viable political opposition that can take power. A viable political opposition is a necessary feature of democracy. As one of my students put it, federalism compels an ongoing political conversation. The historical record proves that American federalism provides an institutional base for opponents to construct political support and alternative governing agendas. In the 2000s, the opponents of unified party control of the national government (first under Republicans, then under Democrats) show that opponents still depend on the states' authority to construct effective political opposition.[14]

Responsiveness

Another argument for federalism is that decentralized power makes government more responsive to citizens. Certainly state governments can be more responsive to regional constituencies than the national government. The diversity of state economic resources, of state ideology, and of state demographics has resulted in state laws that reflect this diversity more than national laws, which necessarily distill the influence of many groups in public policy-making.

However, there is no reason to believe that state governments are any more responsive to their constituents *as a whole* than is the national government. Indeed, there are good reasons to believe that states are sometimes less responsive to the American people. James Madison made an exceptionally powerful argument about the undemocratic consequences of state power in the *Federalist*. Madison cautioned that:

The smaller the society, the fewer probably will be the distinct parties and interests composing it; the fewer the distinct parties and interests, the more frequently will a majority be found of the same party; and the smaller the number of individuals composing a majority, and the smaller the compass within which they are placed, the more easily will they concert and execute their plans of oppression. Extend the sphere, and you take in a greater variety of parties and interests; you make it less probable that a majority of the whole will have a common motive to invade the rights of other citizens; or if such a common motive exists, it will be more difficult for all who feel it to discover their own strength, and to act in unison with each other.[15]

Experience has borne out the wisdom of Madison's observation. Political scientists have shown that, in practice, powerful minorities in some states can dominate policy-making without majority support. Grant McConnell showed that decentralized policy-making often advantaged those minority interests, such as business, with many resources.[16] E.E. Schattschneider argued that a restricted scope of conflict could benefit those with resource advantages by limiting participation in public decisions.[17] Clearly, some interests are able to exercise more powerful control in some states than they can at the national level. In the 2000s, as money continued to flood into political campaigns, these resource advantages seemed increasingly important. It is easy to conclude that the states are more responsive to certain constituencies than the Federal government, but it is very difficult to prove that the states are more responsive to the will of "the people" than the Federal government.

Innovation

Many proponents of federalism argue that the decentralization of power fosters useful policy innovations. Just about every important government effort in the United States was first constructed at the state and local level. These state innovations influenced the design, politics, and implementation of later national initiatives. The most successful state policy experiments often established a practical working model that could function under American circumstances. These successes, in turn, helped attract a supportive constituency within and beyond the state. Richard Nathan took this observation a step further, arguing that the "oscillation of surges of government activism, sometimes from the center and sometimes from the periphery, has impelled the growth of governmental power in a way that would not otherwise have occurred in the individualistic political culture of America ... "[18] Prohibition, unemployment insurance, state anti-discrimination laws, and climate change policy all offer examples.

History shows that there are three limitations to the argument that states serve as "laboratories of democracy" and policy innovation. First, states are not pure "laboratories" that can produce any kind of policy experiment they want. The Constitution removed some of the states' sovereign powers, such as printing money and restricting trade, and exposed them to economic competition with other states. Over time, the states came to rely on their own tax sources and could not rely on the Federal government to bail them out when they were in difficult financial circumstances. The states imposed restrictions on their own fiscal powers with balanced budget requirements.[19] Under these circumstances, the states are strongly biased toward policy experiments that preserve free markets. Political scientist Paul Peterson pointed out that, because of states' exposure to interstate economic competition, the states are better suited to foster economic prosperity than to provide social welfare and equal opportunity policies.[20] Put another way, the states are better suited to develop experiments that promote the first part of Karl Polanyi's "double movement," the expansion of markets, than they are to implement experiments that mitigate the effects of market expansion, the second part of Polanyi's "double movement." Certainly, states have regulated businesses from the beginning. States often enact business regulations in response to popular demands. But a number of these experiments with business regulation—from railroad commissions in the 1800s, to securities regulation in the early 1900s, air pollution restrictions in the 1960s, and carbon emissions limits today—often put a greater burden on out-of-state business interests (such as railroads, oil companies, and auto companies) than on businesses located in the state.

Second, some state policy experiments violate important social values. State policy "laboratories" cooked up many innovative ways to suppress African Americans, from black codes before the Civil War to the Jim Crow laws and voting restrictions after it. More recently, state laws that get "tough" on crime, such as laws that require a prison sentence on a third felony conviction, have resulted in a prison population of two million, a larger prison population than other wealthy industrialized democracies and one heavily populated by blacks and Latinos.[21] There are many other examples. In 1907, Indiana pioneered a state law requiring the sterilization of criminals, rapists, and mental defectives in state custody, and this model compulsory sterilization law spread to a majority of states.[22] In 1922, Oregon enacted a law requiring all children to attend public schools; supported by the anti-Catholic Ku Klux Klan, the law aimed to wreck the Catholic schools.[23] The U.S. Supreme Court, which in other areas was rejecting national rules, applied Constitutional protections to these cases and struck down the compulsory sterilization and public school laws. Ironically, then, one underappreciated consequence of state experimentation may be to accelerate the nationalization of a specific policy issue.

Third, Nathan's assertion that federalism energized active government must be highly qualified when the United States is compared to other nations. Government activism has grown in all wealthy democracies over the last century, whether or not they have federal systems. Comparable nations have governed markets more actively, and mitigated the consequences of markets more extensively, than has the United States. The evidence suggests that federalism has restrained government activism in the United States. In federal systems like the United States, where states have independent revenues and compete with other states for investment and revenues, social welfare programs tend to lag behind programs enacted in other kinds of governments.[24]

Efficiency

Fourth, advocates of American federalism argue that its responsiveness to citizens makes the nation more efficient. Martha Derthick argued that states have a much more practical view of implementing public policy than Federal policy-makers, and that the United States is too big, sprawling, and diverse for national administration. It is essential for states to fill the national government's "performance gaps" and information gaps, so that public policy can work more pragmatically.[25] Paul Peterson argued that states can more effectively guide economic development than the national government.[26] Undoubtedly, there are limits on Federal efficiency and effectiveness. The states' practical experience, and their more immediate knowledge of local conditions, can facilitate policy efficiency and effectiveness.

The view that the states improve government performance has important limitations, however. First, the state governments are not equally efficient. If the Federal government decentralizes policy to some states, they will usually find a way to make it work effectively. But there are other states that routinely fall short. Discretion allows these states to abuse their authority, to waste money, and to administer the program in a way that benefits powerful local constituents rather than ostensible program beneficiaries. In the modern United States, where political contests are fought out via national media, political opponents often use the most exceptional abuses and mistakes to characterize the program, regardless of its other positive achievements (this process occurred in the case of the Comprehensive Employment and Training Act of the 1970s). Second, even if there is no political abuse or outright fraud, decentralized policy results in additional transaction costs, such as negotiation and dispute resolution. High-minded programs can founder on the shoals of divergent goals of state and local government implementation.[27]

Prosperity

Finally, many suggest that federalism in general, and American federalism in particular, promotes national economic prosperity because it protects rules and institutions that promote free markets and inhibit interference with free market processes. Interstate economic competition has limited efforts to interfere with property rights, thereby enriching the nation.

This book provides substantial evidence to support this argument. American federalism clearly has benefited market-driven economic growth, one part of Polanyi's "double movement." But while the American economy has offered tremendous economic opportunity and wealth, it also has created agonizing problems like unemployment, bankruptcy, and destitution. When pressed, most Americans do not support unbridled markets because the consequences are not tolerable. Americans want government to mitigate these consequences; they support Social Security, and insist that government do something about economic recession. Some balance of response to Polanyi's "double movement" is essential to sustain the political system and to meet the minimum requirements of common human decency. This argument about balance is not just a liberal perspective. Some traditional conservatives have argued that unrestricted markets would tear society apart.

In sum, federalism has had benefits for the United States, especially for democracy and prosperity. But these benefits must be weighed against many costs. Whatever its costs and benefits, federalism is an established fact of American life.

Necessary Research

There are many important questions about American federalism that need more study. We need a much better understanding of the effects of a strong national military on federalism. We also need a much better understanding of the effects of federalism on the lives of particular Americans, such as women and Latinos. We have the opportunity to study the impact of federalism on gay rights as that struggle unfolds. We have little systematic evidence about the way the states themselves have influenced the expansion of national rules, by arguing for national Supreme Court rulings, statutes that preempt the states, or other nationalizing actions.

Regionalism conspicuously deserves more systematic analysis. Sectional divisions between the interests of the North, South, and West built upon federalism, and sectional interests used federalism to achieve their goals. This form of sectionalism thrived in the American political system, influenced politics for decades, and continues to play a role in American political development.[28] But the growing prosperity of the South, and the fading of the industrial heartland, has brought these sections closer to parity. Now, the urban–rural dimension of political conflict seems ascendant, and this division cleaves interests in all the states. Meanwhile, a new form of regionalism is thriving. This regionalism, that links smaller groups of states around a more specific policy interest, is best exemplified by the Regional Greenhouse Gas Initiative. Regionalism also is evident in the collective action of state attorneys general. It may be one of the great ironies of American political development that reduced interstate economic differences, post-industrial values, falling communication barriers, and partially nationalized rules, together have enabled like-minded states to better concert their political independence of Washington.

Most of all, we need to step back and develop better normative theories about the basic citizenship rights that must be protected nationally. What are those basic citizenship rights, exactly? What are the "Privileges and Immunities of Citizens in the Several States," that are protected in Article IV, Section 4 of the 1787 Constitution, and evoked again in the Fourteenth Amendment? What would be included in a Bill of Rights for the twenty-first century? More than ever, American federalism requires an explicit national conversation about what exactly must be guaranteed to every American as a right of citizenship. This conversation is long overdue.

The key issue is not whether the states in the abstract can provide better government than the national government, or whether the national government should "return power" to the states in the abstract. The central question turns on specific policy choices: which aspects of a public policy must be uniform everywhere in the United States, and which can vary across the nation? Rather than use the battlefield of federalism to conduct endless and distracting battles over generic principles like "states' rights," the Tenth Amendment or Federal power, Americans must recognize that the true conflicts over federalism turn on which government rules need to be unvarying across the nation, and which can be allowed to vary. Federalism is about unequal and disparate results, as Aaron Wildavsky argued. Americans must articulate more clearly which results they believe should be nationalized and which can be different in different states.

Americans who value democracy must value the very real role that federalism plays by providing safe harbors for a democratic opposition. These Americans must carefully work through their view of which rights are basic, balance the value of rights with the value of democracy, and be very willing to allow the most generous measure of state discretion that they believe is morally consistent with these *basic* rights. In this way, national standards can facilitate state experimentation above a floor of well-conceived rights, and the states can serve as lively polities as well as vehicles for national learning.

Federalism is Making Tomorrow's America

Federalism helped make the United States, and the nation cannot be understood apart from federalism. Federalism will help make the future of the United States. Whether the Obama presidency is eventually viewed as the beginning of a new era in American federalism or as an episode in a continuing conservative trend, federalism will remain a central part of American politics, a powerful weapon for achieving substantive goals.

Beginning a conversation about the basic national standards that are essential for American citizenship would be an important step toward making American federalism a more constructive element of the future political development of the United States. It also is an important task for reconstructing a more inclusive sense of nation, a sense that has been damaged by the polarization of American politics. This discussion can better enable the United States to grapple with the truly daunting problems that it now faces.

American federalism is not just a constraint, it is also a great opportunity. Reflecting on federalism's contribution to the making of America, past, present, and future, is not just an occasion for better understanding the United States. It is a summons to American idealism.

Notes

Chapter 1

1 Ronald L. Watts, "Federalism Today: The Relevance Today of the Federal Idea," paper prepared for the International Conference on Federalism 2002, http://www.forumfed. org/en/federalism/federalismtoday.php (accessed November 8, 2009).

2 Albert Bushnell Hart, *Introduction to the Study of Federal Government* (Boston: Ginn and Company, 1891), 27–48; William H. Riker, *Federalism: Origin, Operation, Significance* (Boston: Little, Brown, 1964), 9, 34–35.

3 Samuel Pufendorf, "Regular States vs. Systems of States," in *Theories of Federalism: A Reader*, eds. Dimitrios Kamris and Wayne Norman (Basingstoke, UK and New York: Palgrave Macmillan, 2005), 35–50.

4 Alfred Stepan, "Federalism and Democracy: Beyond the U.S. Model," in *Theories of Federalism: A Reader*, eds. Dimitrious Karmis and Wayne Norman (Basingstoke, UK and New York: Palgrave Macmillan, 2005), 255–68.

5 Ronald L. Watts, "Comparative Conclusions," in *Distribution of Powers and Responsibilities in Federal Countries*, eds. Akhtar Majeed, Ronald L. Watts, and Douglas M. Brown (Montreal, Canada: McGill-Queens University Press, 2006), 334.

6 Samuel Krislov, "American Federalism as American Exceptionalism," *Publius* 31:1 (Winter, 2001), 9–26.

7 In this book, I use the term "Federal government" as a synonym for the U.S. national government.

8 Ed O'Keefe, "How Many Federal Workers Are There?" *Washington Post*, September 30, 2010, http://voices.washingtonpost.com/federal-eye/2010/09/how_many_federal_workers_ are_t.html (accessed November 23, 2010); U.S. Census Bureau, "Census Bureau Reports State and Local Government Employment Remains at 16.6 Million," August 31, 2010, http://www.census.gov/newsroom/releases/archives/governments/cb10-132.html (accessed November 23, 2010).

9 U.S. Census Bureau, "State and Local Government Spending Increases by 6.5 percent in 2008, Census Bureau Reports," July 14, 2010, http://www.census.gov/newsroom/releases/ archives/governments/cb10–108.html (accessed November 23, 2010); U.S. Office of Management and Budget, *Budget of the United States Government: Historical Tables Fiscal Year 2011*, http://www.gpoaccess.gov/usbudget/fy11/hist.html (accessed November 23, 2010).

10 Barry G. Rabe, "Power to the States: The Promise and Pitfalls of Decentralization," in *Environmental Policy: New Directions for the Twenty-First Century*, eds. Norman J. Vig and Michael E. Kraft (Washington, DC: CQ Press, 2006), 35–36; Environmental Council of the States, "Delegation by Environmental Act," http://www.ecos.org/section/states/ enviro_actlist (accessed January 8, 2011).

11 Delaware Secretary of State, *2005 Annual Report*, http://www.sixwise.com/pdf/2005 DELAWARE doc ar.pdf (accessed February 16, 2010); Bizfilings.com, "Why Incorporate

in Delaware?" http://www.bizfilings.com/Learn_About/Incorporating_In_Delaware (accessed February 16, 2010).

12 U.S. Census Bureau, "Finances of Selected State and Local Government Employee Retirement Systems, Table 1. Cash and Security Holdings for the Quarter Ending June 30, 2010 and Prior Quarters," http://www2.census.gov/govs/qpr/2010/table1.txt, (accessed November 24, 2010).

13 U.S. Department of Education, "Public Elementary and Secondary School Student Enrollment and Staff Counts from the Common Core of Data: School Year 2007–8," November, 2009, http://nces.ed.gov/pubs2010/2010309.pdf (accessed November 13, 2009).

14 Death Penalty Information Center, "Facts about the Death Penalty," http://www.deathpenaltyinfo.org/documents/FactSheet.pdf (accessed March 24, 2011).

15 Congressional Research Service, "National Guard Personnel and Deployments: Fact Sheet," January 17, 2008, http://www.fas.org/sgp/crs/natsec/RS22451.pdf (accessed November 23, 2010).

16 Council of State Governments, "Globalization and Trade," http://www.csg.org/policy/globalization.aspx (accessed December 14, 2010).

17 The four elected presidents who had not won a statewide election were William Howard Taft, Herbert Hoover, Dwight Eisenhower, and George H.W. Bush. Gerald Ford, who succeeded Richard Nixon when Nixon resigned, never won a statewide office, and did not win a presidential election in his own right.

18 Jefferson to Monsieur Destutt De Tracy, letter, January 26, 1811, in *The Writings of Thomas Jefferson*, ed. Paul Leicester Ford (London: G.P. Putnam's Sons, 1904–05), Vol. 9, 308–9.

19 James Madison, *Federalist* 10, in Alexander Hamilton, James Madison, and John Jay, *The Federalist,* ed. Jacob E. Cooke (Middletown, CT: Wesleyan University Press, 1961), 64.

20 Madison, *Federalist* 51, 351.

21 James Bryce, *The American Commonwealth* (London: Macmillan, 1888), Vol. I, 353.

22 Madison, *Federalist* 46, 319–20.

23 Alexis De Tocqueville, *Democracy in America* (Alfred A. Knopf, 1945 [originally 1835 & 1840]), Vol. 1, 163.

24 John D. Nugent, *Safeguarding Federalism: How States Protect their Interests in National Policymaking* (Norman, OK: University of Oklahoma Press, 2009); Kirk Johnson, "States' Rights is Rallying Cry of Resistance for Lawmakers," *New York Times*, March 16, 2010.

25 G. Alan Tarr and Ellis Katz, "Introduction," in *Federalism and Rights*, eds. Ellis Katz and G. Alan Tarr, (Lanham, MD: Rowman & Littlefield, 1996), xi.

26 Madison, *Federalist* 46, 316. See also Alexander Hamilton, *Federalist* 17, 107 and Madison, *Federalist* 45, 313.

27 Bryce, *The American Commonwealth*, Vol. 1, 353; Louis Brandeis in *New State Ice Co. v. Liebmann*, 285 U.S. 262 (1932). See also David Osborne, *Laboratories of Democracy: New Breed of Governor Creates Models for National Growth* (Cambridge, MA: Harvard Business School Press, 1988); Peter Eisinger, *The Rise of the Entrepreneurial State: State and Local Economic Development Policy in the United States* (Madison, WI: University of Wisconsin Press, 1988); Anne O'M. Bowman and Richard C. Kearney, *The Resurgence of the States* (Englewood Cliffs, NJ: Prentice-Hall, 1986); Barry G. Rabe, *Statehouse and Greenhouse: The Stealth Politics of American Climate Change Policy* (Washington, DC: Brookings Institution, 2004); Andrew Karch, *Democratic Laboratories: Policy Diffusion among the American States* (Ann Arbor, MI: University of Michigan Press, 2007).

28 Richard Nathan, "Updating Theories of American Federalism," in *Intergovernmental Management for the Twenty-First Century*, eds. Timothy J. Conlan and Paul L. Posner (Washington, DC: Brookings Institution, 2008), 13–25, quote 16.

29 *The Records of the Federal Convention of 1787*, ed. Max Farrand, 4 vols. (New Haven, CT: Yale University Press, 1937), August 18, II, 331.

30 Tocqueville, *Democracy in America*, Vol. 1, 163.

31 James M. Buchanan and Gordon Tullock, *The Calculus of Consent: Logical Foundations of Constitutional Democracy* (Ann Arbor, MI: University of Michigan Press, 1962), 114.

32 Aaron B. Wildavsky, *Speaking Truth to Power: The Art and Craft of Policy Analysis* (Boston: Little, Brown, 1979), 152.

33 Barry R. Weingast, "The Economic Role of Political Institutions: Market-Preserving Federalism and Economic Development," *Journal of Law, Economics, & Organization* 11:1 (April, 1995), 1–31, quote 4.

34 Edward S. Corwin, "The Passing of Dual Federalism," *Virginia Law Review* 36:1 (February,1950), 1–24.

35 Morton Grodzins, "The Federal System" in *Goals for Americans: The Report of the President's Commission on National Goals* (Englewood Cliffs, NJ: Prentice-Hall, 1960), 265–66. David Walker credits Joseph McLean with the use of the marble cake metaphor in 1952; David B. Walker, *The Rebirth of Federalism: Slouching toward Washington*, 2nd ed. (Chatham, NJ : Chatham House, 2000), 90.

36 Timothy J. Conlan, *From New Federalism to Devolution: Twenty-Five Years of Intergovernmental Reform*, revised ed. (Washington, DC: Brookings Institution, 1998).

37 Deil S. Wright, *Understanding Intergovernmental Relations*, 3rd ed. (New York: Houghton Mifflin Harcourt, 1998).

38 Laurence J. O'Toole, ed., *American Intergovernmental Relations: Foundations, Perspectives, and Issues*, 4th ed. (Washington, DC: CQ Press, 2007); Timothy J. Conlan and Paul L. Posner, eds., *Intergovernmental Management for the 21st Century* (Washington, DC: Brookings Institution, 2008).

39 Harry N. Scheiber, "Federalism and the American Economic Order, 1789–1910," *Law and Society Review* 10:1 (Fall, 1975), 57–118 and "American Federalism and the Diffusion of Power: Historical and Contemporary Perspectives," *University of Toledo Law Review* 9 (Summer 1978), 619–80; Ballard C. Campbell, *The Growth of American Government: Governance from the Cleveland Era to the Present* (Bloomington, IN: Indiana University Press, 1995); William J. Novak, *The People's Welfare: Law and Regulation in Nineteenth Century America* (Chapel Hill, NC: University of North Carolina Press, 1996), Jon C. Teaford, *The Rise of the States: Evolution of American State Government* (Baltimore, MD: Johns Hopkins University Press, 2002); Brian Balogh, *A Government Out of Sight: The Mystery of National Authority in Nineteenth-Century America* (Cambridge and New York: Cambridge University Press, 2009).

40 Alison LaCroix, *The Ideological Origins of American Federalism* (Cambridge, MA: Harvard University Press, 2010); Samuel H. Beer, *To Make a Nation: The Rediscovery of American Federalism* (Cambridge, MA: Belknap Press, 1993). See also Daniel J. Elazar, *Exploring Federalism* (Tuscaloosa, AL: University of Alabama Press, 1987); Dimitrios Karmis and Wayne Norman, eds., *Theories of Federalism: A Reader* (Basingstoke, UK and New York: Palgrave Macmillan, 2005).

41 Riker, *Federalism: Origin, Operation, Significance*. More recent rational choice treatments of federalism include Jenna Bednar, *The Robust Federation: Principles of Design* (Cambridge and New York: Cambridge University Press, 2009), and Mikhail Filippov, Peter C. Ordeshook, and Olga Vitalievna Shvetsova, *Designing Federalism: A Theory of Self-sustainable Federal Institutions* (Cambridge and New York: Cambridge University Press, 2004).

42 Herbert Obinger, Stephan Leibfried, and Francis G. Castles, eds., *Federalism and the Welfare State: New World and European Experiences* (Cambridge and New York: Cambridge University Press, 2005).

43 Jonathan A. Rodden, *Hamilton's Paradox: The Promise and Peril of Fiscal Federalism* (Cambridge and New York: Cambridge University Press, 2006); Kent Eaton, "Federalism in Europe and Latin America: Conceptualization, Causes, and Consequences" *World Politics* 60: 4 (July, 2008), 665–98; Daniel Ziblatt, *Structuring the State: The Formation of Italy and Germany and the Puzzle of Federalism* (Princeton, NJ: Princeton

University Press, 2006); Tulia Falleti, *Decentralization and Subnational Politics in Latin America* (New York: Cambridge University Press, 2010); Anand Menon and Martin A. Schain, eds., *Comparative Federalism: The European Union and the United States in Comparative Perspective* (Oxford and New York: Oxford University Press, 2006); Jan Erk and Wilfried Swenden, *New Directions in Federalism Studies* (Abingdon, UK, and New York: Routledge, 2009).

44 Karen Orren and Stephen Skowronek, *The Search for American Political Development* (Cambridge and New York: Cambridge University Press, 2004), 123.

45 Robert C. Lieberman, *Shifting the Color Line: Race and the American Welfare State* (Cambridge, MA: Harvard University Press, 1998), and *Shaping Race Policy: The United States in Comparative Perspective* (Princeton, NJ: Princeton University Press, 2005).

46 Suzanne Mettler, *Dividing Citizens: Gender and Federalism in New Deal Public Policy* (Ithaca, NY: Cornell University Press, 1998).

47 Kimberley S. Johnson, *Governing the American State: Congress and the New Federalism, 1877–1929* (Princeton, NJ: Princeton University Press, 2007).

48 Richard A. Bensel, *Sectionalism and American Political Development, 1880–1980* (Madison, WI: University of Wisconsin Press, 1984), *Yankee Leviathan: The Origins of Central State Authority in America, 1859–1877* (Cambridge and New York: Cambridge University Press, 1991), and *The Political Economy of American Industrialization, 1877–1900* (Cambridge and New York: Cambridge University Press, 2000).

49 Martha Derthick, *Uncontrollable Spending for Social Services Grants* (Washington, DC: Brookings Institution, 1975), *Up in Smoke: From Legislation to Litigation in Tobacco Politics*, 2nd ed. (Washington, DC: CQ Press, 2004), and *Keeping the Compound Republic: Essays on American Federalism* (Washington, DC: Brookings Institution, 2001).

50 Paul Pierson, *Politics in Time: History, Institutions, and Social Analysis* (Princeton, NJ: Princeton University Press, 2004), 17–53.

51 John Kingdon, *America the Unusual* (New York: St. Martin's, 1999), 7–22; Graham K. Wilson, *Only in America? The Politics of the United States in Comparative Perspective* (Chatham, NJ: Chatham House, 1998), 5–8; Sven Steinmo and Jon Watts, "It's the Institutions, Stupid! Why Comprehensive National Health Insurance always Fails in America," *Journal of Health Politics, Policy and Law* 20:2 (Summer, 1995): 329–72.

52 On the importance of sequence, see Paul Pierson, "Not Just What, but *When*: Timing and Sequence in Political Processes," *Studies in American Political Development* 14:1 (Spring, 2000), 72–92; and the responses to Pierson by Robert Jervis, "Timing and Interaction in Politics: A Comment on Pierson"; Kathleen Thelen, "Timing and Temporality in the Analysis of Institutional Change"; and Amy Bridges, "Path Dependence, Sequence, History, Theory," *Studies in American Political Development* 14:1 (Spring, 2000), 93–112.

53 On institutional change in American Political Development research, see Kathleen Thelen, *How Institutions Evolve: The Political Economy of Skills in Germany, Britain, the United States and Japan* (Cambridge and New York: Cambridge University Press, 2004); Eric Schickler, *Disjointed Pluralism: Institutional Innovation and the Development of the U.S. Congress* (Princeton, NJ: Princeton University Press, 2001); Margaret Weir, "When Does Policy Change? The Organizational Politics of Change," in *Rethinking Political Institutions: The Art of the State*, eds. Ian Shapiro, Stephen Skowronek, and Daniel Galvin (New York: New York University Press, 2006); and James Mahoney and Kathleen Thelen, eds., *Explaining Institutional Change: Ambiguity, Agency, and Power*, (Cambridge and New York: Cambridge University Press, 2009).

Chapter 2

1 Lawrence M. Friedman, *A History of American Law*, 3rd ed. (New York: Touchstone, 2005), 3–53; Robert A. Becker, *Revolution, Reform, and the Politics of American Taxation,*

1763–1783 (Baton Rouge, LA: Louisiana State University Press, 1980); Albert Anthony Giesecke, *American Commercial Legislation before 1789* (New York: Burt Franklin, 1970 [orig. 1910]); Margaret Ellen Newell, "The Birth of New England in the Atlantic Economy: From Its Beginning to 1770," in *Engines of Enterprise: An Economic History of New England,* ed. Peter Temin (Cambridge, MA: Harvard University Press, 2000), 41; Gordon S. Wood, *The Creation of the American Republic, 1776–1787* (Chapel Hill, NC: University of North Carolina Press, 1969), 166–67; Peter C. Ordeshook and Olga Shvetsova, "Federalism and Constitutional Design," *Journal of Democracy* 8:1 (January, 1997), 27–42.

2 Joseph L. Davis, *Sectionalism in American Politics, 1774–1787* (Madison, WI: University of Wisconsin Press, 1977), 16–19; Gary M. Walton and Hugh Rockoff, *History of the American Economy,* 8th ed. (Fort Worth, TX: Dryden Press, 1998), 94–113, 147–50.

3 See comments by Alexander Hamilton, in *The Records of the Federal Convention of 1787* [hereafter, *RFC*], ed. Max Farrand, 4 vols. (New Haven, CT: Yale University Press, 1937), June 29, I, 466, and James Madison, *RFC,* June 30, I, 486–87.

4 Curtis P. Nettels, *The Emergence of a National Economy, 1775–1815* (New York: Holt, Rinehart, and Winston, 1962), 138, 146; Allan Nevins, *The American States during and after the Revolution, 1775–1789* (New York: Macmillan, 1924), 598; Forrest McDonald, *Novus Ordo Seclorum: The Intellectual Origins of the Constitution* (Lawrence, KS: University Press of Kansas, 1985), 217–19; Gary M. Walton and James F. Shepard, *The Economic Rise of Early America* (New York: Cambridge University Press, 1979), 102.

5 Nettels, *The Emergence of a National Economy,* 75–81, 86; Jackson Turner Main, *The Sovereign States, 1775–1783* (New York: New Viewpoints, 1973), 235; David P. Szatmary, *Shay's Rebellion: The Making of an American Insurrection* (Amherst, MA: University of Massachusetts Press, 1980); James Ferguson, *The Power of the Purse: A History of Public Finance, 1776–1790* (Chapel Hill, NC: University of North Carolina Press, 1961), 243–49; Roger H. Brown, *Redeeming the Republic: Federalists, Taxation, and the Origins of the Constitution* (Baltimore, MD: Johns Hopkins University Press, 1993), 83–96, 108–21; Leonard L. Richards, *Shays's Rebellion: The American Revolution's Final Battle* (Philadelphia, PA: University of Pennsylvania Press, 2003).

6 William Pierce to George Turner, May 19, 1787, in *Supplement to Max Farrand's The Records of the Federal Convention of 1787,* ed. James L. Hutson (New Haven, CT: Yale University Press, 1987), 10; Jack N. Rakove, *Original Meanings: Politics and Ideas in the Making of the Constitution* (New York: Alfred A. Knopf, 1996), 33.

7 George Washington to David Stuart, July 1, 1787, *RFC* III, 51–52.

8 David Brian Robertson, *The Constitution and America's Destiny* (Cambridge and New York: Cambridge University Press, 2005), 68–71.

9 Rakove, *Original Meanings,* 31–34; Richard Beeman, *Plain, Honest Men: The Making of the American Constitution* (New York: Random House, 2009).

10 Clinton Rossiter, *1787: The Grand Convention* (New York: Macmillan, 1966), 79–156.

11 James H. Charleton and Robert G. Ferris, eds., *Framers of the Constitution* (Washington, DC: Smithsonian Institution Press, 1986); U.S. Congress, *Biographical Directory of the United States Congress, 1774–1989* (Washington, DC: Government Printing Office, 1989).

12 Ralph Ketcham, *James Madison: A Biography* (Charlottesville, VA: University Press of Virginia, 1971).

13 James Madison, "Vices of the Political System of the United States," in *The Papers of James Madison,* ed. William T. Hutchinson et al., 17 vols. (Chicago: University of Chicago Press, 1975), 9: 348–54; see Richard K. Matthews, *If Men were Angels: James Madison and the Heartless Empire of Reason* (Lawrence, KS: University Press of Kansas, 1995), 178–84.

14 *RFC,* June 7, I, 154.

15 *RFC,* June 28, I, 449.

16 David Brian Robertson, "Madison's Opponents and Constitutional Design," *American Political Science Review* 99:2 (May, 2005), 227–28.

17 *RFC,* June 8, I, 164–65.

18 *RFC*, May 29, I, 20–22.
19 *RFC*, July 5, I, 530.
20 *RFC*, June 18, I, 287.
21 *RFC*, June 8, I, 164.
22 *RFC*, June 30, I, 484–85; July 2, I, 510–11.
23 *RFC*, June 8, I, 167.
24 *RFC*, June 29, I, 461.
25 *Supplement to Max Farrand's The Records of the Federal Convention of 1787*, June 25, 112–13.
26 *RFC*, June 30, I, 492.
27 Wood, *The Creation of the American Republic, 1776–1787*, 527–28; Rakove, *Original Meanings*, 182–84, 188–89.
28 *RFC*, June 18, I, 287.
29 *RFC*, June 8, I, 172.
30 *RFC*, June 29, I, 467.
31 *RFC*, June 6, I, 133.
32 *RFC*, June 16, I, 251.
33 *RFC*, June 7, 1, 152–55.
34 *RFC*, June 21, I, 355.
35 *RFC*, June 25, I, 416.
36 *RFC*, June 29, I, 468–69.
37 *RFC*, July 2, I, 511.
38 Madison to George Washington, April 16, 1787, in *The Papers of James Madison* 9: 383.
39 *RFC*, July 6, I, 551.
40 *RFC,* June 16, I, 17.
41 *RFC*, July 17, II, 25.
42 *RFC*, July 16, II, 17.
43 *RFC*, July 17, II, 25–26.
44 *RFC*, August 8, II, 220.
45 *RFC*, July 13, I, 605.
46 *RFC*, August 22, II, 372.
47 *RFC*, July 12, I, 595–96.
48 *RFC*, August 21, II, 363–64.
49 *RFC*, August 18, II, 332.
50 *RFC*, August 28, II, 437–38.
51 *RFC*, August 18, II, 325.
52 *RFC*, August 18, II, 332–33.
53 *RFC*, August 23, II, 388.
54 *RFC*, August 6, II, 181–83, 187.
55 *RFC,* September 15, II, 640.
56 *RFC*, August 22, II, 367.
57 Compare *RFC*, II, 569 and II, 594. The preamble is at II, 590.
58 *RFC*, August 18, II, 330; September 5, II, 508.
59 *RFC*, August 6, I, 181; August 16, II, 308.
60 *RFC*, September 14, II, 618.
61 *RFC*, August 20, II, 350; August 21, II, 355–56; August 22, II, 366–67.
62 *RFC*, September 15, II, 625.
63 Rakove, *Original Meanings*, 181–88.
64 James Madison, *Federalist* 40 and *Federalist* 45, in Alexander Hamilton, James Madison, and John Jay, *The Federalist,* ed. Jacob E. Cooke (Middletown, CT: Wesleyan University Press, 1961), 261, 311.
65 Madison, *Federalist* 45, 313.
66 "A Landholder" (Oliver Ellsworth), IV, November 26, 1787, http://teachingamerican history.org/library/index.asp?documentprint=1653 (accessed January 2, 2010).

67 Virginia Ratifying Convention, "Proposed Amendments to the Constitution 27 June 1788" in Jonathan Elliot, ed., *The Debates in the Several State Conventions on the Adoption of the Federal Constitution* (New York: Burt Franklin, 1968) 3:657.

68 U.S. House of Representatives, Debates on Amendments to the Constitution, in *The Founders' Constitution*, Vol. 5, *Bill of Rights*, Document 11, http://press-pubs.uchicago. edu/founders/documents/bill_of_rightss11.html (accessed December 15, 2009).

69 John F. Manning "Federalism and the Generality Problem in Constitutional Interpretation," *Harvard Law Review* 122:8 (June, 2009), 2003–69.

70 On the ideas that shaped federalism, see Alison LaCroix, *The Ideological Origins of American Federalism*, (Cambridge, MA: Harvard University Press, 2010).

71 Madison, *Federalist* 51, 351, and *Federalist* 62, 416.

72 "A Freeman" (Tench Cox), II, January 30, 1788, *The Online Library of Liberty*, http://oll.libertyfund.org/?option=com_staticxt&staticfile=show.php%3Ftitle=2069&chapter=156158&layout=html&Itemid=27 (accessed July 7, 2010).

73 Aaron Wildavsky, "Federalism is about Inequality," in *The Costs of Federalism*, eds. Robert T. Golembiewski and Aaron Wildavsky (New Brunswick, NJ: Transaction Books, 1984), 66.

74 Roger Sherman and Oliver Ellsworth to the Governor of Connecticut, letter, September 26, 1787, *RFC* III, 100.

75 Harry N. Scheiber, "Federalism and the American Economic Order, 1789–1910," *Law and Society Review* 10:1 (Fall, 1975), 57–118.

76 For example, a minimum winning coalition of New England and the Middle states would require New Hampshire (with three Representatives and two Senators), Massachusetts (eight Representatives and two Senators), Connecticut (five Representatives and two Senators), New York (five Representatives and two Senators), New Jersey (four Representatives and two Senators), and Pennsylvania (eight Representatives and two Senators), and a Senator from another state, either Rhode Island or Delaware (each with two Senators but only one Representative). This coalition of states would represent fifty-four percent of the House of Representatives, fifty-five percent of the population of the thirteen states according to the 1790 census, and fifty-six percent of the October, 1786 Confederation requisition. A minimum winning coalition that included all the large states would require the unanimous support of Representatives from Virginia (ten Representatives), Pennsylvania (eight), and Massachusetts (eight) and, for example, Maryland (six) and the three states with the smallest representation: Georgia (three), Delaware (one), and Rhode Island (one). This coalition represented about fifty-seven percent of the House of Representatives and of the population of the thirteen states according to the 1790 census.

77 Madison, *Federalist* 51, 350–51.

78 Ronald P. Formisano, "State Development in the Early Republic: Substance and Structure, 1780–1840," in *Contesting Democracy: Substance and Structure in American Political History*, eds. Byron E. Shafer and Anthony Badger (Lawrence, KS: University Press of Kansas, 2001), 11.

79 Herbert Wechsler, "The Political Safeguards of Federalism: The Role of the States in the Composition and Selection of the National Government," *Columbia Law Review* 54:4 (April 1954), 545.

80 Woodrow Wilson, *Constitutional Government in the United States* (New York: Columbia University Press, 1908), 173.

Chapter 3

1 Forrest McDonald, *We the People: The Economic Origins of the Constitution* (Chicago: University of Chicago Press, 1958), 21–37.

2 *The Records of the Federal Convention of 1787* [hereafter, *RFC*], ed. Max Farrand, 4 vols. (New Haven, CT: Yale University Press, 1937), June 6, I, 135–36. These comments anticipate Madison's analysis in *Federalist* 10.

3 *RFC,* June 18, I, 289.

4 James Madison, *Federalist* 51, in Alexander Hamilton, James Madison, and John Jay, *The Federalist,* ed. Jacob E. Cooke (Middletown, CT: Wesleyan University Press, 1961), 353.

5 Madison, *Federalist* 45 and 46, 308–23; see Larry D. Kramer, "Putting the Politics Back into the Political Safeguards of Federalism," *Columbia Law Review* 100:1 (January, 2000), 215–93.

6 V.O. Key, Jr., *Politics, Parties, and Pressure Groups,* 4th ed. (New York: Thomas Y. Crowell, 1958), 6.

7 Aaron Wildavsky, "Federalism is about Inequality," in *The Costs of Federalism,* eds. Robert T. Golembiewski and Aaron Wildavsky (New Brunswick, NJ: Transaction Books, 1984), 55–72.

8 United States Department of Labor, "Comparison of State Unemployment Laws," http://www.workforcesecurity.doleta.gov/unemploy/comparison2009.asp (accessed February 11, 2010).

9 Associated Press, "Abortion Rights Foes Look to Spread Fetal Pain Law," December 9, 2010, http://abcnews.go.com/US/wireStory?id=12358258 (accessed March 30, 2011); Juliet Eilperin, "Environmentalists Plan to Redirect Strategies," *Washington Post,* December 21, 2010, http://www.washingtonpost.com/wp-dyn/content/article/2010/12/20/AR2010122005874.html (accessed December 21, 2010).

10 E.E. Schattschnieder, *The Semisovereign People: A Realist's View of Democracy in America* (New York: Holt, Rinehart, and Winston, 1960).

11 Attorney General of Florida Bill McCullom to Harry Reid, Nancy Pelosi, Mitch McConnell, and John Boehner, January 19, 2010, http://myfloridalegal.com/webfiles.nsf/WF/MRAY-7ZUMNW/$file/HealthCareMemo.pdf (accessed February 11, 2010).

12 Simon Lazarus, "Mandatory Health Insurance: Is It Constitutional?" Issue brief for the American Constitution Society for Law and Policy, December 2009, http://www.nsclc.org/areas/federal-rights/mandatory-health-insurance-is-it-constitutional/at_download/attachment (accessed February 11, 2010).

13 David S. Meyer and Suzanne Staggenborg, "Movements, Countermovements, and the Structure of Political Opportunity," *American Journal of Sociology* 101:6 (May, 1996), 1645.

14 Herbert Wechsler, "The Political Safeguards of Federalism: The Role of the States in the Composition and Selection of the National Government," *Columbia Law Review* 54:4 (April, 1954), 552.

15 Marc Kaufman and Mike Allen, "Cheney Sees Gay Marriage as State Issue: Vice-President Details Differences with Bush," *Washington Post,* August 25, 2004, A01. Bush's running mate, Vice-President Dick Cheney, disagreed with Bush and argued that the legal status of gay marriage should be left to the states.

16 Charles Tilly, *Social Movements, 1768–2004* (Boulder, CO: Paradigm Publishers, 2004); Sidney Tarrow, *Power in Movement: Collective Action, Social Movements and Politics* (Cambridge and New York: Cambridge University Press, 1994).

17 See Chapter 6, below.

18 Meyer and Staggenborg, "Movements, Countermovements, and the Structure of Political Opportunity," 1628–60.

19 Key, *Politics, Parties, and Pressure Groups,* 12; John H. Aldrich, *Why Parties? The Origin and Transformation of Party Politics in America* (Chicago: University of Chicago Press, 1995).

20 Christopher Collier, "The American People as Christian White Men of Property: Suffrage and Elections in Colonial and Early National America," in *Voting and the Spirit of American Democracy: Essays on the History of Voting and Voting Rights in America,* ed. Donald W. Rogers (Urbana, IL: University of Illinois Press, 1992), 19–29.

21 Ibid.; Sean Wilentz, "Property and Power: Suffrage Reform in the United States, 1787–1860, in Collier, *Voting and the Spirit of American Democracy,* 31–42; Alexander Keyssar, *The Right to Vote: The Contested History of Democracy in the United States* (New York: Basic Books, 2000), 26–76.

22 Richard Hofstadter, The *Idea of a Party System: The Rise of Legitimate Opposition in the United States, 1780–1840* (Berkeley, CA: University of California Press, 1968), 206; Alan Ware, "United States: Disappearing Parties?" in *Political Parties: Electoral Change and Structural Response*, ed. Alan Ware (Oxford and New York: Blackwell, 1987), 118).

23 James Bryce, *The American Commonwealth*, (London: Macmillan, 1894), Vol. I, 6; see also Vol. II, 5.

24 Ware, "United States: Disappearing Parties?" 118–19; see also Leon D. Epstein, *Political Parties in Western Democracies*, (New York: Frederick A. Praeger, 1967), 26.

25 Key, *Politics, Parties, and Pressure Groups,* 346; see also E.E. Schattschneider, *Party Government* (New York: Farrar and Rinehart, 1942), 129.

26 Kenneth Janda, "Comparative Political Parties, ed: Research and Theory," *Political Science: The State of the Discipline II*, ed. Ada Finifter (Washington: American Political Science Association, 1993), 163–92.

27 Colin Provost, "When is AG Short for Aspiring Governor? Ambition and Policy Making Dynamics in the Office of State Attorney General," *Publius* 40:4 (Fall, 2010), 597–616.

28 David B. Truman, "Federalism and the Party System," in *American Federalism in Perspective*, ed. Aaron B. Wildavsky (Boston: Little, Brown, 1962), 92.

29 Samuel J. Eldersveld and Hanes Walton, *Political Parties in American Society* (Boston: Bedford/St. Martin's, 2000), 61.

30 For example, John F. Bibby, "Political Parties and Federalism: The Republican National Committee Involvement in Gubernatorial and Legislative," *Publius* 9:1 (Winter, 1978), 229–36.

31 Robert S. Erikson, John P. McIver, and Gerald C. Wright, "State Political Culture and Public Opinion," *American Political Science Review* 81:3 (August, 1987), 797–813.

32 V.O. Key, Jr., *Southern Politics in State and Nation* (New York: Alfred Knopf, 1949).

33 Martin Shefter, *Political Parties and the State: the American Historical Experience* (Princeton, NJ: Princeton University Press, 1994), 61–97.

34 Bryce, *The American Commonwealth*, Vol. II, 21.

35 Stephen Skowronek, *Building a New American State: The Expansion of National Administrative Capacities, 1877–1920* (Cambridge and New York: Cambridge University Press, 1982), 24–31.

36 Elisabeth S. Clemens, *The People's Lobby: Organizational Innovation and the Rise of Interest Group Politics in the United States* (Chicago: University of Chicago Press, 1997), 73, 320; John Gerring, *Party Ideologies in America, 1828–1996* (Cambridge and New York: Cambridge University Press, 1998); Richard S. Katz and Robin Kolodny, "Party Organization as an Empty Vessel: Parties in American Politics," in *How Parties Organize: Change and Adaptation in Party Organizations in Western Democracies*, eds. Richard S. Katz and Peter Mair (Thousand Oaks, CA: Sage, 1994), 31.

37 Ronald P. Formisano, "Deferential-Participant Politics: The Early Republic's Political Culture, 1789–1840," *American Political Science Review* 68:2 (June, 1974), 474, 484.

38 With regard to the nationalization of state debts, see *The Papers of James Madison,* ed. William T. Hutchinson et al., 17 vols. (Charlottesville, VA: University Press of Virginia, 1981), March 1, 1790, Vol. 13, 74, and April 22, 1790, Vol. 13, 167.

39 Madison to Tench Coxe, March 30, 1790, in *The Papers of James Madison,* Vol. 13, 128–29.

40 Madison in the House of Representatives, February 2, 1791, in *The Papers of James Madison,* Vol. 13, 373–75, and February 8, 1791, Vol. 13, 387. See also Jack N. Rakove, *Original Meanings: Politics and Ideas in the Making of the Constitution* (New York: Alfred A. Knopf, 1996), 350–55.

41 Ralph Ketcham, *James Madison: A Biography* (New York: Macmillan, 1971), 317–34.

42 "Consolidation," *National Gazette,* December 5, 1791, *The Papers of James Madison,* Vol. 14, 137–39.

43 The Virginia Resolution, *The Papers of James Madison,* Vol. 17, 188–91.

44 President Andrew Jackson, Veto Message, May 27, 1830, John T. Woolley and Gerhard Peters, *The American Presidency Project,* http://www.presidency.ucsb.edu/ws/index.php?

pid=67036&st=maysville&st1 (accessed January 29, 2010); Sean Wilentz, *The Rise of American Democracy: Jefferson to Lincoln* (New York: Norton, 2005), 327–28.

45 Gerring, *Party Ideologies in America, 1828–1996*, 84, 169–70.

46 Elizabeth Sanders, *Roots of Reform: Farmers, Workers, and the American State, 1877–1917* (Chicago: University of Chicago Press, 1999), 159–60.

47 Gerring, *Party Ideologies in America, 1828–1996*, 232–53.

48 Ibid., 83.

49 Michael Les Benedict, "Abraham Lincoln and Federalism," *Journal of the Abraham Lincoln Association*, 10.1 (1988), http://www.historycooperative.org/journals/jala/10/benedict.html (accessed January 31, 2010).

50 Richard Franklin Bensel, *The Political Economy of American Industrialization, 1877–1900* (Cambridge and New York: Cambridge University Press, 2000).

51 Richard M. Valelly, *The Two Reconstructions: The Struggle for Black Enfranchisement* (Chicago: University of Chicago Press, 2004), 73–148.

52 Progressive Party Platform of 1912, November 5, 1912, John T. Woolley and Gerhard Peters, *The American Presidency Project*, http://www.presidency.ucsb.edu/ws/index.php?pid=29617#axzz1HZlg73EC (accessed January 31, 2010).

53 Gerring, *Party Ideologies in America, 1828–1996,*135–42.

54 Timothy Conlan, *From New Federalism to Devolution: Twenty-Five Years of Intergovernmental Reform* (Washington, DC: Brookings Institution, 1998).

55 Brian J. Glenn and Steven M. Teles, "Introduction: Studying the Role of Conservatives in American Political Development," in *Conservatism and American Political Development*, eds. Brian J. Glenn and Steven M. Teles (Oxford and New York: Oxford University Press, 2009), 3–16.

56 Key, *Politics, Parties, and Pressure Groups*, 23.

57 Arthur F. Bentley, *The Process of Government* (Cambridge, MA: Harvard University Press, 1967 [1908]), 330–99; Mark Petracca, "The Rediscovery of Interest Group Politics," in *The Politics of Interests: Interest Groups Transformed*, ed. Mark Petracca (Boulder, CO: Westview Press, 1992), 3–31; Key, *Politics, Parties, and Pressure Groups*, 14.

58 Alexis De Tocqueville, *Democracy in America* (Alfred A. Knopf, 1945 [originally 1835 & 1840]), Vol. 1, 191.

59 Lance Edwin Davis, Douglass Cecil North, Calla Smorodin, *Institutional Change and American Economic Growth* (Cambridge and New York: Cambridge University Press, 1971), 179.

60 Margaret Susan Thompson, *The "Spider Web": Congress and Lobbying in the Age of Grant* (Ithaca, NY: Cornell University Press, 1986).

61 Robert H. Wiebe, *The Search for Order, 1877–1920* (New York: Hill and Wang, 1967).

62 Clemens, *The People's Lobby*.

63 Mark Petracca, " The Rediscovery of Interest Group Politics," in *The Politics of Interests: Interest Groups Transformed,* ed. Mark Petracca (Boulder, CO: Westview Press), 13–17; Lobbying Database, Opensecrets.org., http://www.opensecrets.org/lobby (accessed February 2, 2010).

64 Kay Lehman Schlozman and John T. Tierney, *Organized Interests and American Democracy* (New York: Harper and Row, 1986), 285; see also David B. Truman, *The Governmental Process: Political Interests and Public Opinion* (New York: Alfred A. Knopf, 1951); Mancur Olson, *The Logic of Collective Action; Public Goods and the Theory of Groups* (Cambridge, MA, Harvard University Press, 1965).

65 Graham K. Wilson, "American Interest Groups in Comparative Perspective," in *The Politics of Interests: Interest Groups Transformed*, ed. Mark Petracca (Boulder, CO: Westview Press: 1992), 80–95.

66 Graham K. Wilson, "Interest Groups and the Constitution," in *The Constitution and American Political Development: An Institutional Perspective*, ed. Peter F. Nardulli (Urbana, IL: University of Illinois Press, 1992), 207–34.

67 Truman, *The Governmental Process*, 94–95, 120.

68 Grant McConnell, *Private Power and American Democracy* (New York: Alfred A. Knopf, 1966), 191–92.

69 Harmon Zeilger, "Interest Groups in the States," in *Politics in the American States: A Comparative Analysis,* eds. Herbert Jacob and Kenneth N. Vines, (Boston: Little, Brown, 1964), 101–47; Anthony J. Nownes, Clive S. Thomas, and Ronald J. Hrebenar, "Interest Groups in the States," in *Politics in the American States,* eds. Virginia Gray and Russell L. Hanson, 9th ed. (Washington, DC: CQ Press, 2008), 98–126.

70 Virginia Gray and David Lowery, "The Institutionalization of State Communities of Organized Interests," *Political Research Quarterly,* 54:2 (June, 2001), 265–84, quote 282.

71 Nownes, Thomas, and Hrebenar, "Interest Groups in the States," 99.

72 Harry N. Scheiber, "Federalism and the American Economic Order, 1789–1910," *Law and Society Review* 10:1 (Fall, 1975), 57–118; William J. Novak, *The People's Welfare: Law and Regulation in Nineteenth-Century America* (Chapel Hill, NC: University of North Carolina Press, 1996), 105–11.

73 Sylvia Bashevkin, "Interest Groups and Social Movements," in *Comparing Democracies: Elections and Voting in Global Perspective,* eds. Lawrence LeDuc, Richard G. Niemi, and Pippa Norris (Thousand Oaks, CA: Sage: 1996), 134–59; Nownes, Thomas, and Hrebenar, "Interest Groups in the States," 117.

74 Sarah McCalley Morehouse, *State Politics, Parties, and Policy* (New York: Holt, Rinehart and Winston, 1981); L. Harmon Zeigler, "Interest Groups in the States," in *Politics in the American States: A Comparative Analysis,* eds. Virginia Gray, Herbert Jacob, and Kenneth N. Vines (Boston: Little, Brown, 1983), 97–132; Nownes, Thomas, and Hrebenar, "Interest Groups in the States," 115–22.

75 J. Rogers Hollingsworth, "The Logic of Coordinating American Manufacturing Sectors," in *Governance of the American Economy,* eds. John L. Campbell, J. Rogers Hollingsworth, and Leon N. Lindberg (New York: Cambridge University Press, 1991), 41–42; Alfred Chandler, *The Visible Hand* (Cambridge, MA: Harvard University Press, 1977) and *The Scale and Scope: The Dynamics of Industrial Capitalism* (Cambridge, MA: Belknap, 1990). David Vogel, "Why Businessmen Mistrust Their State: The Political Consciousness of American Corporate Executives," *British Journal of Political Science* 8:1 (January, 1978), 63.

76 Robert H. Wiebe, "Business Disunity and the Progressive Movement, 1901–14," *The Mississippi Valley Historical Review* 44: 4 (March, 1958), 664–85.

77 Hollingsworth, "The Logic of Coordinating American Manufacturing Sectors," 67.

78 Graham K. Wilson, *Business and Politics: A Comparative Introduction,* 2nd ed. (Chatham, NJ: Chatham House, 1990), 56–57, and "American Interest Groups in Comparative Perspective," 93.

79 Joel Rogers, "Divide and Conquer: Further 'Reflections on the Distinctive Character of American Labor Laws'," *Wisconsin Law Review* 1990:1 (January/February), 1–147; Hans Slomp, *Between Bargaining and Politics: An Introduction to European Labor Relations* (Westport, CT: Praeger, 1996), 1–29.

80 David G. Blanchflower and Richard B. Freeman, "Unionism in the United States and Other Advanced OECD Countries," *Industrial Relations* 31 (1992), 56–79; Franz Traxler, "Collective Bargaining and Industrial Change: A Case of Disorganization? A Comparative Analysis of Eighteen OECD Countries," *European Sociological Review* 12 (1996): 271–87; Hans Slomp, *Labor Relations in Europe: A History of Issues and Developments* (Westport, CT: Greenwood Press, 1990).

81 Joseph B. Rose and Gary N. Chaison, "The State of the Unions in the United States and Canada," *Journal of Labor Research* 6 (Winter, 1985), 97–112; Richard Freeman, "Lessons for the United States," in *Working under Different Rules,* ed. Richard B. Freeman (New York: Russell Sage Foundation, 1994), 223–39.

82 Maurice Duverger, *Political Parties: Their Organization and Activity in the Modern State* (London: Methuen, Ltd., 1964 [1951]), 22–23; see also Werner Sombart, *Why is there No Socialism in the United States?* (London: Macmillan, 1976); Giovanni Sartori, *Parties and Party Systems: A Framework for Analysis* (New York: Cambridge University Press,

1976), 1; Seymour Martin Lipset, *American Exceptionalism: A Double-Edged Sword* (New York: W.W. Norton, 1997).

83 J. David Greenstone, *Labor in American Politics* (New York: Vintage Books, 1969); Taylor E. Dark, *The Unions and the Democrats: An Enduring Alliance*, updated edition (Ithaca, NY: ILR /Cornell University Press, 2001); Margaret Levi, "Organizing Power: Prospects for the American Labor Movement," *Perspectives on Politics* 1:1 (March, 2003), 45–68.

84 Earl Latham, *The Group Basis of Politics: A Study in Basing-Point Legislation* (Ithaca, NY: Cornell University Press, 1952), 36; McConnell, *Private Power & American Democracy*, 339; Theodore J. Lowi, *The End of Liberalism: The Second Republic of the United States*, 2nd ed. (New York: Norton, 1979).

85 Wilson, "American Interest Groups in Comparative Perspective."

86 John P. Heinz, Edward O. Laumann, Robert L. Nelson, and Robert H. Salisbury, *The Hollow Core: Private Interests in National Policy Making* (Cambridge, MA: Harvard University Press, 1993), 301–8; Wilson, "American Interest Groups in Comparative Perspective," 80–95; Anthony King, "The American Polity in the 1990s," in *The New American Political System*, ed. Anthony King, 2nd ed. (Washington: AEI Press, 1990), 296–97).

87 Truman, *The Governmental Process*, 323.

88 Schattschneider, *Party Government*,188; Kay Lehman Schlozman and John T. Tierney, *Organized Interests and American Democracy* (New York: Harper & Row, 1986), 201; Petracca, "The Rediscovery of Interest Group Politics," 26.

89 Schlozman and Tierney, *Organized Interests and American Democracy*, 20.

90 Clive S. Thomas, "Interest Groups in Western Democracies: Contemporary Characteristics and Future Directions," in *First World Interest Groups*, ed. Clive S. Thomas (Westport, CT: Greenwood Press), 219.

91 Barry R. Weingast, "The Economic Role of Political Institutions: Market-Preserving Federalism and Economic Development," *Journal of Law, Economics, & Organization*, 11:1 (April, 1995), 1–31.

Chapter 4

1 Joseph Lowndes, Julie Novkov, Dorian T. Warren, eds., "Race and American Political Development," in *Race and American Political Development* (New York: Routledge, 2008), 1–30.

2 Robert C. Lieberman, *Shaping Race Policy: The United States in Comparative Perspective* (Princeton, NJ: Princeton University Press, 2005), 1.

3 Rogers M. Smith, "Beyond Tocqueville, Myrdal, and Hartz: The Multiple Traditions in America," *American Political Science Review*, 87:3 (September, 1993), 549–66. See also David F. Ericson, *The Debate over Slavery: Antislavery and Proslavery Liberalism in Antebellum America* (New York: New York University Press, 2000), and *The Politics of Inclusion and Exclusion: Identity Politics in Twenty-First Century America* (New York: Routledge, 2010).

4 James L. Sundquist, *Dynamics of the Party System: Alignment and Realignment of Political Parties in the United States*, rev. ed. (Washington, DC: Brookings Institution, 1983), 50–105, 382–93; Keith T. Poole and Howard Rosenthal, *Congress: A Political-Economic History of Roll Call Voting* (New York: Oxford University Press, 1997). Poole and Rosenthal found that race related issues have become increasingly absorbed into the principal dimension since the 1960s (230–32).

5 Colin Gordon maps the historical impact on one city in *Mapping Decline: St. Louis and the Fate of the American City* (Philadelphia, PA: University of Pennsylvania Press, 2008).

6 William Riker, stated this most strongly: "if in the United States one disapproves of racism, one should disapprove of federalism," in *Federalism: Origin, Operation, Significance* (Boston: Little, Brown, 1964), 155.

7 *Barron* v. *Mayor and City Council of Baltimore*, 32 U.S. 243 (1833).

8 Alexander Keyssar, *The Right to Vote: The Contested History of Democracy in the United States* (New York: Basic Books, 2000), 51–60.

9 Rogers M. Smith, *Civic Ideals: Conflicting Visions of Citizenship in U.S. History* (New Haven, CT: Yale University Press, 1997), 132.

10 Douglass C. North, *The Economic Growth of the United States, 1790–1860* (New York: Norton, 1966), 63; James M. McPherson, "Antebellum Southern Exceptionalism: A New Look at an Old Question," *Civil War History* 50:4 (December, 2004), 418–33.

11 Gavin Wright, *Slavery and American Economic Development.* (Baton Rouge, LA: Louisiana State University Press, 2006).

12 Lawrence M. Friedman, *A History of American Law*, 3rd ed. (New York: Touchstone, 2005), 162–63; Gary M. Walton and Hugh Rockoff, *History of the American Economy*, 8th ed. (Fort Worth, TX: Dryden Press, 1998), 283.

13 Walton and Rockoff, *History of the American Economy*, 176–77, 281, 292–95; North, *The Economic Growth of the United States, 1790–1860*, 122 ff.; Stanley L. Engerman, "Slavery and Its Consequences for the South in the Nineteenth Century," in *The Cambridge Economic History of the United States, Vol. II, The Long Nineteenth Century*, eds. Stanley L. Engerman and Robert E. Gallman (Cambridge and New York: Cambridge University Press, 2000), 343.

14 William Goodell, *The American Slave Code in Theory and Practice: Its Distinctive Features Shown by Its Statutes, Judicial Decisions, and Illustrative Face* (New York: American and Foreign Anti-Slavery Society, 1853), http://www.dinsdoc.com/goodell-1-0a.htm (accessed February 22, 2010); Andrew Fede, "Legitimized Violent Slave Abuse in the American South, 1619–1865: A Case Study of Law and Social Change in Six Southern States," *American Journal of Legal History*, 29:2 (April, 1985), 93–150; Sally E. Hadden, *Slave Patrols: Law and Violence in Virginia and the Carolinas* (Cambridge, MA: Harvard University Press, 2001).

15 Donald E. Fehrenbacher, *Slavery, Law, and Politics: The Dred Scott Case in Historical Perspective* (Oxford and New York: Oxford University Press, 1981); Friedman, *A History of American Law*, 157–58.

16 *Annals of Congress*, House of Representatives, 4th Congress, 2nd Session, January 30, 1797, 2018–24, http://lcweb2.loc.gov/cgi-bin/ampage?collId=llac&fileName=006/llac006.db&recNum=251 (accessed February 24, 2010).

17 Walton and Rockoff, *History of the American Economy*, 290–91; Ira Berlin, *Generations of Captivity: A History of African-American Slaves* (Cambridge, MA: Belknap Press, 2003), 167.

18 Robert Pierce Forbes, *The Missouri Compromise and Its Aftermath: Slavery and the Meaning of America* (Chapel Hill, NC: University of North Carolina Press, 2007), 35–43, 118.

19 Forbes, *The Missouri Compromise and Its Aftermath*, 106; McPherson, "Antebellum Southern Exceptionalism."

20 McPherson, "Antebellum Southern Exceptionalism," 421.

21 John C. Calhoun, "South Carolina's Exposition and Protest against the Tariff of 1828," http://www.academicamerican.com/jeffersonjackson/documents/Calhoun1828.htm (accessed February 26, 2010); Daniel Walker Howe, *What God Hath Wrought: The Transformation of America, 1815–1848* (Oxford and New York: Oxford University Press, 2007), 395–410, quote 399. See James H. Read, *Majority Rule versus Consensus: The Political Thought of John C. Calhoun* (Lawrence, KS: University Press of Kansas, 2009).

22 Sundquist, *Dynamics of the Party System*, 61–65.

23 David M. Potter, *The Impending Crisis, 1848–1861* (New York: Harper and Row, 1976), 90–120.

24 McPherson, "Antebellum Southern Exceptionalism," 424; Thomas D. Morris, *Free Men All: The Personal Liberty Laws of the North, 1780–1861* (Baltimore, MD: Johns Hopkins University Press, 1974), 166–85; William E. Nelson, *The Fourteenth Amendment: From Political Principle to Judicial Doctrine* (Cambridge, MA: Harvard University Press, 1988), 34–39.

25 *Dred Scott* v. *John F. A. Sandford,* 60 U.S. 393 (1857).

26 McPherson, "Antebellum Southern Exceptionalism."

27 Gavin Wright, *Old South, New South: Revolutions in the Southern Economy since the Civil War* (New York: Basic Books, 1986), vii, 78, 134, quote 12; Gavin Wright, *Slavery and American Economic Development* (Baton Rouge, LA: Louisiana State University Press, 2006), 70, 124.

28 Keyssar, *The Right to Vote*, 101–4; Richard P. Young and Jerome S. Burstein, "Federalism and the Demise of Prescriptive Racism in the United States," *Studies in American Political Development* 9:1 (1995), 43.

29 Eric Foner, *Reconstruction: America's Unfinished Revolution, 1863–1877* (New York: Harper and Row, 1988); Michael Kent Curtis, *No State Shall Abridge: The Fourteenth Amendment and the Bill of Rights* (Durham, NC: Duke University Press, 1986); Milton R. Konvitz with Theodore Leskes, *A Century of Civil Rights* (New York: Columbia University Press, 1961), 124, 127.

30 Richard M. Valelly, *The Two Reconstructions: The Struggle for Black Enfranchisement* (Chicago: University of Chicago Press, 2004), 28–29.

31 Ibid., 73–120.

32 *The Civil Rights Cases*, 109 U.S. 3 (1883).

33 Konvitz with Leskes, *A Century of Civil Rights*, 156–58.

34 Richard Franklin Bensel, *The Political Economy of American Industrialization, 1877–1900* (Cambridge and New York: Cambridge University Press, 2000), 500–505; Valelly, *The Two Reconstructions*, 94–98.

35 C. Van Woodward, *The Strange Career of Jim Crow*, 2nd rev. ed. (Oxford and New York: Oxford University Press), 97–102.

36 Gunnar Myrdal, *An American Dilemma: The Negro Problem and Modern Democracy* (New York: Harper & Brothers, 1944, 632–33; Davison M. Douglas, *Jim Crow Moves North: The Battle over Northern School Segregation, 1865–1954* (Cambridge and New York: Cambridge University Press, 2005), 61–166.

37 V.O. Key, Jr., *Southern Politics in State and Nation* (New York: Alfred Knopf, 1949), 665.

38 Valelly, *The Two Reconstructions,* 121–31.

39 Keyssar, *The Right to Vote*, 117–62. Meanwhile, several Northern and Western states slowly restricted their electorates through various property, literacy, voter registration, and residency laws aimed at limiting the participation of the urban working class, especially immigrants.

40 *Plessy* v. *Ferguson* 163 U.S. 537 (1896). Similarly, in *Williams* v. *Mississippi*, 170 U.S. 213 (1898), the court unanimously refused to invalidate poll taxes or literacy tests, and positively upheld state voting requirements in *Giles* v. *Harris*, 189 U.S. 475 (1903) and *Giles* v. *Teasley*, 193 U.S. 146 (1904).

41 Kathleen L. Wolgemuth, "Woodrow Wilson and Federal Segregation," *The Journal of Negro History* 44:2 (April, 1959), 158–73.

42 Desmond King, *Separate and Unequal: African Americans and the US Federal Government,* rev. ed. (Oxford and New York: Oxford University Press, 2007), 39–110.

43 Ira Katznelson, *When Affirmative Action was White: An Untold History of Racial Inequality in Twentieth-Century America* (New York: W.W. Norton, 2005), 76–78, quote from Martin Dies (D-Texas), 60.

44 Robert C. Lieberman, *Shifting the Color Line: Race and the American Welfare State* (Cambridge, MA: Harvard University Press, 1998), 7); Suzanne Mettler, *Dividing Citizens: Gender and Federalism in New Deal Public Policy* (Ithaca, NY: Cornell University Press, 1998), 170.

45 King, *Separate and Unequal,*176–204.

46 "National Affairs: Problem No. 1," *Time* Magazine, Monday, July 18, 1938, http://www.time.com/time/magazine/article/0,9171,759988,00.html (accessed March 5, 2010); Bruce Schulman, *From Cotton Belt to Sunbelt: Federal Policy, Economic Development, and the Transformation of the South, 1938–1980* (Durham, NC: Duke University Press, 1994); Philip Selznick, *TVA and The Grass Roots: A Study in the Sociology of Formal Organization* (Berkeley, CA: University of California Press, 1949).

47 Daniel Kryder, *Divided Arsenal: Race and the American State during World War II* (Cambridge and New York: Cambridge University Press, 2000); Katznelson, *When Affirmative Action was White.*

48 Patricia Sullivan, *Days of Hope: Race and Democracy in the New Deal Era* (Chapel Hill, NC: University of North Carolina Press, 1996), 141.

49 Mettler, *Dividing Citizens*, 104–5; Katznelson, *When Affirmative Action was White*, 113–41.

50 Mary L. Dudziak, *Cold War Civil Rights: Race and the Image of American Democracy* (Princeton, NJ: Princeton University Press, 2000).

51 Young and Burstein "Federalism and the Demise of Prescriptive Racism in the United States."

52 Valelly, *The Two Reconstructions*, 149–50.

53 Carol E. Heim, "Structural Changes, Regional and Urban," in *The Cambridge Economic History of the United States, Vol. III, The Twentieth Century*, eds. Stanley L. Engerman and Robert E. Gallman (Cambridge and New York: Cambridge University Press, 2000), 99–105.

54 Kimberley S. Johnson, "Jim Crow Reform and the Democratization of the South," in *Race and American Political Development*, eds. Joseph Lowndes, Julie Novkov, and Dorian T. Warren (London and New York: Routledge, 2008), 155–79.

55 *Smith* v. *Allwright,* 321 U.S. 649 (1944).

56 Gary A. Donaldson, *Truman Defeats Dewey* (Lexington, KY: University Press of Kentucky, 1999).

57 U.S. Department of Labor, *Growth of Labor Law in the United States* (Washington, DC: Government Printing Office, 1967), 224–26.

58 U.S. Department of Labor, *Growth of Labor Law in the United States*, 221–29; Lynn W. Eley and Thomas W. Casstevens, *The Politics of Fair-Housing Legislation; State and Local Case Studies* (San Francisco, CA: Chandler, 1968).

59 Doug McAdam, *Political Process and the Development of Black Insurgency, 1930–1970,* 2nd ed. (Chicago: University of Chicago Press, 1999).

60 *Missouri ex rel. Gaines* v. *Canada,* 305 U.S. 337 (1938), *Sweatt* v. *Painter* 339 U.S. 629 (1950), *McLaurin* v. *Oklahoma State Regents* 339 U.S. 637 (1950); Richard Kluger, *Simple Justice: The History of Brown v. Board of Education and Black America's Struggle for Equality* (New York: Knopf, 1976); Mark V. Tushnet, *The NAACP's Legal Strategy gainst Segregated Education, 1925–1950,* 2nd ed. (Chapel Hill, NC: University of North Carolina Press, 2005).

61 Harrell R. Rodgers, Jr. and Charles S. Bullock, III, *Law and Social Change: Civil Rights Laws and Their Consequences* (New York: McGraw-Hill, 1972), 70–71.

62 Sarah Rowe-Sims, "The Mississippi State Sovereignty Commission: An Agency History," *Mississippi History Now* (September,2002), http://mshistory.k12.ms.us/articles/243/mississippi-sovereignty-commission-an-agency-history (accessed March 22, 2010); Yasuhiro Katagiri, *The Mississippi State Sovereignty Commission: Civil Rights and States' Rights* (Jackson, MS: University Press of Mississippi, 2001), xiii, 4–6, quote 6.

63 "The Southern Manifesto," from *Congressional Record*, 84th Congress, Second Session. Vol. 102, Part 4 (March 12, 1956), 4459–60.

64 Rodgers and Bullock, *Law and Social Change*, 70–71.

65 Taeku Lee emphasizes that ordinary people pushed civil rights in the era in *Mobilizing Public Opinion: Black Insurgency and Racial Attitudes in the Civil Rights Era* (Chicago, IL: University of Chicago Press, 2002); Young and Burstein, "Federalism and the Demise of Prescriptive Racism in the United States," 13.

66 Joseph E. Luders, *The Civil Rights Movement and the Logic of Social Change* (Cambridge and New York: Cambridge University Press, 2010).

67 Valelly, *The Two Reconstructions*, 199–224.

68 Lieberman, *Shaping Race Policy*, 200.

69 Charles S. Bullock and Charles M. Lamb, *Implementation of Civil Rights Policy* (Monterey, CA: Brooks/Cole, 1985), 65; Hugh Davis Graham, *The Civil Rights Era: Origins and*

Development of National Policy, 1960–1972 (Oxford and New York: Oxford University Press, 1990).

70 James R. Ralph, Jr., *Northern Protest: Martin Luther King, Jr., Chicago, and the Civil Rights Movement* (Cambridge, MA: Harvard University Press, 1993).

71 Lieberman, *Shaping Race Policy*, 190–91.

72 Young and Burstein, "Federalism and the Demise of Prescriptive Racism in the United States."

73 *Swann* v. *Charlotte-Mecklenburg Board of Education*, 402 U.S. 1 (1971).

74 J. Anthony Lukas, *Common Ground: A Turbulent Decade in the Lives of Three American Families* (New York: Knopf, 1985); Ronald Formisano, *Boston against Busing: Race, Class, and Ethnicity in the 1960s and 1970s* (Chapel Hill, NC: University of North Carolina Press, 1991).

75 *University of California Regents* v. *Bakke*, 438 U.S. 265 (1978); *Grutter* v. *Bollinger*, 539 U.S. 306 (2003); *Gratz* v. *Bollinger*, 539 U.S. 244 (2003).

76 Robert Pear, "In California, Foes of Affirmative Action See a New Day," *New York Times*, November 7, 1996, http://www.nytimes.com/1996/11/07/us/in-california-foes-of-affirmative-action-see-a-new-day.html?scp=6&sq=california+proposition+209+1996&st=nyt (accessed July 12, 2010); Tamar Lewin, "Michigan Rejects Affirmative Action, and Backers Sue," *New York Times*, November 9, 2006, http://www.nytimes.com/2006/11/09/us/politics/09michigan.html (accessed July 12, 2010).

77 Edward G. Carmines and James A. Stimson, "Racial Issues and the Structure of Mass Belief Systems," *Journal of Politics* 44:1 (February, 1982), 4–5. See also Edward G. Carmines and James A. Stimson, *Issue Evolution: Race and the Transformation of American Politics* (Princeton, NJ: Princeton University Press, 1989); Earl Black and Merle Black, *The Rise of Southern Republicans* (Cambridge, MA: Belknap Press of Harvard University Press, 2002), 28.

78 David Brian Robertson and Dennis R. Judd, *The Development of American Public Policy: The Structure of Policy Restraint.* (Glenview, IL: Scott, Foresman/Little, Brown, 1989), 194–97.

79 Meizhu Lui, "The Wealth Gap Gets Wider," *Washington Post*, March 23, 2009, http://www.washingtonpost.com/wp-dyn/content/article/2009/03/22/AR2009032201506. html (accessed March 10, 2010).

80 Alan Greenblatt, "Race in America" *CQ Researcher*, 13:25 (July 11, 2003), 593–624.

81 Marie Gottschalk, *The Prison and the Gallows: The Politics of Mass Incarceration in America* (Cambridge and New York: Cambridge University Press, 2006), 2. See also Bruce Western, *Punishment and Inequality in America* (New York: Russell Sage Foundation, 2006) and Lisa Miller, *The Perils of Federalism: Race, Poverty, and the Politics of Crime Control* (Oxford and New York: Oxford University Press, 2008).

82 The Gallup organization has for several decades asked the question, "If your party nominated a generally well qualified person for president who happened to be black, would you vote for that person?" In 1958, fifty-three percent said that they would not, and only thirty-seven percent said that they would vote for a qualified black of their own party to be president. That number declined steadily, and by 2007, ninety-four percent were willing to vote for a black candidate, and five percent were not. But five percent of the two hundred and thirteen million Americans eligible to vote in the 2008 presidential election amounts to over ten million voters. Jeffrey M. Jones, "Some Americans Reluctant to Vote for Mormon, 72-Year-Old Presidential Candidates; Strong Support for Black, Women, Catholic Candidates," February 20, 2007, Gallup online, http://www.gallup.com/poll/26611/some-americans-reluctant-vote-mormon-72yearold-presidential-candidates.aspx (accessed July 12, 2010).

83 ABC News, "Fewer Call Racism a Major Problem, though Discrimination Remains," http://abcnews.go.com/images/PollingUnit/1085a2RaceRelations.pdf (accessed March 7, 2010).

84 CNN/Opinion Research Corporation Poll, December 16–20, 2009, http://www.pollingreport.com/race.htm (accessed July 12, 2010).

85 Julie Novkov, *Racial Union: Law, Intimacy, and the White State in Alabama, 1865–1954* (Ann Arbor, MI: University of Michigan Press, 2008).

Chapter 5

1 See Graham K. Wilson, *Only in America: The Politics of the United States in Comparative Perspective* (Chatham, NJ: Chatham House, 1998), 1–16; John W. Kingdon, *America the Unusual* (New York: St. Martin's 1999), 23–84.

2 Graham K. Wilson, *Business and Politics: A Comparative Introduction*, 3rd ed. (New York: Chatham House, 2003), 27.

3 Stanley J. Engerman and Kenneth J. Sokoloff, "Technology and Industrialization, 1790–1914," in *The Cambridge Economic History of the United States, Vol. II, The Long Nineteenth Century*, eds. Stanley L. Engerman and Robert E. Gallman (Cambridge and New York: Cambridge University Press, 2000), 367.

4 Colleen A. Dunlavy, *Politics and Industrialization: Early Railroads in the United States and Prussia* (Princeton, NJ: Princeton University Press, 1994), 4.

5 Karl Polanyi, *The Great Transformation* (New York: Farrar & Rinehart, 1944), 75.

6 Joseph A. Schumpeter, *Capitalism, Socialism, and Democracy* (New York, Harper & Brothers, 1942), 82–83.

7 Polanyi, *The Great Transformation*, 68–76, quote 76.

8 Harold D. Laswell, *Politics; Who Gets What, When, How* (New York: Whittlesey House, 1936).

9 James Madison, *Federalist 10*, in Alexander Hamilton, James Madison, and John Jay, *The Federalist,* ed. Jacob E. Cooke (Middletown, CT: Wesleyan University Press, 1961), 56–65.

10 Richard Franklin Bensel, *The Political Economy of American Industrialization, 1877–1900* (Cambridge and New York: Cambridge University Press, 2000), 510. See also Douglass C. North, *Institutions, Institutional Change, and Economic Performance* (Cambridge and New York: Cambridge University Press, 1990), 108–10.

11 Barry R. Weingast, "The Economic Role of Political Institutions: Market-Preserving Federalism and Economic Development," *Journal of Law, Economics, & Organization*, 11:1 (April, 1995), 1–31.

12 Alexander Hamilton, "Report Relative to a Provision for the Support of Public Credit," in *The Papers of Alexander Hamilton*, ed. Harold C. Syrett, 27 vols. (New York: Columbia University Press, 1963–87), Vol. 6, 51–168, and Alexander Hamilton, "Report on the Subject of Manufactures," December 5, 1791, *The Papers of Alexander Hamilton*, Vol. 10, 230–340; E. James Ferguson, *The Power of the Purse: A History of Public Finance, 1776–1790* (Chapel Hill, NC: University of North Carolina Press, 1961), 256–69, 271, 293–96, 309–11, 314–25.

13 *Fletcher* v. *Peck*, 10 U.S. 87 (1810); *McCulloch* v. *Maryland*, 17 U.S. 316 (1819); *Trustees of Dartmouth College* v. *Woodward*, 17 U.S. 518 (1819), *Gibbons* v. *Ogden*, 22 U.S. 1 (1824).

14 John Lauritz Larson, *Internal Improvement: National Public Works and the Problem of Popular Government in the Early United States* (Chapel Hill, NC: University of North Carolina Press, 2001); Songho Ha, *The Rise and Fall of the American System: Nationalism and the Development of the American Economy, 1790–1837* (London: Pickering & Chatto, 2009); Brian Balogh, *A Government Out of Sight: The Mystery of National Authority in Nineteenth Century America* (Cambridge and New York: Cambridge University Press, 2009), 122–50.

15 In "The Economic Role of Political Institutions," Weingast argued that parties and interest groups have been essential for *sustaining* states' rights and federalism.

16 Larson, *Internal Improvement*, 57–58, 67–69; 139–40; 183–85; James K. Polk, "Veto Message," December 15, 1847, at John T. Woolley and Gerhard Peters, The American Presidency Project, http://www.presidency.ucsb.edu/ws/index.php?pid=67965, accessed July 17, 2010; Franklin Pierce, "Veto Message," August 11, 1856, at The American Presidency Project, http://www.presidency.ucsb.edu/ws/?pid=67736, (accessed April 1, 2010); James Buchanan, "Veto Message," February 24, 1859, The American Presidency Project, http://www.presidency.ucsb.edu/ws/index.php?pid=68368&st=&st1= (accessed July 17, 2010).

17 Robert V. Remini, *Andrew Jackson and the Bank War* (New York: W.W. Norton, 1967).

18 Harry N. Scheiber, "Federalism and the American Economic Order, 1789–1910," *Law and Society Review* 10:1 (Fall, 1975), 71.

19 Harry N. Scheiber, "State Law and 'Industrial Policy' in American Development," *California Law Review*, 75 (1987), 415–44.

20 William J. Novak, *The People's Welfare: Law and Regulation in Nineteenth-Century America* (Chapel Hill, NC: University of North Carolina Press, 1996).

21 Scheiber, "Federalism and the American Economic Order, 1789–1910"; James Willard Hurst, *The Legitimacy of the Business Corporation* (Charlottesville, VA: University Press of Virginia, 1970), 13–57.

22 Scheiber, "State Law and 'Industrial Policy' in American Development," 423; Richard Sylla, "Experimental Federalism: The Economics of American Government 1789–1914," in *The Cambridge Economic History of the United States, Vol. II, The Long Nineteenth Century,* eds. Stanley L. Engerman and Robert E. Gallman (Cambridge and New York: Cambridge University Press, 2000), 524; Susan Hoffmann, *Politics and Banking: Ideas, Public Policy, and the Creation of Financial Institutions* (Baltimore, MD: Johns Hopkins University Press, 2001), 75. Kentucky and Vermont established formidable state-owned central banks.

23 Scheiber, "Federalism and the American Economic Order, 1789–1910," 84, 88, 95, 98.

24 Ibid., 99.

25 Larson, *Internal Improvement*, 76–80, 80; Peter L. Bernstein, *Wedding of the Waters: The Erie Canal and the Making of a Great Nation* (New York: W.W. Norton, 2005); William Cronon, *Nature's Metropolis: Chicago and the Great West* (New York: W.W. Norton, 1991), 60–61.

26 Larson, *Internal Improvement*, 80–107; Scheiber, "Federalism and the American Economic Order, 1789–1910," 97.

27 Colleen A. Dunlavy, *Politics and Industrialization: Early Railroads in the United States and Prussia* (Princeton, NJ: Princeton University Press, 1994); Larson, *Internal Improvement*, 75–80.

28 Frederick Rudolph, *The American College and University: A History* (Athens, GA: University of Georgia Press, 1991[1962]), 51, 185–86.

29 James L. McPherson "Antebellum Southern Exceptionalism: A New Look at an Old Question," *Civil War History* 50:4 (2004), 425.

30 Gavin Wright, *Old South, New South: Revolutions in the Southern Economy since the Civil War* (New York: Basic Books, 1986), 53–54; see also Gavin Wright, *Slavery and American Economic Development* (Baton Rouge, LA: Louisiana State University Press, 2006).

31 Albert Fishlow, "Internal Transportation in the Nineteenth and Early Twentieth Centuries," in *The Cambridge Economic History of the United States, Vol. II, The Long Nineteenth Century,* eds. Stanley L. Engerman and Robert E. Gallman (Cambridge and New York: Cambridge University Press, 2000), 543–643.

32 Alfred D. Chandler, Jr., *The Visible Hand: The Managerial Revolution in American Business* (Cambridge, MA: Harvard University Press, 1977) and *The Scale and Scope: The Dynamics of Industrial Capitalism* (Cambridge, MA: Belknap/Harvard, 1990).

33 Bensel, *The Political Economy of American Industrialization, 1877–1900;* Scheiber, "Federalism and the American Economic Order, 1789–1910," 107.

34 Ibid., 289–354.

35 Bensel, *The Political Economy of American Industrialization, 1877–1900,* 513; Scheiber, "Federalism and the American Economic Order, 1789–1910."

36 Scheiber, "Federalism and the American Economic Order, 1789–1910," 101–2.

37 Sean Patrick Adams, "Promotion, Competition, Captivity: The Political Economy of Coal," *Journal of Policy History* 18:1 (2006), 76.

38 Scheiber, "Federalism and the American Economic Order, 1789–1910," 110–13.

39 Gretchen Ritter, *Goldbugs and Greenbacks: The Antimonopoly Tradition and the Politics of Finance in America, 1865–1896* (Cambridge and New York: Cambridge University

Press, 1999); Elizabeth Sanders, *Roots of Reform: Farmers, Workers, and the American State, 1877–1917* (Chicago: University of Chicago Press, 1999).

40 Hans B. Thorelli, *The Federal Antitrust Policy: Origintion of an American Tradition* (Baltimore, MD: Johns Hopkins University Press, 1955), 79–83; Henry R. Seager and Charles A. Gulick, *Trust and Corporation Problems* (New York: Harper and Brothers, 1929), 53–57.

41 In *Munn* v. *Illinois* 94 U.S. 113 (1877).

42 Wabash, *St. Louis & Pacific Railway Co.* v. *People of State of Illinois*, 118 U.S. 557 (1886).

43 Stephen Skowronek, *Building a New American State: The Expansion of National Administrative Capacities, 1877–1920* (Cambridge and New York: Cambridge University Press, 1982), 121–62; Scott C. James, *Presidents, Parties, and the State: A Party System Perspective on Democratic Regulatory Choice, 1884–1936* (Cambridge and New York: Cambridge University Press, 2000), 36–122; Frank Dobbin and Timothy J. Dowd, "How Policy Shapes Competition: Early Railroad Foundings in Massachusetts," *Administrative Science Quarterly* 42:3 (September, 1997), 501–29; Gerald Berk, *Alternative Tracks: The Constitution of American Industrial Order, 1865–1917* (Baltimore, MD: Johns Hopkins University Press, 1994), 110.

44 U.S. House of Representatives, Committee on the Judiciary, Hearings on *Trust Legislation*, Vol. 2 (Washington, DC: Government Printing Office, 1914), 1197–1217; Seager and Gulick, *Trust and Corporation Problems*, 552–627; Martin J. Sklar, *The Corporate Reconstruction of American Capitalism, 1890–1916: The Market, The Law, and Politics* (New York: Cambridge University Press, 1988), 154–56.

45 Christopher Grandy, *New Jersey and the Fiscal Origins of Modern American Corporation Law* (New York: Garland, 1993), 56; Henry N. Butler, "Nineteenth Century Jurisdictional Competition in the Granting of Corporate Privileges," *Journal of Legal Studies* 14: (January, 1985), 129–66; Seager and Gulick, *Trust and Corporation Problems*, 351–61.

46 William Letwin, *Law and Economic Policy in America: The Evolution of the Sherman Antitrust Act* (Chicago: University of Chicago Press, 1965), 55–70.

47 *U.S.* v. *E.C. Knight* 156 U.S. 1 (1895).

48 Naomi R. Lamoreaux, *The Great Merger Movement in American Business, 1895–1904* (Cambridge and New York: Cambridge University Press, 1985).

49 Grandy, *New Jersey and the Fiscal Origins of Modern American Corporation Law*; Report of the Committee on National Incorporation, *National Association of Manufacturers Proceedings*, 1908, 226–28; Jonathan Chausovsky, "State Regulation of Corporations in the Late Nineteenth Century: A Critique of the New Jersey Thesis," *Studies in American Political Development* 21:1 (Spring, 2007), 30–65.

50 Sklar, *The Corporate Reconstruction of American Capitalism, 1890–1900*.

51 Sanders, *Roots of Reform*, 236–66, 290–97, Marc Allen Eisner, *The State in the American Political Economy* (Englewood Cliffs, NJ: Prentice-Hall, 1995), 106–20; James, *Presidents, Parties, and the State*, 123–99; Gerald Berk, *Louis D. Brandeis and the Making of Regulated Competition, 1900–1932* (Cambridge and New York: Cambridge University Press, 2009), 90–114.

52 Kenneth J. Meier, *The Political Economy of Regulation* (Albany, NY: SUNY Press, 1988); Jonathan R. Macey and Geoffrey P. Miller, "Origins of the Blue Sky Laws," *Texas Law Review* 70:2 (December, 1991), 347 ff.

53 William R. Childs, "State Regulators and Pragmatic Federalism in the United States, 1889–1945," *Business History Review* 75:4 (Winter, 2001), 709.

54 Thomas R. Pegram, *Partisans and Progressives: Private Interest and Public Policy in Illinois, 1870–1922* (Urbana, IL: University of Illinois Press, 1992), 204–5.

55 William R. Childs, *The Texas Railroad Commission: Understanding Regulation in America to the Mid-Twentieth Century* (College Station, TX: Texas A & M University Press, 2005).

56 Gary M. Walton and Hugh Rockoff, *History of the American Economy*, 8th ed. (Fort Worth, TX: Dryden Press, 1998), 516.

57 James T. Patterson, *The New Deal and the States: Federalism in Transition* (Princeton, NJ: Princeton University Press, 1969), 39–40.

58 *A.L.A. Schechter Poultry Corp.* v. *United States*, 295 U.S. 495 (1935).

59 G. John Ikenberry and Theda Skocpol "Expanding Social Benefits: The Role of Social Security," *Political Science Quarterly* 102:3 (Autumn, 1987), 407–11.

60 Childs, "State Regulators and Pragmatic Federalism in the United States, 1889–1945," 705.

61 William M. Emmons III, "Franklin D. Roosevelt, Electric Utilities, and the Power of Competition," *The Journal of Economic History* 53: 4 (December, 1993), 880–907; James, *Presidents, Parties, and the State*, 200–266.

62 Gary D. Libecap, "The Political Economy of Crude Oil Cartelization in the United States, 1933–72," Journal of Economic History 49: 4 (December, 1989), 833–55.

63 James C. Nelson, "The Motor Carrier Act of 1935," *The Journal of Political Economy* 44: 4 (August, 1936), 464–504.

64 Herzel H. E. Plaine, "State Aviation Legislation," *Journal of Air Law and Commerce* 14 (1947), 333ff.; Richard C. Schragger, "The Anti-Chain Store Movement, Localist Ideology, and the Remnants of the Progressive Constitution, 1920–40," *Iowa Law Review* 90 (March, 2005), 1011–93.

65 Childs, "State Regulators and Pragmatic Federalism in the United States, 1889–1945," 731.

66 John Woolley, *The Federal Reserve Bank and the Politics of Monetary Policy* (Cambridge and New York: Cambridge University Press, 1984), 42–44; Allan H. Meltzer, *A History of the Federal Reserve, Vol. 1, 1913–51* (Chicago: University of Chicago Press, 2003). 470–90; Richard H.K. Vietor, "Government Regulation of Business," in *The Cambridge Economic History of the United States, Vol. III, The Twentieth Century*, eds. Stanley L. Engerman and Robert E. Gallman (Cambridge and New York: Cambridge University Press, 2000), 979.

67 Philip Selznick, *TVA and The Grass Roots: A Study in the Sociology of Formal Organization* (Berkeley, CA: University of California Press, 1949).

68 John P. Frendreis and Raymond Tatalovich, *The Modern Presidency and Economic Policy* (Itasca, IL: F.E. Peacock Publishers, 1994), 240; James L. Sundquist, *Politics and Policy: The Eisenhower, Kennedy, and Johnson Years* (Washington: Brookings Institution, 1968); A. James Reichley, *Conservatives in an Age of Change: the Nixon and Ford Administrations* (Washington: Brookings Institution, 1981).

69 Herbert Stein, *The Fiscal Revolution in America*, rev. ed. (Washington, DC: American Enterprise Institute, 1990); "We Are All Keynesians Now," *Time* Magazine, Dec. 31, 1965, http://www.time.com/time/magazine/article/0,9171,842353,00.html (accessed October 12, 2009).

70 Robert Collins, *The Business Response to Keynes, 1929–1964* (New York: Columbia University Press, 1981), 16.

71 Dennis R. Judd and David Brian Robertson, *The Development of American Public Policy: The Structure of Policy Restraint* (New York: Scott, Foresman/Little, Brown, 1989), 326–27.

72 John M. Broder, "Geography is Dividing Democrats over Energy," *New York Times*, January 26, 2009, http://www.nytimes.com/2009/01/27/science/earth/27coal.html (accessed February 3, 2009).

73 Richard A. Harris and Sidney M. Milkis, *The Politics of Regulatory Change: A Tale of Two Agencies*, 2nd ed. (Oxford and New York: Oxford University Press, 1996), quote 9.

74 Theodore J. Lowi, *The End of Liberalism: The Second Republic of the United* States, 2nd ed. (New York: Norton, 1979), 113–15; Harris and Milkis, *The Politics of Regulatory Change*, 22–96.

75 Patrick Nugent, *Safeguarding Federalism: How States Protect their Interests in National Policymaking* (Norman, OK: University of Oklahoma Press, 2009), 168–212.

76 Judd and Robertson, *The Development of American Public Policy,* 339–41; Barry G. Rabe, "Power to the States: The Promise and Pitfalls of Decentralization," in *Environmental Policy: New Directions for the Twenty-First Century*, eds. Norman J. Vig and Michael E. Kraft (Washington, DC: CQ Press, 2006), 35–36.

77 Nugent, *Safeguarding Federalism*, 94–99.

78 Jeff Gerth, "New York Banks Urged Delaware to Lure Bankers," *New York Times*, March 17, 1981, http://www.nytimes.com/1981/03/17/business/19810317BANK.html? ex=1103259600&en=c010543948675c8b&ei=5087 (accessed July 12, 2010).

79 Samuel Issacharoff and Erin F. Delaney, "Credit Card Accountability," *University of Chicago Law Review*, 73:1 (Winter, 2006), 157–82.

80 David J. Vogel, *Fluctuating Fortunes: The Political Power of Business in America* (New York: Basic Books, 1989), 194–99; McGee Young, *Developing Interests: Organizational Change and the Politics of Advocacy* (Lawrence, KS: University Press of Kansas, 2010), 65–82.

81 Monica Prasad, *The Politics of Free Markets: The Rise of Neoliberal Economic Policies in Britain, France, Germany, and the United States* (Chicago: University of Chicago Press, 2006), 62–82.

82 R.J. Moore, "Stopping the States," *National Journal* (July 21, 1990), 1758.

83 Stephen M. Bainbridge, "The Creeping Federalization of Corporate Law," *Regulation* 26:1 (Spring, 2003), 32–39.

84 Peter A. Eisinger, *The Rise of the Entrepreneurial State: State and Local Economic Development Policy* (Madison, WI: University of Wisconsin Press, 1988).

85 James C. Cobb, *The Selling of the South: The Southern Crusade for Industrial Development, 1936–1990*, 2nd ed. (Urbana, IL: University of Illinois Press, 1993); Alberta M. Sbagia, *Debt Wish: Entrepreneurial Cities, U.S. Federalism, and Economic Development* (Pittsburgh, PA: University of Pittsburgh Press, 1996).

86 Kenneth P. Thomas, *Investment Incentives and the Global Competition for Capital* (Basingstoke, UK: Palgrave Macmillan, 2011).

87 Martha Derthick, *Up in Smoke: From Legislation to Litigation in Tobacco Politics*, 2nd ed. (Washington, DC: CQ Press, 2005), 71–92.

88 Erin O'Hara and Larry Rubenstein, *The Law Market* (Oxford and New York: Oxford University Press, 2009).

89 Paul Kanjorski (Chair of the House Subcommittee on Capital Markets, Insurance, and Government Sponsored Enterprises of the U.S. House of Representatives' Committee on Financial Services), interview on CNBC, Thursday, May 14 2009, 7:07am ET, http://www.cnbc.com/id/15840232?video=1123593035&play=1 (accessed May 15, 2009).

90 Opening Statement, Chairman Paul E. Kanjorski, Subcommittee on Capital Markets, Insurance, and Government Sponsored Enterprises, Hearing on "How Should the Federal Government Oversee Insurance?" May 14, 2009, http://www.house.gov/apps/list/hearing/financialsvcs_dem/09_05_14_pek_opening_for_insurance_reg_reform_hearing.pdf (accessed May 15, 2009).

91 Michael Powell, Danny Hakim, and Louise Story, "For Cuomo, Financial Crisis is His Political Moment," *New York Times*, March 21, 2009, http://www.nytimes.com/2009/03/21/nyregion/21cuomo.html?_r=1 (accessed April 16, 2010).

92 On varieties of capitalism, see Peter A. Hall and David Soskice, eds., *Varieties of Capitalism: The Institutional Foundations of Comparative Advantage* (Oxford and New York: Oxford University Press, 2001).

93 David Vogel, "Why Businessmen Distrust Their State: The Political Consciousness of American Corporate Executives," *British Journal of Political Science* 8:1 (January, 1978), 53–54.

94 Ibid.; David J. Vogel, *National Styles of Regulation: Environmental Policy in Great Britain and the United States* (Ithaca, NY: Cornell University Press, 1986), 343. See also Childs, "State Regulators and Pragmatic Federalism in the United States, 1889–1945," 738.

95 On the role of federalism, see Cathie Jo Martin and Duane Swank, "The Political Origins of Coordinated Capitalism: Business Organizations, Party Systems, and State Structure in the Age of Innocence," *American Political Science Review*, 102:2 (May, 2008), 181–98; Peter A. Swenson, "Varieties of Capitalist Interests: Power, Institutions, and the Regulatory Welfare State in the United States and Sweden," *Studies in American Political Development* 18 (Spring, 2004) 1–29.

Chapter 6

1 Morton J. Keller, *Regulating a New Economy: Public Policy and Economic Change in America, 1900–1933* (Cambridge, MA: Harvard University Press, 1990), and *Regulating a New Society: Public Policy and Social Change in America, 1900–1933* (Cambridge, MA: Harvard University Press, 1994); Jon C. Teaford, *The Rise of the States: Evolution of American State Government* (Baltimore, MD: Johns Hopkins University Press, 2002); Ballard C. Campbell, *The Growth of American Government: Governance from the Cleveland Era to the Present* (Bloomington, IN: Indiana University Press, 1995).

2 Marc Allen Eisner, *The State in the American Political Economy* (Englewood Cliffs, NJ: Prentice-Hall, 1995), 100.

3 Price Fishback, "The Progressive Era," in *Government and the American Economy: A New History*, ed. Price Fishback et al. (Chicago: University of Chicago Press, 2007), 289.

4 Richard Hofsteader, *The Age of Reform* (New York: Alfred A. Knopf, 1956), 185–96.

5 Robert H. Wiebe, *The Search for Order* (New York: Hill and Wang, 1967); Daniel T. Rodgers, *Atlantic Crossings: Social Politics in a Progressive Age* (Cambridge, MA: Belknap/Harvard, 1998).

6 Alonzo Hamby, "Progressivism: A Century of Change and Rebirth," in *Progressivism and the New Democracy*, ed. Sidney M. Milkis and Jerome M. Mileur. (Amherst, MA: University of Massachusetts Press, 1999), 40–80. See also Marc Allen Eisner, *The American Political Economy: Institutional Evolution of Market and State* (New York: Routledge, 2011), 42–44.

7 Sheldon D. Pollack, *War, Revenue, and State Building: Financing the Development of the American State* (Ithaca, NY: Cornell University Press, 2009), 242–53; Teaford, *The Rise of the States*, 56–59; David Brian Robertson and Dennis R. Judd, *The Development of American Public Policy: The Structure of Policy Restraint* (Glenview, IL: Scott, Foresman/Little, Brown, 1989), 35–36.

8 Douglas Brinkley, *The Wilderness Warrior: Theodore Roosevelt and the Crusade for America* (New York: Harper, 2009).

9 Daniel P. Carpenter, *The Forging of Bureaucratic Autonomy: Reputations, Networks, and Policy Innovation in Executive Agencies, 1862–1928* (Princeton, NJ: Princeton University Press, 2001); David Brian Robertson, "Policy Entrepreneurs and Policy Divergence: John R. Commons and William Beveridge," *Social Service Review* 62:3 (September, 1988), 504–31; Kenneth Finegold, *Experts and Politicians: Reform Challenges to Machine Politics in New York, Cleveland, and Chicago* (Princeton, NJ: Princeton University Press, 1995).

10 Teaford, *The Rise of the States*, 11, 59–68, 77–80; Campbell, *The Growth of American Government*, 62; Margaret Weir, "States, Race, and the Decline of New Deal Liberalism," *Studies in American Political Development* 19:2 (Fall, 2005), 161; Robert H. Weibe, *Businessmen and Reform: A Study of the Progressive Movement* (Cambridge, MA: Harvard University Press, 1962); Dennis R. Judd, *The Politics of American Cities: Private Power and Public Policy*, 3rd ed. (Glenview, IL and Boston: Scott, Foreman/Little, Brown, 1988), 102–9.

11 Alexander Keyssar, *The Right to Vote: The Contested History of Democracy in the United States* (New York: Basic Books, 2000), 142–43.

12 Alan Ware, *The American Direct Primary: Party Institutionalization and Transformation in the North* (Cambridge and New York: Cambridge University Press, 2002); John D. Buenker, "The Urban Political Machine and the Seventeenth Amendment," *Journal of American History*, 56:2 (September, 1969), 305–22.

13 Thomas Goebel, *A Government by the People: Direct Democracy in America, 1890–1940* (Chapel Hill, NC: University of North Carolina Press, 2002); David D. Schmidt, *Citizen Lawmakers: The Ballot Initiative Revolution* (Philadelphia: Temple University Press, 1989).

14 Daniel Wirls, "Regionalism, Rotten Boroughs, Race, and Realignment: The Seventeenth Amendment and the Politics of Representation," *Studies in American Political Development* 13:1 (Spring, 1999), 1–30.

15 Teaford, *The Rise of the States*, 12–16; Weir, "States, Race, and the Decline of New Deal Liberalism," 165. According to Teaford, in Vermont, the most extreme example, each town had one representative in the lower house, so that the 61 residents of Somerset and the 14,590 residents of Burlington each elected one state Representative.

16 Weir, "States, Race, and the Decline of New Deal Liberalism," 165.

17 *New State Ice Co.* v. *Liebmann*, 285 U.S. 262 (1932).

18 David Brian Robertson, *Capital, Labor, and State: The Battle for American Labor Markets from the Civil War to the New Deal* (Lanham, MD: Rowman and Littlefield, 2000), 17–18.

19 F.B. Gordon, "Georgia's Tempting Invitation to Mill-man and Immigrant," *American Industries*, 3:2 (September 1, 1904), 13.

20 Gerald Berk, *Louis Brandeis and the Making of Regulated Competition, 1900–1932* (Cambridge and New York: Cambridge University Press, 2009); Robertson, "Policy Entrepreneurs and Policy Divergence."

21 Robertson, *Capital, Labor, and State*, 37–93.

22 Eugene Staley, *History of the Illinois State Federation of Labor* (Chicago: University of Chicago Press, 1930), 561–62; Philip Taft, *Labor Politics American Style: The California State Federation of Labor* (Cambridge, MA: Harvard University Press, 1968); John R. Commons, "European and American Unions," in John R. Commons, *Labor and Administration* (New York: Macmillan, 1913), 154.

23 Robertson, *Capital, Labor, and State*, 37–55, 131–33.

24 Gerald G. Eggert, *Steelmakers and Labor Reform, 1886–1923* (Pittsburgh, PA: University of Pittsburgh Press, 1981), 34–38.

25 Robertson, *Capital, Labor, and State*, 95–151, 257–79.

26 Theda Skocpol, *Protecting Soldiers and Mothers: The Political Origins of Social Policy in the United States* (Cambridge, MA: Belknap, 1992), 326; Paula Baker, "The Domestication of Politics: Women and American Political Society, 1780–1920," *American Historical Review* 89:3 (June, 1984), 620–64.

27 Lawrence M. Friedman, *A History of American Law*, 3rd ed. (New York: Touchstone, 2005), 146–48.

28 Eleanor Flexner and Ellen Fitzpatrick, *Century of Struggle: The Woman's Rights Movement in the United States*, enlarged ed. (Cambridge, MA: Belknap, 1996), 208–17; Suzanne M. Marilley, *Woman Suffrage and the Origins of Liberal Feminism in the United States, 1820–1920* (Cambridge, MA: Harvard University Press, 1996).

29 Baker, "The Domestication of Politics," 637; Richard F. Hamm, *Shaping the Eighteenth Amendment: Temperance Reform, Legal Culture, and the Polity, 1880–1920* (Chapel Hill, NC: University of North Carolina Press, 1995), 24.

30 Flexner and Fitzpatrick, *Century of Struggle*, 171–72; Skocpol, *Protecting Soldiers and Mothers*.

31 Skocpol, *Protecting Soldiers and Mothers*, 333.

32 Baker, "The Domestication of Politics," 641; Elisabeth S. Clemens, *The People's Lobby: Organizational Innovation and the Rise of Interest Group Politics in the United States* (Chicago: University of Chicago Press, 1997), 190).

33 Flexner and Fitzpatrick, *Century of Struggle*, 167–69.

34 Ibid., 169–70.

35 Ibid., 255–317.

36 Cahill, *Shorter Hours*, 112.

37 *Muller* v. *Oregon*, 208 U.S. 412 (1908).

38 Skocpol, *Protecting Soldiers and Mothers*, 373–401; U.S. Bureau of Labor Statistics, *Labor Law of the United States*, Bulletin 148, Vol. 1 (Washington, DC: Government Printing Office, 1914) 6; Elizabeth Brandeis, "Labor Legislation," in John R. Commons et al, *History of Labor in the United States*, Vol. 3 (New York: Macmillan, 1918 and 1935), 474–83.

39 Elizabeth Brandeis, "Labor Legislation," 458–59; Vivien Hart, *Bound by Our Constitution: Women, Workers, and the Minimum Wage* (Princeton, NJ: Princeton University Press, 1994); Skocpol, *Protecting Soldiers and Mothers*, 404.

40 Skocpol, *Protecting Soldiers and Mothers*, 424–79.

41 Ibid., 2.

42 Baker, "The Domestication of Politics," 645; Kathryn Kish Sklar, "Two Political Cultures in the Progressive Era: The National Consumers' League and the American Association for Labor Legislation," in *U.S. History as Women's History: New Feminist Essays,* eds. Linda A. Kerber, Alice Kessler-Harris, and Kathryn Kish Sklar (Chapel Hill, NC: University of North Carolina Press), 36–62.

43 Gretchen Ritter, *The Constitution as Social Design: Gender and Civic Membership in the American Constitutional Order* (Stanford, CA: Stanford University Press, 2006); Eileen McDonagh, *The Motherless State: Women's Political Leadership and American Democracy* (Chicago: University of Chicago Press, 2009).

44 Hamm, *Shaping the Eighteenth Amendment*, 46.

45 *Mugler* v. *Kansas*, 123 U.S. 623 (1887); 135 U.S. 100 (1890).

46 Hamm, *Shaping the Eighteenth Amendment*, 79–86, 92–122.

47 K. Austin Kerr. *Organized for Prohibition: A New History of the Anti-Saloon League* (New Haven, CT: Yale University Press, 1985); Ann-Marie E. Szymanski, *Pathways to Prohibition: Radicals, Moderates, and Social Movement Outcomes* (Durham, NC: Duke University Press, 2003).

48 Hamm, *Shaping the Eighteenth Amendment*, 227–55.

49 Daniel Okrent, *Last Call: The Rise and Fall of Prohibition* (New York: Simon & Schuster, 2010); James Morone, *Hellfire Nation: The Politics of Sin in American History* (New Haven, CT: Yale University Press, 2003), 281–344.

50 The material in this section draws heavily on Robertson, *Capital, Labor, and State*, 152–60.

51 Elizabeth Davidson, *Child Labor Legislation in the Southern Textile States* (Chapel Hill, NC: University of North Carolina Press, 1939), 55; U.S. Industrial Commission, *Final Report*, Vol. 19 (Washington, DC: Government Printing Office, 1902), 922; U.S. Commissioner of Labor, *Report on the Condition of Woman and Child Wage Earners in the United States*, U.S. Senate Document 61–645 (Washington: Government Printing Office, 1910), Vol. 1, 187–97, 357–96, and Vol. 6, 45, 134–35; Stephen B. Wood, *Constitutional Politics in the Progressive Era: Child Labor and the Law* (Chicago: University of Chicago Press, 1968), 3–8.

52 Walter Trattner, *Crusade for the Children: A History of the National Child Labor Committee and Child Labor Reform in America* (Chicago: Quadrangle Books, 1970), 45–67, 70, 105–7, 115; William F. Ogburn, *Progress and Uniformity in Child-Labor Legislation: A Study in Statistical Measurement* (New York: Columbia University, 1912), 203–5.

53 House Committee on Labor, *Child-Labor Bill*, Report No. 1400, 63rd Congress, 3rd session (February 13, 1915), 7–8.

54 *Congressional Record,* January 26, 1916, 1584; *Congressional Record*, August 7, 1916, 12208.

55 Trattner, *Crusade for the Children*, 126–27; Wood, *Constitutional Politics in the Progressive Era*, 41–42, 83, 87–93.

56 *Hammer* v. *Dagenhart,* 247 U.S. 251 (1918).

57 Wood, *Constitutional Politics in the Progressive Era*, 206–9, 220–21, 260–74.

58 *Bailey* v. *Drexel Furniture Company,* 259 U.S. 20 (1922).

59 Trattner, *Crusade for the Children*, 163–67; Wood, *Constitutional Politics in the Progressive Era*, 267–74.

60 W. Brooke Graves, *Uniform State Action: A Possible Substitute for Centralization* (Chapel Hill, NC: University of North Carolina Press, 1934); William Graebner, "Federalism in the Progressive Era: A Structural Interpretation of Reform," *The Journal of American History* 64:2 (September, 1977), 331–57; John D. Nugent, *Safeguarding Federalism: How States Protect Their Interests in National Policymaking* (Norman, OK: University of Oklahoma Press, 2009), 77–88.

61 Kimberley S. Johnson, *Governing the American State: Congress and the New Federalism* (Princeton, NJ: Princeton University Press, 2006), 9.

62 Ibid., 161.

63 Richard F. Weingroff, "The Federal Highway Administration at 100," U.S. Department of Transportation, http://www.tfhrc.gov/pubrds/fall93/p93au1.htm (accessed May 23, 2010).

64 Michael R. Fein, *Paving the Way: New York Road Building and the American State, 1880–1956* (Lawrence, KS: University Press of Kansas, 2008), 145–46.

65 Donald D. Lescohier, "Working Conditions," in John R. Commons et al., *History of Labour in the United States* (New York: Macmillan, 1918 and 1935), Vol.3, 281–83; Lawrence A. Cremin, *The Transformation of the School: Progressivism in American Education, 1876–1957* (New York: Alfred A. Knopf, 1962), 38–39; Larry Cuban, "Enduring Resiliency: Enacting and Implementing Federal Vocational Education Legislation," in Harvey Kantor and David B. Tyack, *Work, Youth, and Schooling: Historical Perspectives on Vocationalism in American Education* (Stanford, CT: Stanford University Press, 1982), 45–78; Regina Werum, "Sectionalism and Racial Politics: Federal Vocational Policies and Programs in the Predesegregation South," *Social Science History* 21 (Fall, 1997), 399–453.

66 Elizabeth Sanders, *Roots of Reform: Farmers, Workers, and the American State, 1877–1917* (Chicago: University of Chicago Press, 1999), 314–37.

67 Jess Gilbert and Carolyn Howe, "Beyond 'State vs. Society': Theories of the State and New Deal Agricultural Policies," *American Sociological Review* 56:2 (April, 1991), 204–20; Grant McConnell, *The Decline of Agrarian Democracy* (New York: Atheneum [1953] 1969).

68 *Commonwealth of Massachusetts* v. *Mellon*, 262 U.S. 447 (1923).

69 Skocpol, *Protecting Soldiers and Mothers*, 480–524; Johnson, *Governing the American State*, 136–50.

70 See Johnson, *Governing the American State*, 119. In the 1920s, the states themselves undertook another period of investment in roads that rivaled the canal building era. Teaford, *The Rise of the States*, 96–119, and Fein, *Paving the Way*, 77–129.

71 Harry N. Scheiber, "Federalism and the American Economic Order, 1789–1910," *Law and Society Review* 10:1 (Fall. 1975), 108–9.

72 Terry Sanford, *Storm over the States* (New York: McGraw-Hill, 1967), 80.

73 Hamby, "Progressivism: A Century of Change and Rebirth," 47.

74 Florence Kelley, "The Federal Government and the Working Children," *Annals* 27 (February, 1906), 289–92.

Chapter 7

1 Lizabeth Cohen, *Making a New Deal: Industrial Workers in Chicago, 1919–1939*, new ed. (Cambridge and New York: Cambridge University Press, 2008), 240–43; Michael R. Fein, *Paving the Way: New York Road Building and the American State, 1880–1956* (Lawrence, KS: University Press of Kansas, 2008), 141–42.

2 Michael A. Bernstein, *The Great Depression: Delayed Recovery and Economic Change in America, 1929–1939* (Cambridge and New York: Cambridge University Press, 1987); Marc Allen Eisner, *The State in the American Political Economy* (Englewood Cliffs, NJ: Prentice-Hall, 1995), 160–62; Peter Temin, "The Great Depression," in *The Cambridge Economic History of the United States, Vol. III, The Twentieth Century*, eds. Stanley L. Engerman and Robert E. Gallman (Cambridge and New York: Cambridge University Press, 2000), 302–5; Gary M. Walton and Hugh Rockoff, *History of the American Economy*, 8th ed. (Fort Worth, TX: Dryden Press, 1998), 515–29.

3 William E. Leuchtenburg, *Franklin D. Roosevelt and the New Deal, 1932–1940* (New York: Harper and Row, 1963), 18.

4 Ballard C. Campbell, *The Growth of American Government: Governance from the Cleveland Era to the Present* (Bloomington, IN: Indiana University Press, 1995), 85.

5 Campbell, *The Growth of American Government*, 86–87; James T. Patterson, *The New Deal and the States: Federalism in Transition* (Princeton, NJ: Princeton University Press, 1969), 39–40.

6 Patterson, *The New Deal and the States*, 20–44.

7 Ibid., 39.

8 Jon C. Teaford, *The Rise of the States: Evolution of American State Government* (Baltimore, MD: Johns Hopkins University Press, 2002), 131–37.

9 Teaford, *The Rise of the States*, 124–29, 152–57; David B. Walker, *The Rebirth of Federalism: Slouching toward Washington*, 2nd ed. (Chatham, NJ: Chatham House, 2000), 98.

10 Teaford, *The Rise of the States*, 122–24; Patterson, *The New Deal and the States*, 37–40; Udo Sautter, *Three Cheers for the Unemployed: Government and Unemployment before the New Deal* (Cambridge and New York: Cambridge University Press, 1991), 279–91; Ann E. Geddes, *Trends in Relief Expenditures, 1910–1935* (Washington: Works Progress Administration, 1937), 91–92.

11 David Brian Robertson and Dennis R. Judd, *The Development of American Public Policy: The Structure of Policy Restraint* (New York: Scott, Foresman/Little, Brown, 1989), 98; Wisconsin Legislative Interim Committee on Unemployment, *Report* (Madison, WI: Wisconsin Industrial Commission, 1931), 41–42.

12 James L. Sundquist, *Dynamics of the Party System: Alignment and Realignment of Political Parties in the United States*, rev. ed. (Washington: Brookings Institution, 1983), 200–203.

13 Ibid., 214–39; David Plotke, *Building a Democratic Political Order: Reshaping American Liberalism in the 1930s and 1940* (Cambridge and New York: Cambridge University Press, 1996), 144–56; Daniel J. Tichenor, "The Presidency and Interest Groups: Allies, Adversaries, and Policy Leadership," in *The Presidency and the Political System*, 9th ed., ed. Michael Nelson (Washington: CQ Press, 2010), 272–75.

14 Franklin D. Roosevelt, "Call for Federal Responsibility," October 13, 1932, http://www.columbia.edu/~gjw10/fdr.newdeal.html (accessed June 9, 2010).

15 U.S. Department of Commerce, *National Economic Accounts, Table 3.2*, "Federal Government Current Receipts and Expenditures," http://www.bea.gov/national/nipaweb/TableView.asp?SelectedTable=87&ViewSeries=NO&Java=no&Request3Place=N&3Place=N&FromView=YES&Freq=Year&FirstYear=1929&LastYear=1940&3Place=N&Update=Update&JavaBox=no#Mid (accessed June 13, 2010); U.S. Census Bureau, *Government Employment & Payroll*, http://www.census.gov/govs/apes (accessed June 28, 2010).

16 Peter H. Irons, *The New Deal Lawyers* (Princeton, NJ: Princeton University Press, 1982), 86–107.

17 Franklin D. Roosevelt, Press Conference, May 31, 1935, John T. Woolley and Gerhard Peters, *The American Presidency Project*, http://www.presidency.ucsb.edu/ws/index.php?pid=15065 (accessed June 13, 2010).

18 *N.L.R.B.* v. *Jones & Laughlin Steel Corp.*, 301 U.S. 1 (1937); *Wickard* v. *Filburn*, 317 U.S. 111 (1942).

19 Stephen Gardbaum "New Deal Constitutionalism and the Unshackling of the States," *University of Chicago Law Review* 64:2 (Spring, 1997), 483–566.

20 Budget of the United States Government, 2005, *Historical Table 17.1—Total Executive Branch Civilian Employees, 1940–2003*, http://www.gpoaccess.gov/usbudget/fy05/sheets/hist17z1.xls (accessed June 13, 2010).

21 Patterson, *The New Deal and the States*, 127, 171.

22 Sidney Milkis, *The President and the Parties: The Transformation of the American Party System since the New Deal* (Oxford and New York: Oxford University Press, 1993), 77–97; Susan Dunn, *Roosevelt's Purge: How FDR Fought to Change the Democratic Party* (Cambridge, MA: Belknap Press, 2010).

23 Margaret Weir, "States, Race, and the Decline of New Deal Liberalism," *Studies in American Political Development* 19:2 (Fall, 2005), 166–67; Patterson, *The New Deal and the States*, 180–91.

24 Plotke, *Building a Democratic Political Order,* 137.

25 Milkis, *The President and the Parties,* 52–97; Tichenor, "The Presidency and Interest Groups: Allies, Adversaries, and Policy Leadership," 272–75.

26 Franklin D. Roosevelt, *Looking Forward* (New York: Simon & Schuster, 2009), xii.

27 Arthur M. Schlesinger, Jr., *The Politics of Upheaval* (Boston: Houghton Mifflin, 1960), 385–423.

28 Schlesinger, *The Politics of Upheaval,* 409–23. Roosevelt had defended states' rights as Governor of New York; see Franklin D. Roosevelt's "Radio Address on States' Rights," March 20, 1930, in Franklin D. Roosevelt, *The Public Papers and Addresses of Franklin D. Roosevelt,* Vol. 1 (New York: Random House, 1938), 569–75.

29 U.S. Department of Commerce, *National Economic Accounts, Table 3.2,* "Federal Government Current Receipts and Expenditures," http://www.bea.gov/national/nipaweb/TableView. asp?SelectedTable=87&ViewSeries=NO&Java=no&Request3Place=N&3Place=N&From View=YES&Freq=er&FirstYear=1929&LastYear=1940&3Place=N&Update=Update& JavaBox=no#Mid (accessed June 13, 2010).

30 John Joseph Wallis, "The Birth of the Old Federalism: Financing the New Deal, 1932–40," *Journal of Economic History* 44:1 (March, 1984), 139–59.

31 David B. Truman, *The Governmental Process: Political Interests and Public Opinion* (New York: Knopf, 1951) 469–72, 487.

32 Deil S. Wright, *Understanding Intergovernmental Relations,* 3rd ed. (Pacific Grove, CA: Brooks/Cole, 1988), 13.

33 Calvin B. Hoover, "I. The Agricultural Adjustment Act: Principles, Practices and Problems," in J. Henry Richardson, "The 'New Deal' in the United States," *The Economic Journal* 44:176 (December, 1934), 567–90.

34 Grant McConnell, *Private Power & American Democracy* (New York: Vintage, 1966), 235; Kenneth Finegold and Theda Skocpol, *State and Party in America's New Deal* (Madison, WI: University of Wisconsin Press, 1995), 112–14; Adam D. Sheingate, *The Rise of the Agricultural Welfare State: Institutions and Interest Group Power in the United States, France, and Japan* (Princeton, NJ : Princeton University Press, 2001), 109–10.

35 Finegold and Skocpol, *State and Party in America's New Deal,* 112–14; Sheingate, *The Rise of the Agricultural Welfare State,* 109–17.

36 *United States* v. *Butler,* 297 U.S. 1 (1936); Sheingate, *The Rise of the Agricultural Welfare State,* 115; Theodore Saloutos, *The American Farmer and the New Deal* (Ames, IA: Iowa State University Press, 1982), 236–53.

37 Sheingate, *The Rise of the Agricultural Welfare State,* 143. In *Mulford* v. *Smith,* 307 US 38 (1939), the Supreme Court upheld the 1938 act; three years later, it held the law constitutional even for a small amount of crop production not destined for interstate commerce.

38 John Joseph Wallis, "The Political Economy of New Deal Fiscal Federalism," *Economic Inquiry* 29:3 (July, 1991), 512; James S. Olson, *Herbert Hoover and the Reconstruction Finance Corporation* (Ames, IA: Iowa State University Press, 1977).

39 Wallis, "The Birth of the Old Federalism."

40 Jeff Singleton, *The American Dole: Unemployment Relief and the Welfare State in the Great Depression* (Westport, CT: Greenwood Press, 2000); Edward Amenta, *Bold Relief: Institutional Politics and the Origins of Modern American Social Policy* (Princeton, NJ: Princeton University Press, 1998); Jonathan R. Kesselman, "Work Relief Programs in the Great Depression," in *Creating Jobs,* ed. John L. Palmer (Washington, DC: Brookings Institution, 1978), 158.

41 Patterson, *The New Deal and the States,* 74–105; Wallis, "The Birth of the Old Federalism," 158–59.

42 Kimberley S. Johnson, *Governing the American State: Congress and the New Federalism* (Princeton, NJ: Princeton University Press, 2006), 132–33; Fein, *Paving the Way,* 139–59.

43 Kesselman, "Work Relief Programs in the Great Depression," 158.

44 Patterson, *The New Deal and the States*, 74–85.

45 Franklin D. Roosevelt, "Message to Congress on the Objectives and Accomplishments of the Administration," June 8, 1934, John T. Woolley and Gerhard Peters, *The American Presidency Project*, http://www.presidency.ucsb.edu/ws/print.php?pid=14690 (accessed June 22, 2010). On Roosevelt's preference for state collaboration, see Arthur Altmeyer, *The Formative Years of Social Security* (Madison, WI: University of Wisconsin Press, 1966), 11, 17, 19.

46 Altmeyer, *The Formative Years of Social Security*, 11; Robertson and Judd, *The Development of American Public Policy*, 212–18; Suzanne Mettler, *Dividing Citizens: Gender and Federalism in New Deal Public Policy* (Ithaca, NY: Cornell University Press, 1998), 53–62.

47 Mettler, *Dividing Citizens*, 64–67.

48 Edwin Amenta, *When Movements Matter: The Townsend Plan and the Rise of Social Security* (Princeton, NJ: Princeton University Press, 2006).

49 Abraham Holtzman, *The Townsend Movement: A Political Study* (New York: Bookman Associates, 1963), 88.

50 Robertson and Judd, *The Development of American Public Policy*, 214–16; Mettler, *Dividing Citizens*, 64–69.

51 Daniel Nelson, *Unemployment Insurance: The American Experience, 1915–1935* (Madison, WI: University of Wisconsin Press, 1969); David Brian Robertson, *Capital, Labor, and State: The Battle for American Labor Markets from the Civil War to the New Deal* (Lanham, MD: Rowman & Littlefield, 2000), 245–48.

52 U.S. Social Security Administration, "Historical Background and Development of Social Security," http://www.ssa.gov/history/briefhistory3.html (accessed June 23, 2010); Theda Skocpol, *Protecting Soldiers and Mothers: The Political Origins of Social Policy in the United States* (Cambridge, MA: Belknap, 1992), 472. Alabama, Georgia, South Carolina, Kentucky, and New Mexico provided no support for mothers' pensions. Robert B. Irwin and Evelyn C. McKay "The Social Security Act and the Blind," *Law and Contemporary Problems* 3:2 (April, 1936), 271–78.

53 Robertson and Judd, *The Development of American Public Policy*, 114.

54 See, for example, Susan Stein-Roggenbuck, *Negotiating Relief: The Development of Social Welfare Programs in Depression-Era Michigan, 1930–1940* (Columbus, OH: Ohio State University Press, 2008).

55 Johnson, *Governing the American State*, 150–54; Katharine F. Lenroot, "Maternal and Child Welfare Provisions of the Social Security Act," *Law and Contemporary Problems* 3:2 (April, 1936), pp. 253–62.

56 Edwin Witte, *The Development of the Social Security Act* (Madison, WI: University of Wisconsin Press, 1963), 187–88; Altmeyer, *The Formative Years of Social Security*, 57–58, 261; Daniel Hirshfeld, *The Lost Reform: The Campaign for Compulsory Health Insurance in the United States from 1932 to 1943* (Cambridge, MA: Harvard University Press, 1970); Colin Gordon, *Dead on Arrival: The Politics of Health Care in Twentieth Century America* (Princeton, NJ: Princeton University Press, 2003), 16–21; Paul Starr, *The Social Transformation of American Medicine* (New York: Basic Books, 1982), 267–86.

57 Wallis, "The Political Economy of New Deal Fiscal Federalism"; Patterson, *The New Deal and the States*, 50–55; Altmeyer, *The Formative Years of Social Security*, 36.

58 Lenroot, "Maternal and Child Welfare Provisions of the Social Security Act"; Patterson, *The New Deal and the States*, 36–37; Johnson, *Governing the American State*,151–55; F. Douglas Southfield and William Keck, *Principles of Public Health Practice*, 2nd ed. (Clifton Park, NY: Thomson/Delmar Learning, 2002), 20–21.

59 Mettler, *Dividing Citizens*, 81–84, 156–57. Michael Katz, *In the Shadow of the Poorhouse: A Social History of Welfare in America* (New York: Basic Books, 1986), 244–45.

60 Leo Troy and Neil Heflin, *U.S. Union Sourcebook: Membership, Finances, Structure, Directory* (West Orange, NJ: Industrial Relations Data and Information Services, 1985), Table 3 63.

61 Robertson, *Capital, Labor, and State*, 199–201, 261–62.
62 James A. Gross, *Broken Promise: The Subversion of U.S. Labor Relations Policy, 1947–1994* (Philadelphia, PA: Temple University Press, 1995); Joel Rogers, "Divide and Conquer: Further 'Reflections on the Distinctive Character of American Labor Laws,'" *Wisconsin Law Review* (1990), 117–23; Janice A. Klein and E. David Wanger, "The Legal Setting for the Emergence of the Union Avoidance Strategy," in *Challenges and Choices Facing American Labor*, ed. Thomas A. Kochan (Cambridge: MIT Press, 1985), 75–88.
63 Theodore J. Lowi, *The End of Liberalism: The Second Republic of the United States* (New York: Norton, 1979), 54.

Chapter 8

1 Mark Baldassare, *Trouble in Paradise: The Suburban Transformation in America* (New York: Columbia University Press, 1986), 6–8.
2 National Center for Health Statistics, *Vital Statistics of the United States, 1995*, preprint of vol. II, Mortality, Part A, life tables (Hyattsville, MD: Government Printing Office, 1998), http://www.cdc.gov/nchs/data/lifetables/life95_2.pdf (accessed July 1, 2010); Claudia Goldin, "Labor Markets in the Twentieth Century," in Stanley L. Engerman and Robert E. Gallman, *The Cambridge Economic History of the United States, Vol. III, The Twentieth Century* (Cambridge, and New York: Cambridge University Press, 2000), 549–623.
3 Ronald Inglehart, *Culture Shift in Advanced Industrial Society* (Princeton, NJ: Princeton University Press, 1990).
4 Keith E. Whittington, "'Interpose Your Friendly Hand': Political Supports for the Exercise of Judicial Review by the United States Supreme Court," *American Political Science Review* 99:4 (November, 2005), 586–87.
5 Martha Derthick, "Crossing Thresholds: Federalism in the 1960s," in *Integrating the Sixties: The Origins, Structures, and Legitimacy of Public Policy in a Turbulent Decade*, ed. Brian Balogh (University Park, PA: Penn State University Press, 1996), 75.
6 Hugh Heclo, "The Sixties' False Dawn: Awakenings, Movements, and Postmodern Policy-Making," in *Integrating the Sixties: The Origins, Structures, and Legitimacy of Public Policy in a Turbulent Decade*, ed. Brian Balogh (University Park, PA: Penn State University Press, 1996), 34–63; James Morone, *Hellfire Nation: The Politics of Sin in American History* (New Haven, CT: Yale University Press, 2003), 407–49.
7 John Gerring, *Party Ideologies in America, 1828–1996* (Cambridge and New York: Cambridge University Press, 1998), 232–53; James L. Sundquist, *Politics and Policy: The Eisenhower, Kennedy, and Johnson Years* (Washington, DC: Brookings Institution, 1968), 240–68; Bruce Miroff, *The Liberals' Moment: The McGovern Insurgency and the Identity Crisis of the Democratic Party* (Lawrence, KS: University Press of Kansas, 2007); Stephen Skowronek, *The Politics Presidents Make: Leadership from John Adams to Bill Clinton* (Cambridge, MA: Belknap Press, 1997), 325–60.
8 David B. Walker, *The Rebirth of Federalism: Slouching toward Washington*, 2nd ed. (Chatham, NJ : Chatham House, 2000), 124.
9 "Time Essay: The Marble-Cake Government Washington's New Partnership with the States," May 27, 1966, http://www.time.com/time/magazine/article/0,9171,835637,00.html (accessed July 5, 2010). See Deil S. Wright, *Understanding Intergovernmental Relations*, 3rd ed. (Monterey, CA: Brooks/Cole, 1988), 13.
10 Walker, *The Rebirth of Federalism*, 124.
11 Wright, *Understanding Intergovernmental Relations*, 367–73; Walker, *The Rebirth of Federalism*, 125; Advisory Commission on Intergovernmental Relations (ACIR), *Regulatory Federalism: Policy, Processes, Impact and Reform*, Report A-95 (Washington: ACIR, 1984).
12 David B. Walker, *Toward a Functioning Federalism* (Cambridge, MA: Winthrop, 1981), 193–96.

13　Donald H. Haider, *When Governments Come to Washington: Governors, Mayors, and Intergovernmental Lobbying* (New York: Free Press, 1974), 55.

14　Thomas J. Anton, *American Federalism and Public Policy: How the System Works* (New York: Random House, 1989); Donald C. Baumer and Carl E. Van Horn, *The Politics of Unemployment* (Washington, DC: Congressional Quarterly, 1985).

15　Terry Sanford, *Storm over the States* (New York: McGraw-Hill, 1967).

16　Haider, *When Governments Come to Washington*, 1–41.

17　Timothy J. Conlan, "Congress and the Contemporary Intergovernmental System," in *American Intergovernmental Relations Today: Perspectives and Controversies,* ed. Robert Jay Dilger (Englewood Cliffs, NJ: Prentice-Hall, 1986), 104.

18　R. Douglas Arnold, "The Local Roots of Domestic Policy," in Thomas E. Mann and Norman J. Ornstein, eds., *The New Congress* (Washington, DC: American Enterprise Institute, 1981), 268; John E. Chubb, "Federalism and the Bias for Centralization," in *The New Direction in American Politics*, eds. Jon E. Chubb and Paul E. Peterson (Washington, DC: Brookings Institution, 1985), 281–86; Gary W. Copeland and Kenneth J. Meier, "Pass the Biscuits, Pappy: Congressional Decision-Making and Federal Grants," *American Politics Research* 12:1 (January, 1984), 3–21; Robert M. Stein and Kenneth N. Bickers, *Perpetuating the Pork Barrel: Policy Subsystems and American Democracy* (Cambridge and New York: Cambridge University Press, 1997).

19　Mark H. Rose, *Interstate: Express Highway Politics, 1939–1989* (Knoxville, TN: University of Tennessee Press, 1990), 85–95; Robert Jay Dilger, "Federalism Issues in Surface Transportation Policy: Past and Present," Congressional Research Service report 7–5700 (January 5, 2010); http://www.policyarchive.org/handle/10207/bitstreams/18824_Previous_Version_2010-01-05.pdf (accessed December 30, 2010), 11–12.

20　Richard Nixon, "Address to the Nation on Domestic Programs," August 8, 1969, John T. Woolley and Gerhard Peters, *The American Presidency Project*, http://www.presidency.ucsb.edu/ws/index.php?pid=2191&st=&st1= (accessed July 6, 2010); Timothy Conlan, *From New Federalism to Devolution: Twenty-Five Years of Intergovernmental Reform* (Washington, DC: Brookings Institution, 1998), 19–35.

21　Samuel Beer, "The Adoption of General Revenue Sharing: A Case Study in Public Sector Politics," *Public Policy* 24:1–2 (Spring, 1976), 127–95; Lawrence D. Brown, "The Politics of Devolution in Nixon's New Federalism," in *The Changing Politics of Federal Grants,* eds. Lawrence D. Brown, James W. Fossett, and Kenneth T. Palmer (Washington, DC: Brookings Institution, 1984), 73–74; Conlan, *From New Federalism to Devolution*, 65–76.

22　Conlan, *From New Federalism to Devolution*, 19–92.

23　Advisory Commission on Intergovernmental Relations, *Regulatory Federalism*, 74–87.

24　Kenneth T. Palmer, "The Evolution of Grant Policies," in *The Changing Politics of Federal Grants*, eds. Lawrence D. Brown, James W. Fossett, and Kenneth T. Palmer (Washington, DC: Brookings Institution, 1984), 36.

25　Frederick C. Mosher, "The Changing Responsibilities and Tactics of the Federal Government," *Public Administration Review* 40:6 (November/December, 1980), 541–48; Donald F. Kettl, *Government by Proxy: (Mis?)managing Federal Programs* (Washington, DC: CQ Press, 1988).

26　Martha Derthick, *Policymaking for Social Security* (Washington: Brookings Institution, 1979); Edward D. Berkowitz, *America's Welfare State: From Roosevelt to Reagan* (Baltimore, MD: Johns Hopkins University Press, 1991); Gary V. Englehardt and Jonathan Gruber, "Social Security and the Evolution of Elderly Poverty," in *Public Policy and the Income Distribution*, eds. Alan J. Auerbach, David Card, and John M. Quigley (New York: Russell Sage Foundation, 2006), 259–87; U.S. Social Security Administration, *Annual Statistical Supplement, 2009*, http://www.ssa.gov/policy/docs/statcomps/supplement/2009/5a.html#table5.a4 (accessed July 30, 2010).

27　David Brian Robertson and Dennis R. Judd, *The Development of American Public Policy: The Structure of Policy Restraint* (New York: Scott, Foresman/Little, Brown, 1989), 219.

28 June Axinn and Herman Levin, *Social Welfare: A History of the American Response to Need* (New York: Dodd, Mead, 1975), 235–36; James T. Patterson, *America's Struggle against Poverty, 1900–1980* (Cambridge, MA: Harvard University Press, 1981), 108. Ribicoff quote in Sundquist, *Politics and Policy*, 126.

29 Jennifer Mittelstadt, *From Welfare to Workfare: The Unintended Consequences of Liberal Reform 1945–1965* (Chapel Hill, NC: University of North Carolina Press, 2005); Derthick, *Uncontrollable Spending for Social Services Grants.*

30 Sundquist, *Politics and Policy*, 134–54; Gareth Davies, *From Opportunity to Entitlement: The Transformation and Decline of Great Society Liberalism* (Lawrence, KS: University Press of Kansas, 1996); Robertson and Judd, *The Development of American Public Policy*, 222–23.

31 Felicia Kornbluh, *The Battle for Welfare Rights: Politics and Poverty in Modern America* (Philadelphia, PA: University of Pennsylvania Press, 2007).

32 James C. Ohls and Harold Beebout, *The Food Stamp Program: Design Tradeoffs, Policy and Impacts*: (Washington, DC: Urban Institute Press, 1993).

33 President's Commission on Income Maintenance Programs, *Poverty amid Plenty: The American Paradox* (Washington, DC: Government Printing Office, 1969), 115.

34 Robertson and Judd, *The Development of American Public Policy*, 226–27.

35 Nixon, "Address to the Nation on Domestic Programs."

36 Brian Steensland, *The Failed Welfare Revolution: America's Struggle over Guaranteed Income Policy* (Princeton, NJ: Princeton University Press, 2008), 28–181.

37 Joseph A. Califano, Jr., *Governing America* (New York: Touchstone, 1981), 320–67; Steensland, *The Failed Welfare Revolution*, 182–218.

38 Jacob S. Hacker, *The Divided Welfare State: The Battle over Public and Private Social Benefits in the United States* (Cambridge and New York: Cambridge University Press, 2002), 85–173; Daniel Béland and Jacob S. Hacker, "Ideas, Private Institutions and American Welfare State 'Exceptionalism': The Case of Health and Old-Age Insurance, 1915–65," *International Journal of Social Welfare* 13:1 (January, 2004), 42–54.

39 Sundquist, *Politics and Policy*, 294–97.

40 Sundquist, *Politics and Policy*, 301–7; Judith D. Moore and David G. Smith, "Legislating Medicaid: Considering Medicaid and Its Origins," *Health Care Financing Review* 27:2 (Winter, 2005–6), 45–52.

41 Robert Stevens and Rosemary Stevens, *Welfare Medicine in America: A Case Study of Medicaid* (New York: Free Press, 1974), 43.

42 Stevens and Stevens, *Welfare Medicine in America*, 51; Sundquist, *Politics and Policy*, 317–21; *Congress and the Nation, 1965–1968*, (Washington, DC: Congressional Quarterly Service, 1969), 751–58; Theodore Marmor, *The Politics of Medicare* (London: Routledge & Kegan Paul, 1970).

43 *Congress and the Nation, 1965–1968*, 667–73, 680–83, 697–99.

44 *Congress and the Nation, 1969–1973* (Washington, DC: Congressional Quarterly Service, 1973), 562–71; John Kingdon, *Agendas, Alternatives, and Public Policies*, 2nd ed. (New York: HarperCollins, 1995), passim.

45 David B. Tyack, Robert Lowe, and Elisabeth Hansot, *Public Schools in Hard Times: The Great Depression and Recent Years* (Cambridge, MA: Harvard University Press, 1984), 92–138; Betty Lindley and Ernest K. Lindley, *A New Deal for Youth: The Story of the National Youth Administration* (New York: Viking, 1938); Neil M. Maher, *Nature's New Deal: The Civilian Conservation Corps and the Roots of the American Environmental Movement* (New York and Oxford: Oxford University Press, 2008), 86–91.

46 Suzanne Mettler, *Soldiers to Citizens: The G.I. Bill and the Making of the Greatest Generation* (Oxford and New York: Oxford University Press, 2005), 42.

47 Sundquist, *Politics and Policy*, 155–70.

48 Sundquist, *Politics and Policy*, 173–80, 211; Joel Spring, *The American School, 1642–2000*, 5th ed. (New York: McGraw Hill, 2001), 369–70, 375.

49 Elizabeth Rose, "Where Does Pre-School Belong? Pre-school Policy and Public Education, 1965–Present," in *To Educate a Nation: Federal and National Strategies for School Reform,*

eds. Carl E. Kaestle and Alyssa E. Lodewick (Lawrence, KS: University Press of Kansas, 2007), 281.

50 Spring, *The American School*, 374–75; Sundquist, *Politics and Policy*, 216–17.

51 *Congress and the Nation, 1973–1976* (Washington, DC: Congressional Quarterly Service, 1977), 377–79, 383, 389–91.

52 Patrick McGuinn, *No Child Left Behind and the Transformation of Federal Education Policy, 1965–2005* (University Press of Kansas, June 2006), 199–202. Maris A. Vinovskis, *From A Nation at Risk to No Child Left Behind: National Education Goals and the Creation of Federal Education Policy* (New York: Teachers College Press, Columbia University, 2009), 12–13.

53 *Congress and the Nation, 1965–1968*, 310, 322–23.

54 *Congress and the Nation, 1969–1972*, 255–86.

55 *Congress and the Nation, 1965–1968*, 309–10.

56 *Congress and the Nation 1973–1976*, 559, 563–64, 604–6.

57 Robertson and Judd, *The Development of American Public Policy*, 326–27.

58 Sundquist, *Politics and Policy*, 331–32.

59 Robertson and Judd, *The Development of American Public Policy*, 334.

60 U.S. Congress, House Committee on Interstate and Foreign Commerce, *Clean Air Amendments of 1970,* House Report 91–1146 (Washington, DC: GPO, 1970).

61 Charles O. Jones, *Clean Air: The Policies and Politics of Pollution Control* (Pittsburgh, PA: University of Pittsburgh Press, 1975), 175–210; Robertson and Judd, *The Development of American Public Policy*, 338–41.

62 U.S. Congress, House Committee on Public Works, *Water Quality Act of 1965*, House Report 89–215 (March 31, 1965), 10.

63 Robertson and Judd, *The Development of American Public Policy*, 337.

64 R. Daniel Kelemen, *The Rules of Federalism: Institutions and Regulatory Politics in the EU and Beyond* (Cambridge, MA: Harvard University Press, 2004), 54.

65 Martha Derthick, "Crossing Thresholds: Federalism in the 1960s," 75–76.

66 Ibid., 78.

67 Jeffrey L. Pressman and Aaron Wildavsky, *Implementation: How Great Expectations in Washington are Dashed in Oakland; or, Why It's Amazing that Federal Programs Work at All, This Being a Saga of the Economic Development Administration as Told by Two Sympathetic Observers Who Seek to Build Morals on a Foundation of Ruined Hopes* (Berkeley, CA: University of California Press, 1973).

Chapter 9

1 David Brian Robertson, "Introduction: Loss of Confidence and Policy Change in the 1970s," in *Loss of Confidence*, ed. David Brian Robertson (University Park, PA: Penn State University Press, 1998), 1–18.

2 Susan J. Tolchin and Martin Tolchin, *Dismantling America: The Rush to Deregulate* (Oxford and New York: Oxford University Press, 1983), 147–88; Cathie Jo Martin, "Business and the New Economic Activism: The Growth of Corporate Lobbies in the Sixties," *Polity* 27:1 (Fall, 1994), 49–76; David Vogel, *Fluctuating Fortunes: The Political Power of Business in America* (New York: W.W. Norton, 1989); McGee Young, *Developing Interests: Organizational Change and the Politics of Advocacy* (Lawrence, KS: University Press of Kansas, 2010), 65–76.

3 James A. Morone, *Hellfire Nation: The Politics of Sin in America* (New Haven, CT: Yale University Press, 2003), 450–92.

4 Donald T. Critchlow, *The Conservative Ascendancy: How the GOP Right Made Political History* (Cambridge, MA: Harvard University Press, 2007); Joseph E. Lowndes, *From the New Deal to the New Right: Race and the Southern Origins of Modern Conservatism.* (New Haven CT: Yale University Press, 2008).

5 Andrew Rich, *Think Tanks, Public Policy, and the Politics of Expertise* (Cambridge and New York: Cambridge University Press, 2004). By 1992, the State Policy Network was founded to aid conservative think tanks in each state. State Policy Network, "About SPN," http://www.spn.org/about (accessed October 15, 2010).

6 Edward I. Koch, "The Mandate Millstone," *Public Interest* (Fall, 1980), 43.

7 Ballard C. Campbell, "Tax Revolts and Political Change," *Journal of Policy History* 10:1 (1998), 169–71.

8 Jane Mansbridge, *Why We Lost the ERA* (Chicago: University of Chicago Press, 1976), 129–48; Ballard C. Campbell, "Tax Revolts and Political Change," in *Loss of Confidence*, ed. David Brian Robertson (University Park, PA: Penn State University Press, 1998), 153–78; Critchlow, *The Conservative Ascendancy*, 162–66.

9 Byron E. Shafer and Richard Johnston, *The End of Southern Exceptionalism: Class, Race, and Partisan Change in the Postwar South* (Cambridge, MA: Harvard University Press, 2006); Earl Black and Merle Black, *The Rise of Southern Republicans* (Cambridge, MA: Belknap, 2002).

10 Ronald Reagan, "Remarks in Atlanta, Georgia, at the Annual Convention of the National Conference of State Legislatures," July 30, 1981, John T. Woolley and Gerhard Peters, The American Presidency Project, http://www.presidency.ucsb.edu/ws/index.php?pid=44131 (accessed September 29, 2010).

11 Ronald Reagan, "Interview with Reporters on Federalism," November 19, 1981, http://www.presidency.ucsb.edu/ws/index.php?pid=43277&st=federalism&st1= (accessed September 29, 2010).

12 J. Mitchell Pickerill and Cornell W. Clayton, "The Rehnquist Court and the Political Dynamics of Federalism," *Perspectives on Politics* 2:2 (June, 2004), 238.

13 Ronald Reagan, "Statement on Signing the Executive Order Establishing the Presidential Advisory Committee on Federalism," April 8, 1981, http://www.presidency.ucsb.edu/ws/index.php?pid=43665&st=federalism&st1= (accessed September 29, 2010).

14 "Executive Order 12612—Federalism," October 26, 1987, http://www.presidency.ucsb.edu/ws/index.php?pid=33607&st=12612&st1= (accessed September 29, 2010).

15 Ronald Reagan, "Address before a Joint Session of the Congress Reporting on the State of the Union," January 26, 1982, The American Presidency Project, http://www.presidency.ucsb.edu/ws/index.php?pid=42687&st=federalism&st1= (accessed September 29, 2010).

16 David B. Walker, *The Rebirth of Federalism: Slouching toward Washington*, 2nd ed. (Chatham, NJ: Chatham House, 2000), 147; Ben Canada, "Federal Grants to State and Local Governments: A Brief History," Congressional Research Service *Report RL30705* (Washington: Congressional Research Service, February 19, 2003), 10, http://lugar.senate.gov/services/pdf_crs/grants/Federal_Grants_to_State_and_Local_Governments_A_Brief_History.pdf (accessed October 1, 2010).

17 Susan B. Hansen, "Extraction: The Politics of State Taxation," in *Politics in the American States: A Comparative Analysis*, 4th ed., eds. Virginia Gray, Herbert Jacob, and Kenneth N. Vines, (Boston, MA: Little, Brown, 1983), 440.

18 Walker, *The Rebirth of Federalism*, 152.

19 Ibid., 156–71.

20 Thomas Gais and James Fossett, "Federalism and the Executive Branch," in *The Executive Branch*, eds. Joel D. Aberbach and Mark A. Peterson (Oxford and New York: Oxford University Press, 2005), 486–522.

21 Carol S. Weissert and William G. Weissert, "Medicaid Waivers: License to Shape the Future of Fiscal Federalism," in *Intergovernmental Management for the Twenty-First Century*, eds. Timothy J. Conlan and Paul L. Posner (Washington, DC: Brookings Institution 2008), 158–65.

22 George W. Bush, "Remarks at the National Governors' Association Conference," February 26, 2001, http://www.presidency.ucsb.edu/ws/index.php?pid=45884&st=federalism&st1= (accessed January 30, 2010).

23 U.S. Office of Management and Budget, *Analytical Perspectives, Budget of the U.S. Government, Fiscal Year 2011* (Washington, DC: U.S. Office of Management and Budget, 2010), 253–54, http://www.whitehouse.gov/sites/default/files/omb/budget/fy2011/assets/spec.pdf (accessed October 1, 2010); U.S. Office of Management and Budget, *Budget of the U.S. Government, Fiscal Year 2011, Table 12.1—Summary Comparison Of Total Outlays For Grants To State And Local Governments: 1940–2015* (Washington, DC: U.S. Office of Management and Budget, 2010), http://www.gpoaccess.gov/usbudget/fy11/hist.html (accessed October 1, 2010).

24 Joseph F. Zimmerman, "Federal Preemption under Reagan's New Federalism," *Publius*, 21:1 (Winter, 1991), 7–28.

25 Ibid.

26 Timothy J. Conlan, "And the Beat Goes On: Intergovernmental Mandates and Preemption in an Era of Deregulation," *Publius* 21:3 (Summer, 1991), 41–53.

27 Ibid. 46–48; Stephen L. Percy, "ADA, Disability Rights, and Evolving Regulatory Federalism," *Publius* 23:4 (Autumn, 1993), 87–105.

28 Timothy J. Conlan and John Dinan, "Federalism, the Bush Administration, and the Transformation of American Conservatism," *Publius* 37:3 (Summer, 2007), 279.

29 Paul L. Posner, "Mandates: The Politics of Coercive Federalism," in *Intergovernmental Management for the 21st Century*, eds. Timothy J. Conlan and Paul L. Posner (Washington, DC: Brookings Institution, 2008), 286–309; National Association of State Budget Officers, *Issue Brief: The REAL ID Act*, March 23, 2006, http://www.nasbo.org/LinkClick.aspx?fileticket=xSl7vPJApBM%3d&tabid=83 (accessed January 2, 2011); Jim VandeHei, "Blueprint Calls for Bigger, More Powerful Government" *Washington Post*, February 9, 2005, 1; http://www.washingtonpost.com/wp-dyn/articles/A9307–2005Feb8.html (accessed January 2, 2011).

30 Steven M. Teles, "Transformative Bureaucracy: Reagan's Lawyers and the Dynamics of Political Investment," *Studies in American Political Development*, 23 (April, 2009), 61–83.

31 J. Mitchell Pickerill, "Leveraging Federalism: The Real Meaning of the Rehnquist Court's Federalism Jurisprudence for States," *Albany Law Review* 66:3 (Spring, 2003), 823–33; see also Kathleen M. Sullivan, "From States' Rights Blues to Blue States' Rights: Federalism after the Rehnquist Court," *Fordham Law Review* 75:2 (November, 2006), 799–813, http://law2.fordham.edu/publications/articles/500flspub9557.pdf (accessed November 27, 2010).

32 Pickerill and Clayton, "The Rehnquist Court and the Political Dynamics of Federalism," 240–41. See also Keith E. Whittington, "Taking What They Give Us: Explaining the Court's Federalism Offensive," *Duke Law Journal* 51:1 (October, 2001) 477–520.

33 Linda Greenhouse, "The Revolution Next Time?" *New York Times*, December 16, 2010; http://opinionator.blogs.nytimes.com/2010/12/16/the-revolution-next-time/ (accessed January 3, 2010).

34 Linda Greenhouse, "5-to-4, Now and Forever; At the Court, Dissent over States' Rights is Now War," *New York Times*, June 9, 2002, http://www.nytimes.com/2002/06/09/weekinreview/nation-5-4-now-forever-court-dissent-over-states-rights-now-war.html (accessed January 13, 2011).

35 Jon C. Teaford, *The Rise of the States: Evolution of American State Government* (Baltimore, MD: Johns Hopkins University Press, 2002), 195–230; Larry Sabato, *Goodbye to Good-Time Charlie: The American Governor Transformed, 1950–1975* (Lexington, MA: Lexington Books, 1978); Ann O'M. Bowman and Richard C. Kearney, *The Resurgence of the States* (Englewood Cliffs, NJ: Prentice-Hall, 1986), 47–106; Walker, *The Rebirth of Federalism*, 264–77.

36 Walker, *The Rebirth of Federalism*, 150.

37 Steven Labaton, "States March into the Breach," *New York Times*, December 8, 1988; Alan R. Gold, "States Working to Avert Eviction of Thousands from Subsidized Units, *New York Times*, March 15, 1989.

38 Bowman and Kearney, *The Resurgence of the States*, 214; Richard P. Nathan, Fred C. Doolittle, and Associates, *Reagan and the States* (Princeton, NJ: Princeton University Press, 1987).

39 Lawrence M. Mead, *Government Matters: Welfare Reform in Wisconsin* (Princeton, NJ: Princeton University Press, 2004); Peter Eisinger, *The Rise of the Entrepreneurial State: State and Local Economic Development Policy in the United States* (Madison, WI: University of Wisconsin Press, 1988), 266–331.

40 David Osborne, *Laboratories of Democracy* (Boston, MA: Harvard Business School Press, 1988).

41 Dale Krane, "The Middle Tier in American Federalism: State Government Policy Activism during the Bush Presidency," *Publius* 37:3 (Summer, 2007), 453–77; Richard Thompson Ford, "The New Blue Federalists: The Case for Liberal Federalism" *Slate*, January 6, 2005, http://www.slate.com/id/2111942 (accessed July 1, 2010). In 2010, nine states provided in-state tuition for undocumented students; Dream Act Portal, In State Tuition, http://dreamact.info/students/in-state (accessed January 3, 2011).

42 John D. Nugent, *Safeguarding Federalism: How States Protect Their Interests in National Policymaking* (Norman, OK: University of Oklahoma Press, 2009), 115–67.

43 Martha Derthick, *Up in Smoke: From Legislation to Litigation in Tobacco Politics*, 2nd ed. (Washington, DC: CQ Press, 2005), 71–92; Michael Powell, "States vs. Wall Street: Crusaders for the Public Purse, in Ohio and Elsewhere," *New York Times*, October 12, 2010, B1.

44 Ann O'M. Bowman, "Horizontal Federalism: Exploring Interstate Interactions," *Journal of Public Administration Research and Theory* 14:4 (2004), 535–46; Council of State Governments, "Interstate Cooperation," http://www.csg.org/policy/interstatecooperation.aspx (accessed October 30, 2010).

45 Barry G. Rabe, "Regionalism and Global Climate Change Policy: Revisiting Multistate Collaboration as an Intergovernmental Management Tool," in *Intergovernmental Management for the Twenty-First Century*, eds. Timothy J. Conlan and Paul L. Posner (Washington, DC: Brookings Institution, 2008), 176–205.

46 National Conference of Commissioners of State Uniform Laws, "NCCUSL Acts—List," http://www.nccusl.org/nccusl/DesktopDefault.aspx?tabindex=0&tabid=65 (accessed October 30, 2010).

47 Richard P. Nathan, "Federalism: The Great 'Composition'," in *The New American Political System*, ed. Anthony King (Washington, DC: American Enterprise Institute, 1990), 233.

48 Richard P. Nathan, "Updating Theories of Federalism," in *Intergovernmental Management for the Twenty-First Century*, eds. Timothy J. Conlan and Paul L. Posner (Washington, DC: Brookings Institution, 2008), 16, 21.

49 Thad Kousser, *Term Limits and the Dismantling of State Legislative Professionalism* (Cambridge and New York: Cambridge University Press, 2005); National Conference of State Legislatures, "State Tax and Expenditure Limits—2008," http://www.ncsl.org/default.aspx?tabid=12633#typesoflimts (accessed October 1, 2010) and "The Term Limited States," http://www.ncsl.org/Default.aspx?TabId=14844 (accessed October 1, 2010).

50 Alan H. Peters and Peter S. Fisher, *State Enterprise Zone Programs: Have They Worked?* (Kalamazoo, MI: W.E. Upjohn Institute, 2002), 1.

51 Pamela Winston, *Welfare Policymaking in the States: The Devil in Devolution* (Washington, DC: Georgetown University Press, 2002), 36.

52 Ron Haskins, "Governors and the Development of American Social Policy," in *A Legacy of Innovation: Governors and Public Policy*, ed. Ethan G. Sribnick (Philadelphia, PA: University of Pennsylvania Press, 2008), 85–86; Lawrence M. Mead, *Government Matters: Welfare Reform in Wisconsin* (Princeton, NJ: Princeton University Press, 2004), 25–30, 37–53.

53 Winston, *Welfare Policymaking in the States*, 37; June Axinn and Mark J. Stern, *Social Welfare: A History of the American Response to Need*, 7th ed. (Boston: Pearson/Allyn Bacon, 2008), 297–98; Haskins, "Governors and the Development of American Social Policy," 87–88.

54 Haskins, "Governors and the Development of American Social Policy," 88; Winston, *Welfare Policymaking in the States*, 35, 49; Weissert and Weissert, "Medicaid Waivers," 160.

55 Haskins, "Governors and the Development of American Social Policy," 89–93; Gene Falk, "Temporary Assistance for Needy Families (TANF): Issues for the 110th Congress," Congressional Research Service, *Report RL34206*, October 9, 2007, 6–8, http://digitalcommons.ilr.cornell.edu/key_workplace/388 (accessed January 1, 2011).

56 Winston, *Welfare Policymaking in the States*, 242–43; TaxCreditResources.org, http://www.taxcreditresources.org/pages.cfm?contentID=39&pageID=12&Subpages=yes#states, (accessed January 1, 2011); National Conference of State Legislators, "Family Cap Policies," http://www.ncsl.org/default.aspx?tabid=16306 (accessed January 1, 2011).

57 Jocelyn M. Johnston, "Welfare Reform: A Devolutionary Success?" in *Intergovernmental Management for the Twenty-First Century*, eds. Timothy J. Conlan and Paul L. Posner (Brookings Institution 2008), 128–30.

58 Winston, *Welfare Policymaking in the States*, 231; "Assessing the New Federalism: Eight Years Later," (Washington, DC: Urban Institute, 2005), 11, http://www.urban.org/UploadedPDF/311198_ANF_EightYearsLater.pdf (accessed July 25, 2010).

59 U.S. Census Bureau, "Income, Poverty, and Health Insurance Coverage in the United States: 2009" Figure 5, 17, http://www.census.gov/prod/2010pubs/p60–238.pdf (accessed January 1, 2011).

60 Timothy J. Conlan, *From New Federalism to Devolution: Twenty-Five Years of Intergovernmental Reform* (Washington, DC: Brookings Institution, 1998), 114.

61 Nathan, *Reagan and the States*, 75–77, 96; Richard P. Nathan, "Federalism and Health Policy," *Health Affairs* 24:6 (2005), 1458–66.

62 Colleen M. Grogan and Vernon K.Smith, "From Charity Care to Medicaid: Governors, States, and the Transformation of American Health Care," in *A Legacy of Innovation: Governors and Public Policy*, ed. Ethan G. Sribnick (Philadelphia, PA: University of Pennsylvania Press, 2008), 216–18.

63 Thomas R. Oliver and Pamela Paul-Shaheen, "Translating Ideas into Actions: Entrepreneurial Leadership in State Health Care Reforms," *Journal of Health Politics, Policy and Law* 22:3 (1997), 729; Weissert and Weissert, "Medicaid Waivers," 162–63.

64 Weissert and Weissert, "Medicaid Waivers," 160.

65 Kaiser Commission on Medicaid and the Uninsured, "The Role of Section 1115 Waivers in Medicaid and Chip: Looking Back and Looking Forward," March 2009, http://www.dhcs.ca.gov/provgovpart/Documents/Waiver Renewal/The Role of Section 1118 Waivers_Mar2009.pdf (accessed January 2, 2011).

66 President George W. Bush had vetoed two efforts to expand the Children's Health Insurance Program after Democrats took control of Congress. David Stout, "Bush Vetoes Children's Health Bill," *New York Times*, October 3, 2007, http://www.nytimes.com/2007/10/03/washington/03cnd-veto.html?_r=1 (accessed January 2, 2011); Robert Pear, "Obama Signs Children's Health Insurance Bill," *New York Times* February 5, 2009, http://www.nytimes.com/2009/02/05/us/politics/05health.html?ref=health (accessed January 2, 2011).

67 National Conference of State Legislatures, "State Legislation and Actions Challenging Certain Health Reforms, 2010," http://www.ncsl.org/?tabid=18906, accessed January 7, 2011.

68 Kaiser Commission on Medicaid and the Uninsured, "Hoping for Economic Recovery, Preparing for Health Reform: A Look at Medicaid Spending, Coverage and Policy Trends Results from a 50-State Medicaid Budget Survey for State Fiscal Years 2010 and 2011," September, 2010 http://www.kff.org/medicaid/upload/8105_ES.pdf (accessed January 2, 2011).

69 Patrick McGuinn, *No Child Left Behind and the Transformation of Federal Education Policy, 1965–2005* (Lawrence, KS: University Press of Kansas, June 2006), 207–13; Jeffrey Henig, "Education Policy from 1980 to the Present: The Politics of Privatization," in *Conservatism and American Political Development*, eds. Brian J. Glenn and Steven M. Teles (Oxford and New York: Oxford University Press, 2009), 292–93.

70 Elizabeth Rose, "Where Does Pre-School Belong? Pre-school Policy and Public Education, 1965-Present," in *To Educate a Nation: Federal and National Strategies for School Reform*, eds. Carl E. Kaestle and Alyssa E. Lodewick (Lawrence, KS: University Press of Kansas, 2007), 281–301.

71 Maris Vinovskis, *From a Nation at Risk to No Child Left Behind: National Education Goals and the Creation of Federal Education Policy* (New York: Teachers College Press, 2009), 15.

72 Henig, "Education Policy from 1980 to the Present," 302–9. By the mid-2000s, however, fewer than 40,000 students were enrolled in voucher programs nationwide.

73 National Commission on Excellence in Education, *A Nation at Risk*, http://www2.ed.gov/pubs/NatAtRisk/index.html (accessed October 17, 2010).

74 Vinovskis, *From a Nation at Risk to No Child Left Behind*, 19, 24, 56–84.

75 Ibid., 158–70; Wong, "Accountability and Innovation," 107–8.

76 Posner, "Mandates," 290.

77 Vinovskis, *From a Nation at Risk to No Child Left Behind*, 189–92.

78 David Brian Robertson and Dennis R. Judd, *The Development of American Public Policy: The Structure of Policy Restraint* (New York: Scott, Foresman/Little, Brown, 1989), 343–49.

79 Ibid., 346–47; Barry Rabe, "Power to the States: The Promise and Pitfalls of Decentralization," in *Environmental Policy in the 1990s*, eds. Norman J. Vig and Michael E. Kraft (Washington, DC: CQ Press, 1997), 35–39.

80 Barry Rabe, "Environmental Policy and the Bush Era: The Collision Between the Administrative Presidency and State Experimentation," *Publius* 37:3 (Summer, 2007), 415, 421; U.S. General Accounting Office, "Environmental Protection: Overcoming Obstacles to Innovative State Regulatory Programs," Report GAO-02-268, http://www.gao.gov/new.items/d02268.pdf (accessed January 7, 2010).

81 Rabe, "Environmental Policy and the Bush Era," 421. See also Denise Scheberle, *Federalism and Environmental Policy: Trust and the Politics of Implementation*, 2nd ed. (Washington, DC: Georgetown University Press, 2004).

82 Rabe, "Environmental Policy and the Bush Era," 416–19.

83 Pew Center on Global Climate Change,"Climate Action," http://www.pewclimate.org/states-regions (accessed January 5, 2011).

84 Regional Greenhouse Gas Initiative, http://www.rggi.org/home (accessed January 5, 2011).

85 Rabe, "Environmental Policy and the Bush Era," 413.

86 *Massachusetts* v. *EPA*, 549 U.S. 497 (2007).

87 Bryan Walsh, "Battle Brews over EPA's Emissions Regulations," *Time* Magazine, January 3, 2011, http://www.time.com/time/health/article/0,8599,2040485,00.html#ixzz1A7NXtDVz, (accessed January 4, 2011).

88 Morone, *Hellfire Nation*, 450–92.

89 *Engel* v. *Vitale*, 370 U.S. 421 (1962); *Roe* v. *Wade*, 410 U.S. 113 (1973).

90 Daniel J. Tichenor, "The Presidency and Interest Groups: Allies, Adversaries, and Policy Leadership," in Michael Nelson, ed., *The Presidency and the Political System*, 9th ed., (Washington: CQ Press, 2010), 272–75; Daniel K. Williams, *God's Party: The Making of the Christian Right* (Oxford and New York: Oxford University Press, 2010), 187–211.

91 Guttmacher Institute, "State Policies in Brief," http://www.guttmacher.org/statecenter/spibs/index.html (accessed January 5, 2011).

92 National Conference of State Legislatures, "State Family and Medical Leave Laws that Differ from the Federal FMLA," http://www.ncsl.org/Portals/1/documents/employ/fam-medleave.pdf (accessed January 5, 2011).

93 J. Mitchell Pickerill and Paul H.S. Chen, "Medical Marijuana Policy and the Virtues of Federalism" *Publius* 38:1 (Winter, 2008), 22–55, 2008; NORML, Active State Medical Marijuana Programs http://norml.org/index.cfm?Group_ID=3391 (accessed January 5, 2011).

94 Guttmacher Institute, "State Policies in Brief."

95 See Jeffrey R. Lax and Justin H. Phillips, "Gay Rights in the States: Public Opinion and Policy Responsiveness," *American Political Science Review* 103:3 (August, 2009), 367–86.

96 Human Rights Campaign, Map of State Laws and Policies, http://www.hrc.org/about_ us/state_laws.asp (accessed January 5, 2010).

Chapter 10

1 Wayne Slater, "Analysis: Perry's 'States' Rights' Battle Cry Evokes History that Could Damage His Message," *Dallas Morning News*, November 19, 2010, http://www.dallasnews.com/sharedcontent/dws/news/texassouthwest/stories/DN-perry_19tex.ART0.State.Edition 1.4b7d22a.html (accessed November 24, 2010).

2 Bill Bartel, "Cuccinelli Shines among GOP Stars at Tea Party Rally," *The Virginian-Pilot*, October 10, 2010, http://hamptonroads.com/2010/10/tea-party-activists-treat-cuccinelli-rock-star (accessed November 24, 2010).

3 Ginger Gibson, "Delaware Politics: Can the Tea Party Movement Win in the First State? Hard Times Again Produce Populist Backlash," *The News Journal*, September 12, 2010, http://www.delawareonline.com/article/20100912/NEWS02/9120361/Delaware-politics-Can-the-tea-party-movement-win-in-the-First-State- (accessed November 24, 2010).

4 See the work of Michael S. Greve at the American Enterprise Institute http://www.aei.org/scholar/24; (accessed November 24, 2010); the Cato Institute federalism webpage, http://www.cato.org/federalism (accessed November 24, 2010); and the State Policy Network, http://www.spn.org (accessed November 24, 2010).

5 10th Amendment Task Force, http://robbishop.house.gov/10thAmendment/News/DocumentSingle.aspx?DocumentID=201773 (accessed November 24, 2010); "Pledge to America," http://pledge.gop.gov/ (accessed November 24, 2010).

6 John MacMullin, "Repeal the 17th Amendment," The Tenth Amendment Center website, http://www.tenthamendmentcenter.com/2008/10/24/repeal-the-17th-amendment (accessed November 30, 2010).

7 Richard P. Nathan, "Federalism and Health Policy," *Health Affairs* 24:6 (2005), 1458–66; "Updating Theories of American Federalism," in *Intergovernmental Management for the Twenty-First Century*, eds. Timothy J. Conlan and Paul L. Posner (Washington, DC: Brookings Institution, 2008), 13–25.

8 Dale Krane, "The Middle Tier in American Federalism: State Government Policy Activism during the Bush Presidency," *Publius* 37:3 (July, 2007), 453–77.

9 Margot Roosevelt, "Prop. 23 Battle Marks New Era in Environmental Politics," *Los Angeles Times*, November 4, 2010, http://articles.latimes.com/2010/nov/04/local/la-me-global-warming-20101104 (accessed November 27, 2010).

10 John Dinan, "The State of American Federalism 2007–8: Resurgent State Influence in the National Policy Process and Continued State Policy Innovation," *Publius* 38:3 (July, 2008), 381–415.

11 Kathleen M. Sullivan, "From States' Rights Blues to Blue States' Rights: Federalism after the Rehnquist Court," *Fordham Law Review* 75:2 (November, 2006), 810–13; Richard Thompson Ford, "The New Blue Federalists," *Slate*, January 6, 2005, http://www.slate.com/id/2111942 (accessed July 1, 2010). See also comments by Joel Rogers at the Conference on "Taking Back America, 2008—The New Green Deal," March 18, 2008, video on the Campaign for America's Future website, http://ourfuture.org/video/tba-2008-new-green-deal (accessed November 27, 2010), comments begin at 39:20. See also home page of the Progressive States Network, http://www.progressivestates.org (accessed January 7, 2011).

12 In *Federalism: Political Identity and Tragic Compromise* (Ann Arbor, MI: University of Michigan Press, 2008), Malcolm Feeley and Edward L. Rubin take this argument to its

logical conclusion: that federalism is an appendage from the past that is no longer meaningful in the United States.

13 Robert A. Schapiro's *Polyphonic Federalism: Toward the Protection of Fundamental Rights* (Chicago: University of Chicago Press, 2009), 6, 54–91, discusses this point from the perspective of public law. Thanks to John Nugent for bringing this perspective to my attention. See also Ellis Katz and G. Alan Tarr, eds., *Federalism and Rights* (Lanham, MD: Rowman & Littlefield, 1996).

14 Robert A. Schapiro develops one perspective on the value of federalism for democracy in *Polyphonic Federalism*.

15 James Madison, *Federalist* 10, in Alexander Hamilton, James Madison, and John Jay, *The Federalist*, ed. Jacob E. Cooke (Middletown, CT: Wesleyan University Press, 1961), 63–64.

16 Grant McConnell, *Private Power & American Democracy* (New York: Alfred A. Knopf, 1966), summarized on 104–5. See also David B. Truman, *The Governmental Process: Political Interests and Public Opinion* (New York: Alfred A. Knopf, 1951), 323.

17 E.E. Schattschneider, *The Semisovereign People: A Realist's View of Democracy in America* (New York: Holt, Rinehart and Winston, 1960), 6.

18 Richard P. Nathan, "Updating Theories of Federalism," in *Intergovernmental Management for the Twenty-First Century*, eds. Timothy J. Conlan and Paul L. Posner (Washington, DC: Brookings Institution, 2008), 16, 21.

19 Jonathan A. Rodden, *Hamilton's Paradox: The Promise and Peril of Fiscal Federalism* (Cambridge and New York: Cambridge University Press, 2006).

20 Paul E. Peterson, *The Price of Federalism* (Washington, DC: Brookings Institution, 1995); see also Thomas Anton, "New Federalism and Intergovernmental Fiscal Relationships: The Implications for Health Policy," *Journal of Health Politics, Policy and Law*, 22:3 (June, 1997), 701–2.

21 Bruce Western, *Punishment and Inequality in America* (New York: Russell Sage Foundation, 2006).

22 Mark H. Haller, *Eugenics: Hereditarian Attitudes in American Thought* (New Brunswick, NJ: Rutgers University Press, 1963), 50.

23 Paula Abrams, *Cross Purposes: Pierce v. Society of Sisters and the Struggle over Compulsory Public Education* (Ann Arbor, MI: University of Michigan Press, 2009).

24 Herbert Obinger, Stephan Leibfried, and Francis G. Castles, eds., *Federalism and the Welfare State: New World and European Experiences* (Cambridge and New York: Cambridge University Press, 2005); Ellen M. Immergut, "Political Institutions," in *The Oxford Handbook of the Welfare State*, eds. Francis G. Castles, Stephan Leibfried, Jane Lewis, Herbert Obinger, and Christopher Pierson (Oxford and New York: Oxford University Press, 2010), 237.

25 Martha Derthick, *Keeping the Compound Republic: Essays on American Federalism* (Washington, DC: Brookings Institution, 2001), 40, 52–53.

26 Peterson, *The Price of Federalism*, 18–27.

27 Jeffrey L. Pressman and Aaron Wildavsky, *Implementation: How Great Expectations in Washington are Dashed in Oakland; or, Why It's Amazing that Federal Programs Work at All, This Being a Saga of the Economic Development Administration as Told by Two Sympathetic Observers Who Seek to Build Morals on a Foundation of Ruined Hopes* (Berkeley, CA: University of California Press, 1973).

28 Richard Franklin Bensel, *Sectionalism and American Political Development, 1880–1980* (Madison, WI: University of Wisconsin Press, 1984); *Yankee Leviathan: The Origins of Central State Authority in America, 1859–1877* (Cambridge and New York: Cambridge University Press, 1990); and *The Political Economy of American Industrialization, 1877–1900* (Cambridge and New York: Cambridge University Press, 2001).

Index